AF324715

PSEUDO-ZENO

ANONYMOUS PHILOSOPHICAL
TREATISE

PHILOSOPHIA ANTIQUA

A SERIES OF STUDIES
ON ANCIENT PHILOSOPHY

FOUNDED BY J.H. WASZINK AND W.J. VERDENIUS

EDITED BY

J. MANSFELD, D.T. RUNIA
J.C.M. VAN WINDEN

VOLUME LXXXIII

M.E. STONE AND M.E. SHIRINIAN

PSEUDO-ZENO

ANONYMOUS PHILOSOPHICAL
TREATISE

PSEUDO-ZENO

ANONYMOUS PHILOSOPHICAL TREATISE

BY

M.E. STONE AND M.E. SHIRINIAN

TRANSLATED WITH THE COLLABORATION

OF

J. MANSFELD AND D.T. RUNIA

BRILL

LEIDEN · BOSTON · KÖLN

2000

This book is printed on acid-free paper.

Library of Congress Cataloging-in-Publication Data

The Library of Congress Cataloging-in-Publication Data is also available.

Die Deutsche Bibliothek – CIP-Einheitsaufnahme

Pseudo-Zeno : Anonymous philosophical treatise / by M.E. Stone and M.E. Shirinian. Transl. with the collaboration of J. Mansfeld and D.T. Runia. – Leiden ; Boston ; Köln : Brill
(Philosophia antiqua ; Vol. 83)
ISBN 90–04–11524–2

ISSN 0079-1687
ISBN 90 04 11524 2

PRINTED IN THE NETHERLANDS

CONTENTS

PART TWO
TEXT AND CRITICAL APPARATUSES

PART THREE
TRANSLATION

PART FOUR
INDEXES AND TOOLS

PREFACE

This book is the product of a team of scholars, working during the academic year 1997-1998 at the Netherlands Institute of Advanced Studies in Wassenaar. We wish to express our appreciation to NIAS and its staff who provided us with ideal working conditions. The members of the group resident at NIAS were M.E. Stone and J.J.S. Weitenberg (directors), Th.M. van Lint, G. Muradyan, D.T. Runia, M.E. Shirinian and J.W. Wesselius. In addition, J. Mansfeld worked with the group, though he was not resident. Under a grant from NWO, Dr. Peter Robinson assisted the group in computer applications.

In the 1980's M.E. Stone and J. Mansfeld began jointly to prepare an English translation of a Greek philosophical treatise which had survived only in Armenian. Stone knew Armenian but not ancient philosophy and Mansfeld's skills were complementary. Although a brief report on this project was published,[1] in fact Stone and Mansfeld only managed to prepare a preliminary translation of about a quarter of the work, basing themselves on the text then available. Their work, however, provided a basis for the formation of the group at NIAS in 1997-1998.

The project, as it developed at NIAS, became the preparation of a new edition, using the computer program Collate written by Peter Robinson. This program enabled us to produce a full edition, and the materials prepared for Collate also serve as the basis of an electronic edition of the work. Collate outputs the edition in an electronic form. Its results are included in this book as the text and two apparatuses and, in addition, the electronic edition will contain transcriptions and scans of the individual manuscripts, a full KWIC concordance of the book, Arevšatyan's Russian translation and some further resources. The book also contains a translation into English with annotations, a number of indexes, a concordance of the Armenian text, and a detailed word-list of the English translation.

---

[1] M.E. Stone and J. Mansfeld, "Compte rendu préliminaire sur la traduction anglaise de la composition *De Natura* attribuée à Zeno stoïcus," *Newsletter of Association Internationale des Etudes Arméniennes*, 19 October 1993 (1993) 4-6.

The project was carried out under the overall direction of M.E. Stone. M.E. Shirinian worked together with him on most parts of it and they are co-authors of this book. Stone was responsible for the preparation of the edition, for the stemmata and part of the Introduction, including the stemmatics, for the textual commentary, and for the indexes. He also entered the Armenian text of pseudo-Zeno into the computer. M.E. Shirinian was responsible for checking the collations of the text and manuscripts and the critical apparatuses, for revising the textual commentary, for retranslating some of the technical terms and neologisms into Greek, for participating in the revision of the translation and for writing the basic part of the introduction. She also entered the text of the Russian translation made by S.S Arevšatyan into the computer.

J.J.S. Weitenberg prepared the Armenian Concordance; G. Muradyan checked the collations and participated in the revision of the translation.

The translation presented a major problem. The text is particularly difficult and knowledge both of Armenian and of ancient philosophy is required. This procedure was followed. A first draft was prepared, including the prior Stone-Mansfeld material, by van Lint, Weitenberg and Stone. D.T. Runia participated in the revision of substantial parts of this first draft together with M.E. Shirinian and G. Muradyan. It was J. Mansfeld, however, who worked with M.E. Stone on preparing the fully revised draft. Mansfeld's contribution was very valuable indeed. Stone then revised this draft a second time and Mansfeld annotated the newly revised translation from the point of view of ancient philosophy, and worked through the whole once more.

Together with this, it should be emphasized that while we present the text, apparatuses and other Armenological aspects of the work as definitive, this is not the case for the translation. The translation is the best we can do, but many points remain obscure and many statements remain puzzling. Nonetheless, we venture to offer it to the learned world as a working document and hope that it will stimulate further study of published and unpublished philosophical texts in Armenian and their contribution to the study of ancient philosophy as well as of the learned tradition of Armenia.

The Armenian philosophical tradition has been little utilized by students of ancient philosophy. The following incident recounted by M.E. Shirinian is typical.

The first time I heard of the Armenian translation of (pseudo-)Zeno was while I was studying Classics and was asked about it (I did not know much about it at that time). Then one of our professors explained that the work is clearly not an Armenian translation of Zeno the Stoic and the conclusion that there is "nothing interesting in it" was in air. From that time I became very interested in this translation and promised myself that some day I would deal with it to see what it really was.

Such views may explain why, after L. Xač'ikyan's publication of the *editio princeps* of the Armenian text of pseudo-Zeno in 1950, it received almost no attention from students of ancient philosophy. After its translation into the Russian by S.S. Arevšatyan in 1965,[2] the single exception was the fine, pioneering study by E.G. Schmidt in 1960.[3]

Indeed, as a whole, philosophical writings in Armenian remain relatively unknown to the specialists in Greek philosophy. It is regrettable that certain critical editions of Greek texts do not even mention the existence of an Armenian version, which is often older than the most ancient preserved Greek manuscripts. One wonders how a new edition of Porphyry's *Isagoge*, containing a substantial discussion of its reception in Latin West and Arabic East, says not a single word about the early Armenian translation of this work and the rich tradition of commentaries on it in Armenian.[4] A repertory of published Armenian translations of Greek works was recently published by C. Zuckerman,[5] but many works remain unstudied in manuscript form.[6]

---

[2] S.S. Arevšatian, "Zeno the Stoic's Treatise 'On Nature' and its Ancient Armenian Translation," *Banber Matenadarani* 3 (1956) 315-342 (in Russian).

[3] E.G. Schmidt, "Die altarmenische 'Zenon'-Schrift," *Abhandlungen der deutschen Akademie der Wissenschaften zu Berlin: Klasse für Sprachen, Literatur und Kunst,* Jahrgang 1960, Nr. 2 (1961) 5-50.

[4] A. De Libera and A.-Ph. Segonds, *Porphyre: Isagoge, Greek & Latin Lesetext,* with transl., introd. & notes, (Paris, 1998). D. Gutas, *Greek Thought, Arabic Culture. The Graeco-Arabic Translation Movement in Baghdad and Early Abbasid Society (2nd-4th/8th-10 centuries)* (London/New York, 1998) is an impressive study of the Syriac and especially the Arabic translation movements. Yet he is silent on the Armenian. His only remark on Armenia is on p. 139 where he tells us that the Syro-Palestinian Greek, Qusta ibn Luqa (after 900 C.E.) first worked in Baghdad and "eventually... went to Armenia where he continued to ply his trade."

[5] Constantine Zuckerman, *A Repertory of Published Armenian Translations of Classical Texts* (Jerusalem, 1995). This is also posted on the Jerusalem Armenian Studies Internet site at http://unixware.mscc.huji.ac.il/ ~armenia.

[6] At the initiative of Association Internationale des Etudes Arméniennes, Dr. M. Papazian (University of Virginia) is pursuing a preliminary study of one manuscript, rich in philosophical writings.

As noted above, the study of these Armenian philosophical texts faces two hurdles: it requires an expert in ancient philosophy and it also requires a knowledge not just of classical Armenian but of the special dialect of the Hellenizing school.[7] An individual with these qualifications, working at the intersection of Armenology and history of philosophy, is scarcely to be found. Pseudo-Zeno is a truly difficult text demanding repeated investigation; not only is every other word a technical term, but a philosophical theory hides behind almost each sentence.[8] Considering that, it is obvious how important the work of the philosophers in the team was. The co-operation of J. Mansfeld and D.T. Runia with the Armenologists resident at NIAS provided the necessary knowledge of ancient philosophy.

---

[7] This is discussed below, in the Introduction.

[8] The difficulty of such texts was pointed out in the seventeenth century by the historian Aṙakʻel of Tabriz. He says it is necessary to read them many times in order to understand them: see *History of Aṙakʻel of Tabriz* (Vałaršapat, 1896) 390-413, and particularly 393 (in Armenian).

PART ONE

INTRODUCTION
BIBLIOGRAPHICAL ABBREVIATIONS
SIGLA AND TECHNICAL ABBREVIATIONS

INTRODUCTION

1. *The Title and Author*

The title *Զենոնի, յաղագս բնութեան, Zeno's On Nature* was created by
the first editor of this treatise, L. Xač'ikyan.[1] The attribution *Զենոնի
իմաստասիրի* "of Zeno the Philosopher" is preserved in one manuscript (D),[2] but no manuscript contains *յաղագս բնութեան "On Nature"*.
Xač'ikyan called the title "preliminary" and provided some
arguments for its choice. Our view is that it should be rejected and we
refer to the work as *Anonymous Philosophical Treatise.*

No title at all occurs in the preserved manuscripts, that found in
manuscripts B and D, *յաղագս պիտանացու սեռից* "On Useful Kinds",
referring to the first section but not to the whole writing.[3] Xač'ikyan
thought that, "the chapter *յաղագս ազդմանց* 'On Influences' is very
useful for establishing a preliminary title."[4] From §1.6.9 he acutely
infers that four sections of the work exist (section 1 is not included in
this enumeration). When the listing in §§1.6.9 is aligned with the
contents of the work from section 2 on, the parallel is only perfect in
the first division, the practical (= §2.1.1-3), and there it is only
achieved by regarding §§2.3.4 and 2.3.5 as secondary. Beyond this
division, moreover, some parallels between the second division in
§1.6.9 and sections 3 and 4 may be observed, and again some parallels
to the fourth division in §1.6.9 exist in section 5. Thus, it does seem to
be true that, on the whole, §1.6.9 provides us with an overall listing of
the contents of the treatise from §2.0.0 to the end, though there are
quite a lot of points of difference.

Even if the above observation were quite sound and §§1.6.9-11
contained a completely correct Table of Contents of sections 2-5 of
pseudo-Zeno, Xač'ikyan's assertion that nature is common to these
four divisions is by no means obviously the case.[5] This is, therefore, no

---

[1] L. Xač'ikyan, "The Armenian Translation of Zeno's *Concerning Nature*," *Kitakan
Niwt'eri Zołovacu* 2 (1950) 65-98 (in Armenian): henceforth Xač'ikyan.

[2] The sigla are set forth below, section 8.

[3] Xač'ikyan, 69.

[4] *Ibid.*

[5] It does not seem to us that §1.6.14 proves that the total content is about
nature, as he asserts. In addition, a separate section on nature is named in §1.6.11
and such a section occurs in §5.5.

argument for the title *On Nature,* any more than is the statement that because a writing entitled *On Nature* was ascribed to Zeno "it is natural to suppose that the [Armenian MES] opus was entitled *On Nature*".[6]

Another explanation of Xač'ikyan's action might be the following. In manuscript A, which is a rich collection of philosophical texts, three other works occur on topics also treated by pseudo-Zeno. There are two different works entitled "About Movement" (cf. Pseudo-Zeno §5.7) which are apparently parts of an unknown writing and a writing called "Rhetorician On Nature".[7] Manuscript A entitles pseudo-Zeno's writing "Another Discourse" and Xač'ikyan might have been influenced by the title "Rhetorician On Nature" when he chose the name for the newly discovered anonymous treatise. Indeed, the word "another" indicates that there was a similar work in the manuscript.[8]

Schmidt devotes an excursus to the name Zeno which is associated with this tractate.[9] He thinks that the work may have been written by an Armenian, who attributed it to Zeno because of the lively Zeno tradition that existed in Armenian.[10] We would differ from this conclusion for two reasons. First, we see no reason to assume that the book was composed in Armenian. To the contrary, it is quite clear that it was translated into Armenian from Greek and there seems to be no evidence that an Armenian wrote the Greek text. Second, for some reason Schmidt says that both manuscripts B and D witness the name Zeno (p. 45). In fact, and this should be stressed, the name Zeno is only found in manuscript D, the latest of the four manuscripts by some centuries. Consequently, the attribution to Zeno seems to us to be secondary in the Armenian tradition, and, adapting Schmidt's comments, we may say that the vitality of the Armenian philosophical tradition may have preserved knowledge of Zeno's name, facilitating

---

[6] *Ibid.,* 70, see further 70-71. There he argues for Zeno the Stoic being the author of the *Vorlage* of the present treatise. It will be evident from our discussion of its intellectual affinities, that this is not the case: see below, 26-28.

[7] This is an anonymous treatise edited by S.S. Arevšatyan, "Two Ancient Philosophical Fragments - 'Rhetorician, On Nature' and 'Philosophical Definitions'," *Banber Matenadarani,* 5 (1960), 371-392.

[8] If this was what happened, however, Xač'ikyan did not say so. We might further remark that many sections of the *Anonymous Treatise* do deal with topics which are the subject of separate works in the list of Zeno the Stoic's writings, such as physics, ethics and logic. These are commonplace philosophical topics, however, so this fact is of no weight.

[9] Schmidt, 45-47.

[10] *Ibid.,* 46.

the false attribution in manuscript D.[11]

In view of all the above considerations, we have chosen to refer to this work simply as pseudo-Zeno's *Anonymous Philosophical Treatise.*

2. *History of Research*

In 1930, Melik'set'-Beg, in "Kistorii tocnyx nauk v Armenii i Gryzii" announced that a translation of περὶ φύσεως, the lost work of Zeno the Eleatic, was to be found in the library of manuscripts in Ējmiacin.[12] This was the short recension of pseudo-Zeno and it was edited by H. Manandian from manuscripts A, B and D and passed on to L. Xač'ikyan for publication. In 1942, in the course of working on a thematic bibliography of the Matenadaran, the Library of Ancient Manuscripts in Erevan, Armenia, Xač'ikyan's attention was drawn to an untitled text in the rich, philosophical manuscript, no. M5254 (our manuscript A), which turned out to be the long recension. Utilizing Manandian's edition of BCD as well as manuscript A, in 1950 Xač'ikyan published the *editio princeps.*

In 1954 M. Shaginian in her book about Armenia which was translated into German, when speaking about the Armenian science and scholarship, mentioned that the Armenian translation of Zeno the Stoic was found in manuscripts of Matenadaran.[13] This information in German language drew the attention of Western scholars to pseudo-Zeno.

In 1956, S.S. Arevšatyan translated Xač'ikyan's text into the Russian with an introduction in which he gave a short excursus on the development of philosophical ideas in Armenia and on Stoic philosophy. He speaks of the difficulty of rendering the work's philosophical terminology, especially terms created by the translator and used only in this text.[14] The need to add explanations of such

---

[11] The number of pseudonymous works in Armenian is very large, as is also true in Greek. Consequently, it is difficult to build much on the attribution of a work in its latest, seventeenth-century manuscript. A natural desire for a major find has, in this instance, led scholarship astray into a barren field of complete speculation.

[12] Xač'ikyan, 66.

[13] M. Schaginian, *Reise durch Sowjetarmenien* (Moskau, 1954) 173 wrote: "Von den Werken des altgriechischen Philosophen Zeno ist bekanntlich nichts erhalten geblieben. Die Mitarbeiter des 'Matenadaran' hegten lange im verborgensten Winkel des Herzens die Hoffnung, dieser ihr Zeno sei jener einzige, - eine natürlich kaum irgendworauf fußende Hoffnung".

[14] Compare the List of Neologisms given below on pp. 253-254.

terminology resulted in the Russian translation being longer than the Armenian original. In his translation, Arevšatyan set passages which he considered to be interpolations inside square brackets. This translation was very important also because it stimulated a review by H. Dörrie in 1957[15] and the research published a decade later by E.G. Schmidt (1961). A review article devoted to E.G. Schmidt's study was written by L. Westerink in 1963.[16]

Dörrie pointed out that the *Anonymous Philosophical Treatise* was not written by Zeno the Stoic,[17] gave a brief summary of the contents of the work stressing elements he identified as Neo-Platonic, and on the basis of the astrological elements proposed a Persian context of transmission.[18] He also mentioned Albinus as a possible source for definitions of philosophy.[19] Later Schmidt remarked that Albinus' *Didascalicu*s indeed has some similarities with pseudo-Zeno, but clearly pseudo-Zeno's definitions of philosophy are closest to David and Elias.[20]

E.G. Schmidt's substantial paper published in 1961 was groundbreaking, because he was the first scholar familiar with both Greek philosophy and Armenian language to examine the work.[21] Schmidt made a careful analysis and showed that the sources of the pseudo-Zeno were dominantly located in the Greek philosophical tradition. We should remark that some of the works cited by Schmidt as sources for pseudo-Zeno also exist in Armenian translations, and that the Armenian tradition is unanimous in identifying David "the Invincible" as an Armenian.[22] His central conclusions show that pseudo-Zeno uses the *Prolegomena* of David, and must be later than that work, which was composed in the mid-sixth century. He concludes "[e]r stammt wohl aus dem 7. Jh.".[23] In addition to adducing many parallels and

---

[15] H. Dörrie, review of *Der Bote aus dem Matenadaran* (i.e., *Banber Matedarani*) 3 (1956) in *Gnomon*, 29 (1957) 445-450.

[16] L.G. Westerink, review of Schmidt in *Mnemosyne* 4.16 (1963) 195-7.

[17] Dörrie, 445.

[18] *Ibid.*, 447-449.

[19] *Ibid.*, 447.

[20] Compare Schmidt, 27-32.

[21] He also knew Russian which helped him to compare the translation made by S.S. Arevšatian with the text.

[22] Compare the observations of B. Kendall and R.W. Thomson, *Definitions and Divisions of Philosophy by David the Invincible Philosopher* (University of Pennsylvania Armenian Texts and Studies, 5; Chico, CA, 1983) xiii-xvii. See also the papers in A.K. Sanjian (ed.), *David Anhaght the 'Invincible' Philosopher* (Studies in Near Eastern Culture and Society, 7; Atlanta, 1986); Zuckerman, 19-20.

[23] Schmidt, 45.

sources, Schmidt also proposes possible Greek parallels to technical terms used in the Armenian translation of pseudo-Zeno.

L.G. Westerink's review is a clear presentation of some of Schmidt's central views with certain critical comments. For example speaking about David: "Freilich kann man die Frage erheben, ob das Verhältnis zu David nicht etwas komplizierter ist als Schmidt (S.32) annimt".[24] He concludes that "die 'Zenon'-Schrift scheidet aus der Geschichte der griechischen Philosophie aus und nimmt einen (bescheidenen) Platz ein im (gleichfalls sehr bescheidenen) philosophischen Schrifttum Armeniens".[25] In this respect he follows the proposal of Schmidt, that the *Anonymous Philosophical Treatise* was composed in Armenian. We have already noted that this is clearly not the case, as is evident from the obviously translated Hellenizing language. So, the place of pseudo-Zeno in the Greek philosophical tradition seems assured.[26]

Finally, a concordance of Xač'ikyan's text was prepared by H. Hovhanessian and published in Erevan in 1978.[27]

3. *Armenian Translations of Philosophical Writings*

The survival in Armenian of the *Anonymous Treatise* by pseudo-Zeno does not surprise those familiar with the Armenian literary tradition. The Armenian alphabet was invented at the beginning of the fifth century CE and the work of translation was coeval with the alphabet. The first work translated into Armenian was also the first written work in that language, that is the translation of the Bible. In the course of the fifth century, abundant translations were made into Armenian, chiefly from Greek and Syriac.[28]

---

[24] Westerink, 196.

[25] *Ibid.*, 196-197.

[26] The two further discussions of pseudo-Zeno do not broach central issues: see Stone and Mansfeld, *Newsletter of Association Internationale des Etudes Arméniennes*, 19 October 1993 (1993) 4-6 and Zuckerman, 34-35.

[27] *Armenian Concordances, 12; Zeno's Booklet On Nature* ed. H. Hovhanessian (Erevan, 1978) (in Armenian). The work is now also included in the Leiden Armenian Data Base edited by J.J.S. Weitenberg.

[28] The most recent major scholarly work enumerating Armenian literary writings is R.W. Thomson, *A Bibliography of Classical Armenian Literature to 1500 A.D.* (Corpus Christianorum; Turnhout, 1995). Older works devoted to Armenian translations and detailed bibliographies of Armenian literature in general are: [G. Zarphanalian], *Մատենադարան Հայկական Թարգմանութեանց Նախնեաց* (Library of Ancient Armenian Translations; Venice, 1889); H.S. Anasyan, *Հայկական*

Armenia, because of its geographic location, was profoundly influenced by these two great Christian cultures, the one to the South and the other to the West. Moreover, the political division of Armenia between the Sasanian and the Byzantine empires enshrined these twin sources in a representative political reality. Yet we should remark that the Byzantine influence was not confined to Armenia Minor, the part under Byzantine rule. It was profoundly felt in the central regions of the Armenian settlement, in Armenia Major.[29] With the loss of political independence in the early fifth century, Armenia nonetheless bid fair for a large measure of cultural independence which was reinforced by the inception of writing in the Armenian language and, after the Council of Chalcedon in 451 CE, gradually led to an ecclesiastical split between the non-Chalcedonian Armenian Church and the Chalcedonian Byzantine Church.[30] The work of translation into Armenian, therefore, began as part of the cultural effort which was coextensive with the Armenian aspirations to preserve their cultural, religious and in the final analysis political independence.

There is a passage in the *Epistle against the Byzantine Philosopher Theophistus*, by the eleventh-century writer Pawłos of Tarawn from which we can learn of the overall attitude of the Armenians to translations. He says:

> You keep saying that Armenians are translating and learning from the Romans and it is not honourable for you [Armenians]. All nations translated the Law and the Prophets from the Hebrews, who now stray in darkness. There are many books in Armenia but the Romans do not translate them, because they are lazy and arrogant. We translate from the Syrians, the Egyptians,[31] the Romans and the Greeks, the writings of the holy fathers or homilies of the holy martyrs. In addition, (we translate) numerous (writings) by the heretics which are

Մատենագիտութիւն (Armenian Bibliology; 2 vols.; Erevan, 1959 & 1976).

[29] In general, on Armenian history see Gérard Dédéyan (ed.), *Histoire des Arméniens* (Toulouse, 1982) and more recently Richard G. Hovannisian ed., *The Armenian People from Ancient to Modern Times: Vol. I: The Dynastic Periods: From Antiquity to the Fourteenth Century; Vol. II: Foreign Dominion to Statehood: The Fifteenth Century to the Twentieth Century* (New York, 1997).

[30] N.G. Garsoïan, "Quelques précisions préliminaires sur le schisme entre les Églises byzantine et arménienne au sujet du concile de Chalcedoine: II La date et les circonstances de la rupture," *L'Armenie et Byzance: Histoire et culture* (Paris, 1966) 99-112.

[31] Perhaps he means the representatives of the old Alexandrian school. Aratus and perhaps Callimachus were translated into the Armenian (see Zuckerman, 12-13). Alternatively he refers to Alexandrians of time of Philo, who of course does not belong to "the holy fathers" or even Hermes Trismegistos.

in accordance with orthodoxy, because St. Athanasius says: "In many cases the heretics confess with us, which we should accept".

Then he adduces metaphorical examples of useful and useless things and concludes: "Similarly, the Armenians choose the useful things from among all unworthy things, neglecting the worthless".[32]

An examination of Armenian translations of Greek philosophical and doxographical writings shows that there was a tradition, indeed a canon of works chosen for the translation:[33] those are mainly the writings of authors who stand at the beginning of Christian thought and Greek Christian Platonism.[34] The translators designed, in the first place, to make the basic works of Christian worship and learning available in the Armenian language. Early on the list of translated works, in addition to the Bible, are such service books as the Missal and the Lectionary. Almost immediately, however, a project of ecclesiastical translation began. The initiators and inventors of the alphabet, St. Sahak Part'ew and St. Mesrop Maštoc' sent students to the great seats of Syriac and Greek culture, Edessa, Alexandria and Byzantium.[35] In addition to the ecclesiastical works mentioned, they translated highly influential patristic writings, such as the Prayers and Commentaries of St. Ephrem Syrus and many works by St. John Chrysostom. The *Hexaemeron* of St. Basil of Caesarea, works of

---

[32] N. Połarian, *Armenian Writers* (Jerusalem, 1971) 209 (in Armenian).

[33] A canon of authors and writings which were accepted by the Armenian Church definitely existed. One such canon is preserved in a very interesting work by the tenth-century author, Samuel Kamṙǰaworec'i. Asserting that Armenians of his time are not well informed about Plato because he is not transmitted with the Gospel, and are ignorant of արհեստից եւ մակացութեանց "arts and sciences", he adduces the list of accepted figures: see Połarian, *Armenian Writers*, 163. The nature and range of the Hellenizing school is discussed by Abraham Terian, "The Hellenizing School: Its Time, Place, and Scope of Activities Reconsidered," *East of Byzantium: Syria and Armenia in the Formative Period* eds. N.G. Garsoïan, T. Mathews, and R.W. Thomson (Washington, 1982) 175-186. See also his comments in Abraham Terian, "Syntactical Peculiarities in the Translations of the Hellenizing School," *First International Conference on Armenian Linguistics: Proceedings*, ed. John A.C. Greppin (Delmar, NY, 1980) 197-207.

[34] These terms for late antique philosophy and doxography are taken from *The Cambridge History of Later Greek and Early Medieval Philosophy* (Cambridge, 1967).

[35] It seems likely that Athens was also on the itinerary of the early Armenian translators. Alexandria has been debated, but the philosophical background of the present treatise speaks for it. Compare also the remarks of Kendall and Thomson, *Definitions and Divisions*, xiv-xvii on Armenian scholars in Alexandria.

Evagrius of Pontus and others enriched Armenian intellectual life. The Aristotelian tradition, perhaps in some modified form, was always potent in the teaching of philosophy in Armenia as is witnessed both by the translations and the commentaries.[36] It should be noted that many among the translated writings are compilatory in character which is in keeping with the founding and buttressing of an intellectual and learned tradition in Armenia.

About a century after the inception of literary activity in Armenian, there developed a style of translation from Greek into Armenian which has been called the "Hellenizing" or the "Hellenophile" style. This type of translation seems to have developed during the attempt to render the lexicon and syntax of Greek as literally as possible. It constrains the Armenian language to conform to the constructions of Greek syntax and, where a construction in Greek is not available in Armenian, the Hellenizing translators created one. It uses very numerous lexical calques, frequently forming neologisms in the Armenian language. The result of this process is a type of Armenian which differs radically from the classical language of the fifth century, and from the clear translation style of, say, the Bible. This Hellenizing language sacrifices the syntax and structure of the classical language on the altar of convoluted literalness. Frequently, works in the Hellenizing style are barely comprehensible in Armenian, unless read with Greek words and syntax in mind.[37]

Naturally, the literalness of the Hellenizing translations, which impedes their readability, enhances their value as witnesses to Greek texts. In recent years scholars have begun to profit from these Armenian translations. Thus we may mention M.E. Shirinian's contribution to Hansen's recent Greek edition of Socrates' *Ecclesiastical History*, G. Bolognesi's utilization of the Armenian version of Aelius Theon's *Progymnasmata*, and A. Tessier's work on the Armenian translation of Aristotle as a witness to the Greek.[38] Observe also that

---

[36] See Zuckerman, 13-15.

[37] The major scholarly works on the Hellenizing school of translators include the following: H. Manandian, Յունաբան դպրոցը եւ նրա զարգացման շրջանները (The Hellenizing School and the Stages of its Development; Vienna, 1928); Hans Lewy, *The pseudo-Philonic De Jona, Part 1* (Studies and Documents; London, 1936) 20-21; S.S. Arevšatyan, "A propos de l'époque de la traduction en arménien des dialogues de Platon," *Banber Matenadarani* 10 (1971) 7-20 (in Armenian with a French résumé); Ch. Mercier, "L'Ecole hellénistique dans la littérature arménienne," *Revue des études arméniennes* NS 13 (1978/1979) 59-75; A. Terian, *East of Byzantium*, 175-186. See also note 33 above.

[38] G.Ch. Hansen and M. Shirinian, *Sokrates Kirchengeschichte* (Berlin, 1995);

Morani's critical edition of Nemesius' *De natura hominis* takes its Armenian translation into account.[39] Considerable benefit may be expected for the study of Greek works from the further serious utilization of their Armenian versions.

Many mysteries still surround the work of the Hellenizing school. It is far from clear why Armenians began to translate in this obscure style and to what end. Scholars are only now focusing on the question of whether stereotypical translations of this type are a totally new phenomenon, or whether they represent a carrying to an extreme of a tendency already present in pre-Hellenizing translations into Armenian. With the continued publication of texts, of bi-lingual concordances and word-lists, it may be expected that the Hellenizing translations as a whole, what is called (somewhat misleadingly) following Manandian's pioneering work, the "Hellenizing School", will yield its secrets.

Pseudo-Zeno is one of a number of philosophical works that were translated into Armenian from Greek, nearly all of which are in the Hellenizing style. Many, but not all of these philosophical works have been published in one or another form, though frequently the editions are very old and not fully critical. Many writings in manuscripts, however, remain unidentified and unpublished, such as a *Notice of Aristotle*,[40] the anonymous *On Nature*,[41] *On Logic*,[42] and

---

Michel Patillon with Giancarlo Bolognesi, *Aelius Théon, Progymnasmata* (Collection des Universités de France, Série grecque, 374; Paris, 1997); A. Tessier, *Il testo di Aristotele e le traduzioni armene* ('Proagones', Studi 17; Padova, 1979); idem, "Some Remarks about the Armenian Translations of Aristotle," *Proceedings of the World Congress on Aristotle (Thessaloniki, August 7-14, 1978),* (Athens, 1982) 94-97.

[39] M. Morani, *Nemesius. De Natura Hominis* (BSB, 6; Leipzig, 1987).

[40] The Matenadaran, Institute of Ancient Manuscripts, in Erevan alone has 43 manuscripts which contain this work, such as nos. M2101, M2373, M1763, M1740 etc. as may be learned from the two volumes of O. Eganyan, A. Zeyt'unyan and P'. Ant'abyan, *Catalogue of Manuscripts of the Maštoc' Matenadaran* (Erevan, 1965 and 1970), Index *s.v.* (in Armenian). This work was ascribed to David Hark'ac'i (sixth century) who was a known figure of the Hellenizing School. It is a commentary on Greek philosophy which presents the different theories of Plato, Aristotle, Anaxagoras etc. It seems to be a translation from Greek as is indicated by its Hellenizing language and unusual technical terms, such as բնայատդական. This is a rare word not found in *NBH* but occuring three times and perhaps rendering Greek ἀκουστικός.

[41] For example Matenadaran nos. M1690, M1713, M2333, M2334, M2342, M4424, etc. These manuscripts include works entitled "On Nature" or "On Nature by another author". The second form of title may occur because a second writing was preserved in the same manuscript as the first one. Such are M2333 and M2334.

[42] Probably a translation, see nos. M1967, M3911, and M4984.

others.[43] Like certain other works preserved in Armenian, the Greek original of pseudo-Zeno has perished. This makes the careful study of the Armenian text doubly important. However, as Arevšatyan already noted, the combination of Hellenizing obscurity and the book's technical character makes the tasks of edition and translation particularly demanding.

In 1995 C. Zuckerman published his *Repertory of Published Armenian Translations of Classical Works*.[44] It will be of interest to non-Armenologists for us to list here the chief philosophical works translated into Armenian and that which follows is freely acknowledged to be heavily dependent on Zuckerman's work. We give the names of the authors and works, followed by the page number in Zuckerman and some comments.[45] However, the following *caveats* should be borne in mind about the list given here. First and foremost, it is a list of published Armenian translations of Classical philosophical works. This means that any translations of unpublished works that exist in manuscripts are not included nor are references to or occasional citations of Classical works in Armenian sources.[46] Second, works belonging to the Classical tradition which are not philosophical in character are excluded from our list: some such are recorded in note 45.[47] Third, this list does not include works which have been heavily Christianized, such as Nemesius of Emesa's *On Human Nature*. Within these limitations, it is hoped that what follows will provide readers of the present volume with a context into which to set pseudo-Zeno's *Untitled Philosophical Treatise*. A more extensive bibliography of editions, translations and scholarly studies, and a discussion of each work, are to be found in Zuckerman's *Repertory*.

---

[43]   The Association Internationale des Etudes Arméniennes has taken the first steps towards the preparation of a list of all the works contained in Armenian manuscripts of predominantly philosophical content.

[44]   The work was published by the Institute of African and Asian Studies of the Hebrew University of Jerusalem. It has been posted and indexed on the Internet site of the Armenian Studies Program of that Institute at http://unixware.mscc. huji.ac.il/~armenia/repertory/ repertory.html.

[45]   We have not included rhetorical works such Aelius Theon's *Progymnasmata* or the *Book of Chreiai*, nor collections of proverbs and fables such as Aesop, nor pseudo-Callisthenes. Fragments of Euclid have been found as well.

[46]   See Zuckerman, 5-6.

[47]   Relatively little is known of the Armenian astrological, medical and mathematical traditions. Translations of additional Classical works may well be discovered in these contexts.

Anonymous Commentaries on Aristotle, *Categories; De Interpretatione* (Zuckerman, pp. 10-11).

> Found in Armenian manuscripts of Aristotle, these two works are similar in style and language and generally attributed to one author. Older attributions to David the Invincible and Iamblichus have been contested.

Anonymous Treatises, *Rhetor, On Nature* and *Philosophical Definitions* (Zuckerman, p. 11).

> S. Arevšatyan edited two short philosophical texts with a brief introduction and a translation into Russian.[48] The two texts provide some basic philosophical definitions. The second text often furnishes alternative definitions of one and the same notion, quoting Plato, Aristotle and sometimes the Stoics or Zeno by name.

Apophthegmata Philosophorum (Zuckerman, p. 12).

> An Armenian compilation of sentences and anecdotes attributed to Greek philosophers adapted from the Greek collections. Not published in full.

Aratus of Soloi (Zuckerman, pp. 12-13).

> An Armenian text exists closely resembling verses 50-251 of Aratus' Διοσημεῖαι or Προγνωστική. In addition, a small fragment exists entitled *On the Single Sphere by Aratus*, which describes an astronomical appliance reproducing the sphere of Zodiac, perhaps extracted from Aratus' lost Κανών.

Aristotle, *Categories; De Interpretatione* and **pseudo-Aristotle**, *De Virtutibus et Vitiis; De Mundo* (Zuckerman, pp. 13-15).

> The Aristotelian tradition played a central role in Armenia. Original treatises and commentaries, notably by David of Alexandria, were translated from the Greek. The number of manuscripts perhaps explains why no critical editions yet exist. A full critical edition of *De Virtutibus et Vitiis* is being prepared by M.E. Shirinian.

David, *Definitions and Divisions of Philosophy; On Aristotle's Categories; On Porphyry's Isagoge; On Aristotle's Analytics* (Zuckerman, pp. 19-21).

---

[48] S.S. Arevšatyan, "Two Ancient Philosophical Fragments – 'Rhetor, On Nature' and 'Philosophical Definitions'," *Banber Matenadarani* 5 (1960) 371-392 (in Russian).

Arevšatyan has edited and translated these works into Russian and he considers these alone to be genuine works of David. Thomson and Kendall have translated the *Definitions* into English. The Armenian tradition considered David to be one of the earliest group of Armenian translators and attributed numerous works to him. The author appears to be a disciple of Olympiodorus of Alexandria and has affinities with him and his pupil Elias. The *Commentary on the Analytics* survives only in Armenian translated from the Greek.

Dionysius Thrax, *Ars Grammatica* (Zuckerman, pp. 21-23).

This is considered by many to be the first Hellenizing translation of the late fifth or sixth century. The Armenian version became very important in the medieval grammatical tradition which has been studied by Ervine.[49]

Hermes Trismegistos, *Definitions* (Zuckerman, pp. 24-25).

This work belongs to the Hellenistic Hermetic tradition and only fragments of its Greek original survive. The final chapter is a shortened adaptation of the early eighth-century Armenian translation of Nemesius' *On Human Nature,* chapter 5. It has been edited and translated by Mahé.[50]

Paulus of Alexandria (Zuckerman, p. 25).

A fragment of Εἰσαγωγική by Paulus of Alexandria, a late fourth century pagan astrologer, is preserved in Armenian. This comprises the introduction and most of the chapter on the Zodiac.

Plato, *Euthyphro, Apology; Timaeus; Laws; Minos* (Zuckerman, pp. 26-28).

An Armenian translation of these dialogues is preserved in a single manuscript from the late sixteenth or seventeenth century. The date of the translation, attributed to Grigor Magistros (eleventh century), is itself contested, and some consider it to be later.

---

[49] R. Ervine, *Yovhannēs Erznkac'i Pluz's* Compilation of Commentary on Grammar (Ph.D. Thesis, Columbia University, 1988).

[50] J.-P. Mahé, *Hermès en Haute-Egypte,* vol. 2 (Bibliothèque copte de Nag Hammadi, Section "Textes," 7; Québec, 1982). The Greek fragments were published by J. Paramelle and J.-P. Mahé, "Nouveaux parallèles grecs aux *Définitions* hermétiques arméniennes," *Revue des études arméniennes* NS 22 (1990-1) 115-134. J.-P.Mahé informs me that his English translation of the Greek and Armenian *Definitions* will appear in London, 1999 (letter of 23.12.1998).

Porphyry, *Isagoge* (Zuckerman, p. 28).

The Armenian translation is traditionally attributed to David the Invincible Philosopher. David's Greek commentary on the *Isagoge* was also translated into Armenian and no doubt contributed to the popularity of the treatise.

Proclus Diadochus, *Elements of Theology* (Zuckerman, p. 29).

Unlike all other texts in this survey, the translation of Proclus produced in 1248 by the monk Siměon of Garni was made through the intermediary of a Georgian translation.

Secundus Taciturnus (Zuckerman, pp. 29-30).

The Armenian *Life and Sayings* of Secundus is a faithful reproduction of the Greek text of this late second-century popular treatise. Dashian sets the date of the translation in the seventh century at the latest. Some of Secundus' sayings were integrated into the collection of *Apophthegmata Philosophorum*.

Sextus, *Sentences* (Zuckerman, pp. 30-31).

The *Sentences* of Sextus is an early Christian adaptation of a collection of mainly Pythagorean sapiential sayings. Of the two Armenian versions, a corpus of about 180 sentences is transmitted and published among the works of Evagrius of Pontus. The translation is made into good literary Armenian and might be as early as the fifth century.

4. *The Character of pseudo-Zeno's Anonymous Philosophical Treatise*

The writing is a compendium or epitome of philosophical theories which were widespread in Greco-Roman literature. Many examples could be cited and we shall mention some which have Armenian translations (as a rule made in Hellenizing style) as representatives of the type.

Pseudo-Aristotle, *De Virtutibus et Vitiis* can be considered to be a compendium of mainly Aristotelian ethical views. The *De Mundo*, also ascribed to Aristotle, on the other hand, is a treatise with literary pretensions which provides a summary of Peripatetic cosmology much coloured by later thought and containing references to ancient authorities. The *Book of the Chreiai* is a compendium on rhetoric.[51] It

---

[51] This work is a collection of rhetorical exercises or *progymnasmata* with their definitions. The major part of these goes back to Aphthonius.

can be compared with pseudo-Zeno because it too was translated from a lost Greek original,[52] and is a compendium. These compendia are translated in an abrupt and difficult Hellenizing style. They are all text-books for or summaries of specific fields of learning.

a. *Christian Character*

There are Christian features in the work as we have it. In principle, the Christianizing passages might be explained by editorial activity in Greek or Armenian[53] or might be interpolations.[54] However, it is equally possible that they were original. To prove that the author was a Christian, it is necessary to demonstrate that at least some of the explicitly Christian material cannot be removed from its context without damaging it irreparably. In fact, this is our conclusion and the evidence is set forth here.

There are a number of very explicit Christian passages throughout the work. In other cases, there is clear reference to biblical ideas and language. In assessing the weight of these passages, moreover, it should be remembered that we are dealing with a philosophical treatise, not a theological work.

§1.1.3 "the firmament of the watery vault" is biblical, based on Genesis 1:6-7.

§1.1.4 "the constitutor and the habitation of reptiles and of the enormous marine animals" is biblical, see Genesis 1:21.

§1.6.16 "according to faith, according to hope, according to love" is derived from 1 Corinthians 13:13, 1 Thessalonians 1:3 and 5:8. Here, the words from "Again, man ....love" express the tripartite division of man, already discussed in the obscure §1.6.14.

§2.5 seems to be different in character and may be from a different source, so much weight cannot be given to the last phrase of §2.5 "and the Word of God is Lord."

§3.1.5-7 deals with the definitions of philosophy. In §3.1.5 it is sixfold; in §3.1.6 it is fourfold and there the Pythagorean love of four is

---

[52] There is some discussion between G. Muradyan (editor of Armenian text) and S.P. Cowe as to whether it was all translated or only partly. Cowe considers the whole writing to be translated from a Greek imitator of Aphthonius. See G. Muradyan, Դիրք Պիտոյից (Erevan, 1993) reviewed by S.P. Cowe in *Le Muséon* 108 (1995) 200-205.

[53] See Xač'ikyan, 27

[54] See Arevšatyan, 322.

mentioned; §3.1.7 returns to six definitions again, concluding that six is made of two threes and is half a dozen. Then he goes on to the tetraktys (§3.1.8), with this four following the six as in §3.1.5 and §3.1.6. A discussion of the tens in §3.1.9 leads into a discussion of the even-oddness of three. This even-oddness is taken as the relationship with God (see notes on the translation) an the passage concludes with its only explicitly Christian phrase "who is the first and the last" (§3.1.10).[55]

§5.9 which is climactic in the book, is *On the Infinite*. From §5.9.4 to the end it is explicitly Christian throughout. §§5.9.4 – 5.9.6 deal with the Trinity, drawing together speculations about the tetrad and the Trinity. This is the same play that was made in §§3.1.5ff. but here the Christian language is explicit. The understanding we would propose of the last part of §5.9 is that the Trinity underlies all the constitutive divisions of the philosophical discourse which preceded, so that, as §5.9.8 says, philosophy is left "to those who are going to be penalised in this world." The philosophized Trishagion in §5.9.6 is a striking example of this attitude.

§6.1.1 is of course doxological and could well be secondary.

Taking these passages as a whole, it seems to us that what is implicit in §§3.1.5ff is made explicit in Christian language in §§5.9.4ff.

A further, broader consideration is also relevant. In the literary structure we have a number of significant subscriptions of sections. The major ones are §§1.6.16-17 which is the conclusion to the Useful Kinds; §4.3.5 which contains two parts: (a) a summary of subjects of Categories concluding with the words "in the existent" and (b) a larger conclusion, which reads "the second part, etc. (p. 27)." We think this "second part" is all of §2.0.0 to §4.3.5. The third major subscription is in §§5.9.8ff. which is also the conclusion of the whole book.

So we have three major parts:

    a. Useful kinds §§1.0.0-1.6.17

    b. Logic, etc., etc. §§2.0.0-4.3.5

    c. Cosmology and perhaps ethics §§5.0.0-5.9.8

If this is correct, then this structure is Trinitarian. According to §1.6.18 end, section a is "definitions of the first thing/word of the triad" = Christ; in section b, §4.3.5 "speaking with God" = God the

---

⁵⁵ The theme of the ὁμοίωσις θεῷ which dominates the rest of this chapter is not necessarily Christian.

Father; in §5.9.4 "the one which goes forth" = the Holy Spirit, see "spirit hovering" in Genesis 1 and further the whole remainder of this section. This conclusion, if correct, supplements the detailed indications given above.

We may conclude, therefore, that author was a Christian philosopher of the late sixth century or a little later. He is writing in the tradition of ancient philosophy, but does so as a Christian and shows an integration of Christian and philosophical concepts, but in a very restrained way.

b. *Translated from Greek*

Above, in section 2 we alluded to the opinion of Schmidt and Westerink that pseudo-Zeno was composed in Armenian, and we dissented from it. Indeed, pseudo-Zeno's *Untitled Philosophical Treatise* is clearly a translation made from Greek. This is evident from its Hellenizing language and unique neologisms created by the translator, mainly rendering Greek compound words. Most of them are technical terms which were needed to communicate the scholarly ideas with which the treatise deals. A complete list of the words unique to pseudo-Zeno is given at the end of the present book.

In addition to these general considerations, there are a couple of specific points at which the Armenian is only explicable as a mistranslation of Greek or as a faithful translation of an inner-Greek corruption. These are discussed in the Notes on the Translation of paragraphs §3.1.4 and §§5.5.1-5.

It is appropriate to consider why pseudo-Zeno's *Anonymous Philosophical Treatise* was chosen for translation. It formed part of the deliberate construction of an Armenian-language intellectual context, based on the achievements of Greco-Roman science and philosophy, with which to buttress Armenian Christian ideology.[56] After the Council of Chalcedon in 451 and the subsequent process of division between the Armenian and Byzantine churches,[57] it became even

---

[56] The Armenians, to establish their own historiography in the context of religious historical writing, widely used early Greek historiography. This is clear in medieval Armenian histories, most strikingly, perhaps, in *History of the Armenians* attributed to Moses of Xorēn, but in many other sources as well. See for an English translation R.W. Thomson, *Moses Khorenatsi: History of the Armenians* (Harvard Armenian Texts and Studies, 4; Cambridge, MA, Harvard, 1978).

[57] See the recent article by N. Garsoïan, "La date." For previous views consult Karekin Sarkissian, *The Council of Chalcedon and the Armenian Church* (New York,

more pressing for Armenia, which encountered political problems expressed through confessional controversies, to have a strong philosophical background for dogmatic debates. An example of this is *The Refutation of Heresies* (also called *de Deo*) by Eznik Kołbac'i: the dates for this writing proposed by different scholars vary from the fifth to the sixth century.[58] The work of pseudo-Zeno, like many other works of the Hellenizing school, containing concise information from different sciences, provided an appropriate intellectual background for Christian ideas.

c. *Style*

Since pseudo-Zeno's difficult style is one of its foremost characteristics, its causes should be further considered. In part, it may be due to this not being a polished literary work, but merely notes for a larger work or a summary of a lecture course in philosophy, or some similar document. Indeed, J. Mansfeld believes that "what we have here is a first draft, a collection of notes made for a series of lectures with the intention of turning them into a book, an intention never realized".[59] In addition, the difficult language of pseudo-Zeno might also result from its complex subject matter. The work covers diverse fields of learning which were expressed mainly by technical terms and many technical terms could be understood in different senses in the various sciences. The accumulation of this terminology, often little explained, sometimes renders the work incomprehensible unless the intellectual context is known from other sources. For example in §3.1.4 we find the mysterious phrase "Whence is 'definition' known? — From the agrarian proof". "The agrarian proof" can be understood against the background of David, *Prol.* 15.11-12 and similar material in Elias.[60] If we did not have those parallels, this rendering would be completely incomprehensible.

Moreover, the very Hellenizing language itself adds a further layer of obfuscation to that already engendered by the summary

---

1965).

[58] L. Mariès and Chr. Mercier, *Eznik, De Deo* (Patrologia Orientalis, 28.4; Paris, 1959). The extensive literature on this work is listed by R.W. Thomson, *A Bibliography of Classical Armenian Literature to 1500* (Corpus Christianorum; Turnhout, 1995), 117-121.

[59] Personal communication.

[60] See Schmidt, 28 and notes on our translation.

presentation, the technical terminology and the obscurity of part of
the intellectual background. Its stereotypical character is so dominant
that the sense of many expressions can only be perceived through the
Greek original. Since pseudo-Zeno lacks a Greek text, sometimes the
interpretation of a passage depends on hypothetical retroversion into
Greek. Nonetheless, Hellenizing translations are very literal and do
not usually add to or omit from their Greek originals, so we may
assume that this obscure style faithfully reflects that of the Greek
original, the style of which was typical for the Greek compilers,
commentators and other authors in the early Christian centuries.[61]

d. *Hellenizing Morphological and Syntactic Features*

The Hellenizing School, as we observed in section 3, created not only
lexical neologisms[62] but also new grammatical forms, since its imita-
tion of Greek was on lexical, morphological and syntactical levels. In
pseudo-Zeno we have examples of the obscure diction created by this
process, such as the following expressions. These and others like
them signalled in the Notes on the Translation, are not readily
comprehensible in Armenian.

a. §3.2.1 *զայլմէցն*, which could be considered as a composition from
ablative singular of pronoun *այլ* - *այլմէ* + the ending of genitive or
ablative plural *-ցն*. This might be retroverted as *τῶν (περὶ) ἄλλου.
With its initial *զ-* (*nota accusativi*) compare also unusual use of *nota
accusativi* in §5.2.3 *զանդրէն* "from there, from it" (literally "from this
place"); §4.2.5 *ի զինչէումն* "in quiddity"; §4.2.2 *զենթակայէ* "from
subject" or "from person".

b. Twice the translator uses a literal rendering of the Greek πέφυκε +
infinitive to mean "he used to": §5.3.7 *բնաւորեցաւ գոլ* "he used to be"
and §1.2.2 *բնաւորեցան գոլ* "they used to be".

c. Often translators of Hellenizing School rendered one Greek word
by hendiadîs, using two Armenian words in an attempt to make the
meaning of the Greek more explicit. Examples are: §1.5.7 *գոյգ եւ բաւ
կշռով*, "according to an equally balanced"; §1.5.10 *պատերազմունք
մարտիցն*, "wars and battles," etc.

---

[61] It can be observed in the writings of pseudo-Aristotle, Elias, Albinus, Ammonius, Galenus and others.

[62] A list of *hapaxlegomena* and *dislegomena* in pseudo-Zeno is to be found at the
end of the present book. The number of them is striking.

d. There are words which the translator did not translate but just transliterated: e.g., §2.5 *միմոսութիւն* from the Greek μιμήσις.[63]

e. *Structure and Content*

Pseudo-Zeno survives in two recensions, one long and the other short. The long recension is almost double the length of the short recension. It seems clear that the additional material preserved in the long recension is nearly all original, but that the order of the material in the long recension is confused. This point was already appositely made by Xač'ikyan.[64] He also realised that in §1.6 and particularly in §§1.6.9-11 the listing of the four parts of erudition with their subdivisions is equally a table of contents of the latter part of the book.[65] This "table of contents" covers all the material from our §2 to the end, except for two paragraphs, §2.4 which occurs only in the long recension and §2.5 which occurs only in the short recension. We have included them both in our text, for completeness' sake, but they are most probably secondary. The whole of part 1 is not included in §1.6, but clearly must have preceded it.

In order to present this situation more clearly, we give the text of §§1.6.9-11 and following each subdivision we write the number of the paragraph of pseudo-Zeno in which that subdivision is explicated. We italicise those section titles that are missing from the short recension.

From this table it is immediately clear that the contents of parts 2–4 of the book correspond, with some differences of order, to the list in §§1.6.9–11, and the same order is also preserved in the parts of the text that survive in the manuscripts of the short recension.[66]

1.6.9 *But erudition (ἐπιστήμη) is art and it is divided into four species,*

into the practical,	2.1–2.3
and into the reasonable,	3.1–3.3 (with some disruption of order)
into the theoretical	4.1–4.3
and into the comprehensible.	5.1–5.9

---

[63] The word *կազդեանց* in §2.1.1 has no meaning in Armenian. Judging from the context it could be the proper name, perhaps transliterated, but from what?

[64] Xač'ikyan, 67.

[65] *Ibid.*

[66] Even though B and C are lacunose at the end, we consider it most likely that they reflect a recension of the same scope as manuscript D. See below on this. Schmidt has also discussed these issues on pp. 8-14.

And the practical (πρακτικόν),

into administrative (οἰκονομικόν),	2.1.0
into moral (ἠθικόν),	2.2.0
and into political (πολιτικόν).	2.3.0

And the reasonable (λογικόν),

into the demonstrating (ἀποδεικτικόν)	*3.2.0*
into the dialectical (διαλεκτικόν),	*3.2.2*
into the sophistical (σοφιστικόν),	*3.3.0*
into the divisible (διαιρετικόν),	*3.1.0*
into the analytical (ἀναλυτικόν),	*3.3.2*
into the definitional (ὁριστικόν).	*3.1.0*

1.6.10 *And the theoretical, by means of which (is) the searchable,*

into the intentional,	*4.1.0?*
into the inseparable definition,	*4.2.0*
into the categories of beings,	*4.2.8*
into the opposites,	*4.3.0*
into a cause of ascription, under which, partly (is) reference,	*4.3.2*
into the quality of the dogmatic.	*4.3.3*

1.6.11 *To the comprehensible (belong):*

evil and good,	*5.1.0*
time,	*5.3.0*
perfection,	*5.2.0*
beginning and end,	*5.4.0*
nature,	*5.5.0*
definitional and efficient, being,	*5.6.0*
matter and movement,	*5.7.0*
void,	5.8.0
infinity.	*5.9.0*

Xač'ikyan compares this four-fold division of philosophy with that of Elias, saying:

> Moreover, Elias' *Commentary on the Categories of Aristotle* was very widely known in Armenian philosophical literature and influenced a number

of philosophical treatises and commentaries. In that work philosophy is divided into three parts and not into four as in our work: 'philosophy is divided into three—the theoretical, the practical and the rational'. Zeno's fourth division is 'the intelligible'.[67]

f. *Structure of the Text according to the Manuscripts*

Only manuscript A preserves an almost complete copy. Its sections, however, are in a different order to that found in manuscripts BCD (given immediately above), and are set forth here:

0.0.0	1.2.0-4
	1.3.0-5
5.1.1-10	1.4.0-11
5.2.0-12	1.5.0-14
	1.6.0-18
2.0.0-1	
2.0.1	5.4.0-8
2.1.1	5.5.0-5
2.2.0-3	
2.3.0-7	3.1.0-16
2.4.0-2	3.2.0-3
2.4.1-2	3.3.0-2
5.3.0-9	5.6.0-4
1.0.0-1	4.1.0-3
1.1.1-6	4.2.0-15
4.3.0-5	5.9.0-8
5.7.0-4	6.1.1
5.8.0-2	

---

[67] *Ibid.* Xač'ikyan (see p. 67), guided by his view that the work was written by Zeno, then proceeds to explain how its putative later editor structured Zeno's original writing according to his own quadripartite division of philosophy, itself a development of a tripartite division found in Elias' *Commentary on Aristotle*, etc. The first part of the book, "On the Useful Kinds" is, according to him, another piece of Zeno's writing, and §1.6.4 is a bridging passage. All this discussion becomes superfluous once Zeno's authorship is rejected.

An examination of this order shows no particular rationale, and it contradicts the order of the sections set forth in §§1.6.9-11. What is clear is that the whole of part 1, i.e., §§1.0-1.6 has been displaced from the beginning. Parts 2, 3 and 4 follow sequentially, but between them sections of part 5 are interspersed. Even these sections of part 5 are sequential in occurrence.[68] A comparison of this table with the above list of contents reveals no relationship between the sections omitted from manuscripts BCD in the process of abbreviation and the order of the sections in A or between that order and the minor differences of the order in BCD §§1.6.9-11.

Manuscripts BCD all have the same shortened text-form, except that manuscripts B and C are both incomplete at the end. Manuscripts B and D run from the beginning to the end of §2.3.7. Next comes *յաղագս Բովանդակութեան* "On Content" (§2.5.0). B has been taken as the base of collation of this section; B's title for it adds the words *յայլ գրոց* "from another manuscript". Clearly B and D have a common *Vorlage*, and it may be that this title of B in §2.5.0 came from that *Vorlage*. In that case, the scribe of the *Vorlage* presumably drew this section from a manuscript other than his exemplar. His original probably came to an end with §2.3.7 and he then found another copy from which he continued in §2.5.0.

Manuscript C stops altogether with §1.6.0 in the middle of a sentence. A small colophon ensues. Because it shares a hyparchetype with BD and a hyp-hyparchetype with D, its original may be assumed to have contained the same span of text as BD.

Thus the book starts with the "Necessary Kinds" (part 1), which are cosmology, geometry, arithmetic, astrology, medicine. Then ensue the four parts of "Erudition" (cf. §1.6.9): the practical (pseudo-Zeno part 2), the reasonable (pseudo-Zeno part 3), the theoretical (pseudo-Zeno part 4), and the comprehensible (pseudo-Zeno part 5). Thus, one major division of this treatise is into two: On Necessary Kinds (part 1) and "Erudition" (parts 2-5). This is the structure inferred by Xač'ikyan from §§1.6.9-11 and supported, directly and indirectly, by the contents of the manuscripts. However, as we showed above, in section 4a of this Introduction, attention to the subscriptions of the sections reveals another structure which is Trinitarian in character. Both structures seem to exist in the book simultaneously.

---

[68] In the electronic edition of this text, a full transcription of manuscript A showing its foliation is to be found.

Since, within each part and each section, the author is enumerating the divisions of his particular topic, it is tempting to attempt to draw a "tree" of parts, groups, subgroups etc. Schmidt did this to some measure, comparing in tabular form the ways that philosophy was divided by Aristotelians and Platonists with that in pseudo-Zeno.[69] Were it feasible to map out all this "genealogy" of the Necessary Kinds and of Erudition, further subtleties of the presentation might emerge and different parts of the work might illuminate one another. In fact, however, the structure of the thought is not so rigorous as to make this type of complete schematic presentation feasible.

5. *Sources Utilized by pseudo-Zeno*

Lists of sources utilized by pseudo-Zeno were made by L. Xač'ikyan,[70] S. Arevšatyan[71] and E.G. Schmidt.[72] The notes on the translation, given below, make no claim to being an exhaustive commentary on pseudo-Zeno from the perspective of the history of philosophy. However, in them the sources and parallels judged most clearly relevant have been noted. The range of these sources, incidentally, puts the final nail of anachronism into the coffin of Zeno's proposed authorship of the work.

The following are the chief sources cited in our Notes on the Translation. Those authors whose names are emphasized seem to be known to pseudo-Zeno, while ideas of the others are to be found in indirect transmission or similar ideas to his occur in their works.

Aristotle (directly or through an epitome or commentaries)
Bible (see above, section 4a)
David, *Prolegomena, Commentaries* (?)
Dionysius Thrax
Divisiones Aristotelae

---

69 Schmidt, 14-16.

70 Xač'ikyan, 73-76. Xač'ikyan mainly compared this text with those preserved in ancient Armenian translation, so, he does not cite any Greek texts directly.

71 S.S. Arevšatyan, 319-321. Arevšatyan tends to see elements of Stoic philosophy in pseudo-Zeno. For example, he points to ideas of the four original elements of the universe, the unity of universe or the negation of the void.

72 Passim.

Elias, *Prolegomena*
Epicurus, *Epistula Pythoclem* (?)
Lucretius (?)
Περὶ κόσμου (?)
Plato, *Phaedo, Timaeus*
Porphyry
"The Pythagoreans" (named in the text)
Seneca, *Naturales Quaestiones*

As is clear from the above, there are Platonic and Neoplatonic ideas
in this work. However, pseudo-Zeno mainly reflects philosophical
ideas of the Aristotelian tradition. As a proof one can cite many
points of dependence on different works of Aristotle and on commentaries on them, which are given in the Notes on the Translation.
The Pythagoreans are the only Greek philosophers named by pseudo-
Zeno (§3.1.6). His love of arithmology is doubtless drawn from a
Pythagoreanizing tradition.[73]

The question may be posed of the translator's technique at points
at which pseudo-Zeno is citing a Greek source, well known in
Armenian. Did he simply translate the Greek text of pseudo-Zeno that
he had before him, including its citations, or did he consult existing
Armenian translations of the sources cited by pseudo-Zeno?[74]
Certainly the majority of the sources cited by pseudo-Zeno were
translated directly from Greek as integral parts of the work. However,
in a few instances, the translator used existing Armenian translations
of the sources. Most such cases are common *topoi* which may be found
all over Armenian philosophical literature, translated and original.[75]
Consequently, it is difficult to determine their precise source.

For example, in the case of the list of the eight parts of speech
(§2.3.4), the translator might have drawn directly on the Armenian
version of Dionysius Thrax or else on one of many other Armenian
authors who have exactly the same passage.[76] Since this is a list of

---

[73] See D.J. O'Meara, *Pythagoras Revived: Mathematics and Philosophy in Late
Antiquity* (Oxford, 1989) who shows to what extent Pythagoreans like Nicomachus
of Gerasa influenced later Platonism via Iamblichus.

[74] Indeed, the matter is even more complex. Because such citations are usually
replete with technical terms, and since there were stereotyped translations for the
technical terms, in fact an new translation might be more or less *litteratim* identical
with an existing one.

[75] See the dictum discussed in the next paragraph.

[76] Nicolas Adontz, *Denys de Thrace et les Commentateurs Arméniens: traduit du russe*
(Bibliothèque arménienne de la Fondation Calouste Gulbenkian; Louvain, 1970),

eight parts of speech using their Greek and Armenian names, it would have been surprising to find differences in it.[77] In §3.1.14 we find the famous but spurious definition attributed (by the late commentators) to Aristotle of philosophy as τέχνη τεχνῶν καὶ ἐπιστήμη ἐπιστημῶν. This definition is already found (without being attributed) in Philo of Alexandria in the first century CE, *De specialibus legibus* IV.156.[78] It is very common among the Greek late Neoplatonists: Proclus (once), Ammonius (four times), Asclepius (three times), Olympiodorus (once), Philoponus (twice), Simplicius (once), David (twenty-three times in the *Prolegomena* alone), Elias (four times) and is also found in Armenian sources like the Armenian translation of David's *Prolegomena*.[79] In this case, the Armenian of pseudo-Zeno is *verbatim* identical with David. It might have been borrowed straight from this Armenian translation or it might have been a *topos* of the Armenian school tradition. Note that in most of the authors cited (and not only in David) the definition is found together with other definitions of philosophy, just as in pseudo-Zeno.

6. *Date*

The works of David and Elias seem to provide a *terminus post quem* for pseudo-Zeno because pseudo-Zeno clearly used both of them. So, pseudo-Zeno was probably composed in the sixth century or later in Greek and subsequently translated into the Armenian. Schmidt holds it to have been composed in the seventh century, but a late sixth-century date is also possible.[80]

Greek §11 = Armenian §12.12.

[77] The list of ten categories cited in §4.2.8 is very similar. It is found elsewhere in manuscript A, fol. 222v, titled "10 Categories of Aristotle."

[78] In Philo, it refers not exactly to philosophy, but to the art of government. It recurs in the Emperor Julian's Εἰς τοὺς ἀπαιδεύτους κύνας §3 (without being attributed, and together with the "becoming like a god" definition), and in the Desert Father, Isidore of Pelusium (ca. 365-ca. 435), *Epist.* Lib. V, no. CLVIII in Migne, *PG*, p. 1637. In Isidore it is not attributed to anyone in particular either, but it is listed together with definitions of philosophy attributed to Pythagoras, Plato and Chrysippus. It was also known to the Christian authors Gregory Nazianzus (once), Didymus Caecus (once) and John of Damascus (seven times).

[79] Frequently, see B. Kendall and R.W. Thomson, *Definitions and Divisions of Philosophy by David the Invincible Philosopher* (University of Pennsylvania Armenian Texts and Studies, 5; Chico, CA, 1983), e.g., 56ff.

[80] Schmidt, 45.

L. Xač'ikyan is disposed to think that it was translated at the beginning of seventh century because he regarded its translation as belonging to the third period of the Hellenizing School's activity. This third period provides the date mentioned.[81] S.S. Arevšatyan assumes that it was translated in sixth-seventh centuries by a Christian translator and then edited by a monastic scribe in the thirteenth-fourteenth centuries.[82]

7. *Significance of the Translation*

Pseudo-Zeno did not circulate widely in Armenia. Three of the four manuscripts which have survived are of the thirteenth-fourteenth centuries. No earlier manuscript of or reference to the work has been found. Since it was most likely translated in the seventh century, the inception of the surviving manuscript tradition in the high middle ages is doubtless due to the "university" tradition of Armenian monastic learning at that time.[83] That tradition came to include pseudo-Zeno, to some extent at least, in its curriculum.

8. *The Manuscripts and the Edition*

The Contents of the Manuscripts

As is noted above, pseudo-Zeno survives in long and the short recensions. The long recension is preserved in a single manuscript, while three copies of the short recension survive. The *New Dictionary of the Armenian Language (NBH)* published in Venice in 1836 cites

---

[81] Xač'ikyan also says that pseudo-Zeno precedes the work of Anania Širakac'i (c. 600-c.670) though he does not explain the reason for this statement. See Xač'ikyan, 76. Recent scholarship has called into question the division of the Hellenizing school into clearly datable schools.

[82] Arevšatyan, 321-322. Presumably behind this view stands his need to explain the Christian elements in a philosophical work he supposed to be pagan.

[83] See Xač'ikyan, 77 and Arevšatyan, 321. A long citation from pseudo-Zeno is found in a degree thesis of one of the pupils of Gladzor University; Matenadaran manuscript M631, 89v-90r of the fifteenth century, cited by Xač'ikyan, *ibid.*

phrases from pseudo-Zeno in its entries for certain words. Pseudo-Zeno is cited by *NBH* under the title *Տօնական*, "Festal Calendar". Such citations are found, for example, with the words *եռակաբար*, *անկրական*, *Համեստական* and *պադպաջմունք*. We can infer, therefore, that a manuscript of the *Տօնական* "Festal Calendar" preserved in the library of manuscripts in Venice contains a copy of pseudo-Zeno. Unfortunately, our approaches to the Library of the Mechitarist Fathers to obtain a copy of this manuscript have not been successful. Judging from the citations contained in *NBH*, Xač'ikyan concluded that this fifth manuscript was of the short recension.[84]

Long Recension:

A Matenadaran manuscript M5254 of 1280 CE from the Monastery of Deǰjut (Armenia)[85] copied by the scribe Geworg.

The contents of the manuscript indicate the context in which pseudo-Zeno was transmitted. This is an important collection of theological, scholastic and philosophical works and contains, *inter alia*:

> 125v-131v: Yovhannēs Sarkawag "On Angular Numbers"; 133r-135r: The "Cause" of Nemesius' "On Nature"; fols. 181v: Discourse from Another Writing; 182v-190r: A Small Discourse from the Physiologus; 190r-202v: Discourse of Philo; 202v-204r: Philosophy about Divinity; 217v-217v: Aristotle, *Peri hermeneias*; fols. 212v-220v: Rhetorician, "On Nature";[86] fols. 220v-222v: Philosophical Definitions;[87] fols. 222v: 10 Categories of Aristotle; 223r-223v: About the Movements; 223v-227r: Commentary on Aristotle's Categories; 227v: The "Tree" (the ten Aristotelian categories) of Philosophy; 231r-237r: From the medical book "On the Nature of Man"; 237r-237v: About the Movement; 238v-256r: Another Discourse (i.e., pseudo-Zeno); 256r-256v: On the Categories; 256v: The Book of Essences by David the Philosopher.[88]

Short Recension:

B Matenadaran manuscript M627 of 1314 CE, copied by the scribe

---

[84] Xač'ikyan, 66.

[85] Apparently identical with Deǰjnuti Vank', no. 676 in Michel Thierry, *Répertoire des monastères arméniens* (Corpus Christianorum; Turnhout, 1993).

[86] This short philosophical text with the following one was preserved presumably in a twelfth-century compilation of translated philosophical treatises (both of them are Hellenizing translations). Both those texts are edited by S. S. Arevšatian ("Two Ancient Philosophical Fragments - 'Rhetorician, On Nature' and 'Philosophical Definitions' ") and with a brief introduction and translation into Russian are published in *Banber Matenadarani*, 5 (1960) 371-392. See Zuckerman, 11-12.

[87] See note 86.

[88] See the detailed listing in Xač'ikyan, 77-79. The scribe's colophon does not indicate anything about the purpose for which the manuscript was copied.

Xačik in Čanči Xur.

This manuscript contains *inter alia*:

> 205-213: Explanations of Aristotle, *de mundo*; 213-236v: Explanations of
> Porphyry; 236v-261v: Explanations of *Categories* of Aristotle; 262-269:
> Explanations of *Book of Definitions*; 269v-275v: Concerning Knowledge
> of Useful Kinds (i.e., pseudo-Zeno).

C Matenadaran manuscript M3487 of 1389 CE copied by the known
scribe Jacob of Crimea in the region Toxat' (Eutokia, Ekedia) in the
Church of Kabos. This manuscript contains:

> pp. 4-95: Short Miscellany concerning the soul and its virtues; pp. 97-
> 165: Concerning the virtues of the soul; pp. 166-276: Concerning the
> nature of angels; pp. 278-287: pseudo-Zeno, without a title.

D Matenadaran 1823 of 1731 copied by the scribe Mesrob in
Ējmiacin.

This manuscript contains:

> 13-231v: Commentary on the Books of Proclus by Bishop Simeon of
> Gaṙni; 231v-245v: Mattēos *vardapet* on the Hexaemeron at the request
> of Sargis the Monk; Aristotle *Analytica,* etc.; 386-392v: Concerning the
> Useful Kinds of Zeno the Philosopher.

No other copies are known to exist in the Matenadaran or other
libraries except for the copy mentioned above that was in Venice in
the first half of the nineteenth century.

Manuscript A

This is the fullest manuscript of the *De natura*. It is the sole witness to
the text for a substantial number of the sections of the work. In the
editio princeps, Xač'ikyan used the text of this manuscript for much of
the book, but rearranged the order of the sections. A discussion of
the sections of the work surviving in all four manuscripts is given
below.

The title of the work in A is simply *Այլ բան* "Another Discourse". In
the section titles in the last part of the work, the last word is usually
առանձին "a separate section". This may indicate that these sections
came from another source. Such instances are §§5.3.0, 5.4.0, 5.5.0 etc.
The following are the general scribal characteristics of A and a record
of abbreviations and scribal phenomena which have not been
included in the edition itself.

Numerals are usually abbreviated. We note the following abbreviations and give some instances of each.

Ա	առաջին	3.1.3 4.2.2 5.2.2 5.3.5 5.4.3 5.6.2 5.7.3
Բ	երկու	1.6.16 5.6.1
Բ	երկրորդ	3.1.4 4.2.8 5.3.6 5.6.3 5.7.4 5.9.3
Բին	երկրորդին	5.9.2
Գ	երիս	1.5.2
Գից	երից	1.3.1
Գ	երրորդ	1.1.3 5.2.6 5.3.7 5.4.5
գԳորդ	գերրորդ	1.3.3
Դ	չորք	1.5.1 4.1.1 4.2.12
Դ	չորս	3.1.1 3.1.2 3.1.6 4.2.3 4.2.10
Դ	չորրորդ	5.1.2 5.2.8 5.3.8
Դանկին	չորեքանկին	1.1.5
Ե	հինգ	4.2.4
Ե	հինգերորդ	1.1.5 5.1.5 5.2.9
Զ	վեց	1.0.1 1.1.1 1.4.11 2.3.2 3.1.5 3.1.7 3.1.7 4.3.4
վեցդ	վեցերորդ	1.1.6
Զեակն	վեցեակն	1.6.16
Զեկին	վեցեկին	5.9.1
Է	եւթն	1.3.3 1.3.5
Ը	ութ	2.3.4
ԲԺան	երկուտասան	1.4.4
ԲԺանեկին	երկուտասանեկին	3.1.7
ԺԳիցն	երեքտասանիցն	5.3.4
ԹԺեակն	իննետասաներեակն	5.3.3
ԻՉիւք	քսանութիւք	5.3.3

However, numerals are not always abbreviated, so at §3.1.6 we may observe չորից written in full.

In addition the following unusual abbreviations should be noted:

գն	գլուխն	1.4.7
պն	պարանոցն	1.4.7
ոն	ուսն	1.4.7
լն	լանջքն	1.4.8
ձ	ձեռն	1.4.8 1.4.8

ծխ	ծախ	1.4.9
են	երանքն	1.4.9
քն	քարձքն	1.4.10
թն	թաթք	1.4.10
բա	բաժանի	3.1.2

Preservation The manuscript is lacunose in a number of places and damage has carried away part of the text, e.g., on fols. 245-246. There are places throughout the manuscript where the ink has faded or rubbed.

Corrections There are a number of corrections and different signs of correction in the manuscript. On fol. 248v a dot above a letter marks a correction below the line. In §§3.1.4, 4.2.5 erasure is marked by two dots above the letter to be erased and one below. A single dot above and below the letter marks an erasure in §5.9.2. In §4.2.11 the erasure of a *p* is marked by two horizontal dots above the letter, differing from the previously mentioned dots.

Titles Groups of three dots are written over words in titles, which titles are also written in a smaller script. On fol. 254v we see groups of three rising dots over a subscription, similarly on fol. 255r. On fol. 255v a title is marked by a diamond of four dots above and below it. On fol. 241r the scribe starts using a new, or different, stylus.

Orthography The orthography is generally standard, though there are often omissions of intervocalic *yi*. The copyist proof-read his manuscript and corrected it, most often *inter lineas*, so §§3.1.5, 3.1.7, 5.4.6, 5.9.2 etc. These cases are noted in the second apparatus.

*Manuscript **B***

The manuscript is incomplete. Moreover, there is a displacement of one folio, perhaps due to an error in the course of renovation or rebinding. Present fol. 274r-v should follow present 271r. The manuscript has many corrections of scribal errors *prima manu*, often interlinear. It seems to have been copied rather carelessly. It has been copied by more than one scribe, though there is no indication of a change of exemplar.

The paper seems to have soaked up the ink and on the photographs one may discern the writing, in mirror form, of the other side of the folio or of the facing page. This characteristic of the paper probably explains the unclear and blurred character of some of the writing.

The abbreviation mark is sometimes omitted, thus on *թնութեան* in §1.5.4, *առողջութթ* §1.5.7, and in many other cases. Two dots indicate an erasure in §2.3.2. As has been noted in the Textual Commentary, **B** tends to shorten words to one syllable, or to omit a final syllable of words with no marking.

It is clear that the *Vorlage* of **B** was itself damaged. On occasion the scribe of **B** has left a *vacat*, where he could not decipher his *Vorlage*. Moreover, sometimes the letters preceding or following such a *vacat* are read incorrectly, indicating that in the *Vorlage* only part of the letter survived and the scribe made a wrong guess at it.

Manuscript **B** runs from the beginning to the end of §2.3.7. Next comes *Յաղագս բովանդակութեան* "On Content" (§2.5.0). This section survives only in **B** and **D**; we have used **B** as the base of collation for it. **B**'s title of *Յաղագս բովանդակութեան* "On Content" has the additional words *յայլ գրոց* "from another manuscript" or "writing". Clearly **B** and **D** had a common *Vorlage*, and it may be that this title of §2.5.0 in **B** came from that *Vorlage* and reflects its scribe's activity. His original came to an end with §2.3.7 and he then found another copy from which he continued in §2.5.0.

B has ideograms for *աշխարհ* in §1.3.4 1.4.1 and for *աստղ* in §1.4.4.

Numerals are abbreviated, and the following instances serve as examples. This is quite commonplace.

Դից	չորից	1.4.1
Ջ	վեց	1.4.11
Է	եւթն	1.3.5bis

Manuscript C

The manuscript is incomplete: see above. At the end there is a colophon: *զյակոբ որիմեցի սպասաւոր բանին աղաչեմ յիշել ի տէր* "I beg to remember Jacob of the Crimea, servant of the Word, to the Lord." According to N. Bogharian, *Հայ Գրողներ* (*Armenian Writers*), Jerusalem, 1971, Jacob lived between 1350 and 1426. Scribe and author, he was trained by Geworg Erznkac'i. In 1389 he lived in Kapos Vank' were he copied a *Miscellany* for Abraham the priest. He also lived in Mecop' in 1416 and died in Arclē in 1426. In 1415 he edited the sermons of Vardan Arewelc'i. He is the author of *Canons on the*

Marriage of Minors, A Commentary on the Calendar, a small work on geometry; Sermons for Good Friday, on Repentance and on the Transfiguration; a Synopsis of Nehemiah, Tobit and Maccabees; and a poem on Saint Sargis. Thus he was a considerable author of wide interests, as well as a copyist.

The manuscript has an ideogram for *որպէս* and abbreviations of numerals, of which the following are examples:

Ղ	*շորք*	1.5.1
Ղ	*շորս*	1.6.9
Ջ	*վեց*	1.4.11
Է	*եւթն*	1.3.5bis
Թձ	*երկոտասան*	1.4.5

Manuscript **D**

The manuscript is incomplete. Dittography may be observed in §1.6.13. In §5.8.2 it has the ideogram for *որպէս* and in §4.2.5 a superfluous *ն* is marked by a dot above it. The letters *եւ* are frequently ligatured and numerals are abbreviated, as in the following examples:

Բ	*երկուս*	§4.2.10
Գ	*երրորդ*	4.2.10
Ղ	*շորս*	§1.6.9
Ղ	*շորք*	1.5.1 4.2.12
Ե	*հինգ*	4.2.4
Ջ	*վեց*	1.4.11
Ջեկի	*վեցեկի*	§5.9.1
Է	*եւթն*	1.3.5bis
ղ	*տասն*	4.2.8
Թղ	*երկոտասան*	1.4.4

Relationship between the Manuscripts

The manuscripts fall into two groups, **A** and **BCD**. **A** is distinguished from **BCD** by some overall factors and by a series of readings.

1. **A** has substantially more text than do **BCD**. **C** is incomplete, breaking off at the bottom of a page. The following is a list of blocks missing in the various manuscripts.

*Manuscripts **ABCD***

The following sections are supplied by the editors and are missing from all manuscripts.

2.1.0 3.0.0 4.0.0 5.1.0

*Manuscript **A***

Section 0.0.0 follows 4.3.5

The order of the text in **A** is quite different to that in **BCD**. Those three manuscripts have the identical order of text and the same quantity of text as long as they run parallel. Since **C** breaks off early, in §1.6.9, its evidence is not sustained throughout. **BD** run together until **B** breaks off in §4.2.8 and thereafter **D** continues on its own as the sole representative this group. As far as can be determined, these manuscripts contained the following sections of text and in the following order.[89]

§§1.0.0-2.3.7 2.5.0-5 4.2.0-15 5.8.0-5.9.2.

Since **C** had already stopped at §1.6.9, we cannot determine whether the sections numbered §§2.5.0- 2.5.5, which do not occur in **A**, were actually in **C**, but this is most likely. After §4.2.8 where **B** stops, the only witnesses are **A** and **D**, and substantial parts of the text do not occur in **D**. All the text in **BCD** also occurs in **A**, except for §2.5.0-5.

In view of this, it seems to be likely that **BCD** go back to a common hyparchetype, which was shorter than **A** and in a different order. Xačik'yan followed the order of **BCD** and the contents of **A**. The order of text that he adopted is discussed above (see pp. 21-23). The absence of sections is indicated in the apparatus criticus, at the beginning of the variants for each section.

If the first bifurcation is accepted on these grounds, the question still remains of the relationship of **A** with each of **B**, **C** and **D** and with groups of them, and of **BCD** among themselves. The substantial variants, not including purely orthographic and technical phenomena, were taken from the collations output generated by Collate and the data set so created was manipulated with two different programs to produce stemmata. They produced the following

---

[89] Manuscript C does not have the section titles. It leaves blanks for their rubrication, which was never effected.

stemmata which are the most likely reflection of the readings. It will be observed that although the graphic representation is different, the actual manuscript relationships exhibited by the two stemmata are very similar. The same manuscript relations were also uncovered and will be demonstrated using traditional methods.

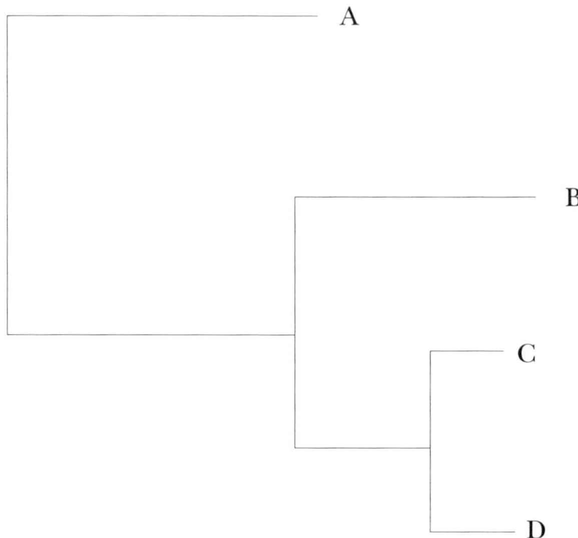

It will be observed that in the following stemma, expression is given to some ambiguities in the relationship of the manuscripts by the box in the middle of the stemma. Were the relationship completely unambiguous, this would not be a box but a single line. These ambiguities are presented in the lists of readings below.

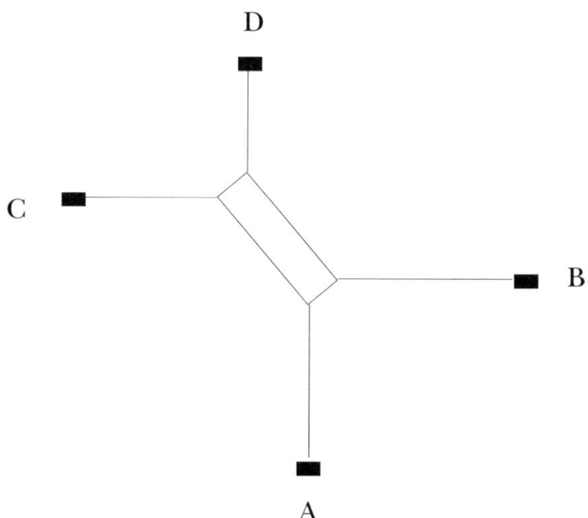

Readings Demonstrating the Bifurcation **A:BCD**

In addition to the considerations of contents and block order noted above, the following readings were noted:

A : BCD

1.1.4 *մարմնական*] *մարմնոյ* BCD

1.2.1 *բնականութեան*] *բնակութեան* BCD

1.2.3 *եւ եղծումն*] omitted BCD

1.3.2 *բացերեւեցան*] *բացերեւեցան* BCD

1.3.2 *ի*] omitted BCD

1.3.3 *է*] omitted BCD

1.4.3 *բոլորակ*] *բոլոր* BCD

1.5.10 *Հարկաբար*] *Հարկաւորաբար* BCD

1.6.4 *ի*] omitted BCD

1.6.4 *ձեռի*] *ձեռ* BCD

1.6.6 *ի վերայ*] omitted BCD

1.6.6 *ախտաստացականից*] *ախտաստացականի* BCD

Less convincing, but still possibly significant readings, are the following.[90]

1.1.6 *փորուած*] *փորուածս* BCD

1.1.6 *բնակութիւն*] *բնակութիւնք* BCD

1.4.3 *ձեւ*] *ձեւս* BCD

1.4.11 *եկաւորի*] *եկաւոր* BCD

These are instances in which the text = **BCD** and **A** is in the apparatus
A: BCD

1.1.1 *տրամագծին*] *անփոփոխ* added A

1.1.1 *փոփոխեալ*] omitted A

1.1.2 *բաղկացեալ*] *պարփակեալ* added A

1.1.7 *աստեղատանցն*] *աստեղացն* A

1.2.3 *Հանդիպին նորին*] *Հետեւին* A

1.3.1 *շրջանք*] *զ* added A

1.3.4 *յորս*] *յոր* A

1.3.5 *այսորիկ լուանթագն*] omitted A

1.3.5 *լուսաբերն լուսինն*] *եւ այլքն* A

1.4.2 *իսկ*] *եւ* A

1.4.2 *գանագանեալք*] *գանագանեալ* A

1.4.4 *չափի*] *վաթսուն* added A

1.4.5 *Հաստարակածիր*] *իսկ* added A

1.4.6 *Հող*] *Հողմ* A

1.4.6 *Հաստարակածիր*] *Հաստարակածք* A

1.4.7 *որ է*] *եւ* A

1.4.7 *որ է*] *եւ* A

1.4.7 *որ են*] *եւ* A

1.4.7 *որ է*] *եւ* A

1.4.8 *եղադացող*] *եղադացիք* A

1.4.8 *յունաց եւ*] omitted A

---

[90] The following are readings involving the addition or omission of the suffixed article. These may be found in all manuscript combinations and are too commonplace to have conjunctive significance:

1.4.5 *խեզգետի*] *խեզգետին* BCD

1.4.6 *Հող*] *Հողն* BCD

1.5.8 *արգանդի*] *արգանդին* BCD

1.5.11 *կենացն*] *կենաց* BCD

1.6.9 *տնաւրինական*] *տնաւրինականն* BCD

1.6.9 *քաղաքական*] *քաղաքականն* BCD

1.6.9 *յապացուցական*] *յապացուցականն* BCD

1.6.9 *տրամաբանական*] *տրամաբանականն* BCD

1.4.9 *սրունքն*] *կիլիկեցիք կը կարինճ լիտալացող եւ աւան* A
1.4.10 *որ են*] *եւ* A
1.4.10 *եւ ծունկքն*] *սրունքն* A
1.4.10 *եւ*] *որ* A
1.5.2 *եւ*] omitted A
1.5.3 *նիւթոյ ի*] *նիւթի* A
1.5.3 *Հոսմանէ*] *Հոսման* A
1.5.3 *կրից*] *խառնից* A
1.5.3 *խառնից*] *կրից* A
1.5.4 *այլ*] omitted A
1.5.4 *բնութեան*] omitted A
1.5.4 *անթուելի*] *անթնդելի* A
1.5.5 *եւ*] omitted A
1.5.5 *ուկերք եւ*] *ուկր* A
1.5.7 *եւ*] *են* A
1.5.7 *լինի*] omitted A
1.5.8 *գրտոյ*] *գրոյ* A
1.5.10 *բնութենէն*] *են* added A
1.5.12 *շրջագայութենէ*] *շրջագայէ* A
1.5.14 *բատ*] omitted A
1.6.1 *են որ*] *որք* A
1.6.1 *որ*] *որք* A
1.6.3 *երակի բաժանի*] *եռ*[   ]*նի* A
1.6.3 *գոյն*] *եւ* added A
1.6.3 *իսկ շորից*] [   ] A
1.6.3 *կապոյտ սատ*] [   ]*ս* A
1.6.3 *բաղկանան ի*] [   ] A
1.6.4 *բաժանականին*] [   ]*կանին* A
1.6.4 *երկարն եւ*] *եւ երկարն եւ* A
1.6.6 *եւ*] *է* added A
1.6.7 *բանական*] *բնական* A
1.6.7 *բանական*] *բնական* A
1.6.8 *տեսլենէն*] *են* added A
1.6.9 *գործնական*] *գործական* A
1.6.9 *ի բարոյական*] [   ]*արոյական* A
1.6.9 *ի*] omitted A
1.6.9 *ի*] omitted A
1.6.9 *ի*] omitted A

Addition or omission of *-ն* etc. article **BCD** :: **A**

1.1.4 *մեծամեծաց*] *մեծամեծացն* A

1.1.4 *կենդանեացս*] *կենդանեաց* A

1.1.5 *երկրիս*] *երկիրս* A

1.1.6 *կապուած*] *կապուածս* A

1.2.2 *իմացս*] *իմաց* A

1.3.1 *ունայնին*] *ունայնի* A

1.3.1 *տեսակս*] *տեսակ* A

1.3.3 *երկնիցն*] *երկնից* A

1.4.7 *ցատակից*] *ցատակիցն* A

1.4.7 *խեցգետինն*] *խեցգետին* A

1.5.3 *Հոգւոյ*] *Հոգւոյն* A

1.5.3 *մարմնոյ*] *մարմնոյն* A

1.5.7 *մաղձն*] *մաղձ* A

1.5.7 *արիւնն*] *արիւն* A

1.5.10 *վարք*] *վարքն* A

1.5.14 *անեղին*] *անեղի* A

1.6.3 *խառնուածք*] *խառնուածքն* A

1.6.6 *գերագունին*] *գերագունի* A

1.6.9 *գործնականն*] *գործական* A

A :: **BD** where **C** is not extant

1.6.17 *ունել*] *ունելի* A

1.6.17 *գշարժմունս*] *շարժմունս* A

1.6.18 *որոշմանց*] *որոշման* A

2.3.1 *նախադրի*] *նախադրի* A

2.3.2 *Համեմատութեանց*] *Համեմատութեան* A

2.3.3 *ըստ*] omitted A

2.3.4 *բայ*] *եւ* added A

2.3.5 *աղոյ*] *ուղա* A

2.3.7 *բաժանին*] *բաժանեն* A

2.3.7 *պարսավել*] *պարսաւել* A

4.2.0 *եւ*] omitted A

4.2.2 *որ*] *ոչ* added A

4.2.2 *գենթակայէ*] *է* added A

4.2.4 *ինքեան*] *ինքեանց* A

4.2.4 *տեսակագոյնք*] *տեսագոյնք* A

4.2.4 *սեռականագոյնք*] *եռականագոյնք* A

4.2.4 *եւ*] omitted A

4.2.5 *սահմանաւ ունի*] *սահմանին ի* A

4.2.5 *իբրեւ*] *իբր* A
4.2.5 *սահմանի*] *է* added A
4.2.6 *գոյացութիւն*] *գոյութիւն* A

A : **BD** where **C** is not extant: addition or omission of the article *-ն*, etc.

1.6.10 *կացադրութիւնս*] *կացադրութիւն* A
1.6.18 *ժամուց*] *ժամուցն* A
2.1.1 *ճոխութեան*] *ճոխութեանն* A
2.2.2 *սովորութեան*] *սովորութեանն* A
2.2.3 *կենդանեաց*] *կենդանեացն* A
2.3.5 *բանն*] *բան* A
2.3.6 *քաղաքավարականն*] *քաղաքավարական* A
2.3.7 *բաղխոճականն*] *բախոճականն* A
2.3.7 *յատենականն*] *յատենական* A
2.3.7 *կացրդականն*] *կացրդական* A
2.3.7 *բաղխոճականն*] *բախոճական* A
2.3.7 *կացրդականն*] *կացրդական* A
4.2.4 *գոյացութեան*] *գոյացութեանն* A

Cases of **A** : **D** where **BC** are not extant:

4.2.10 *յոլովութեան*] *յոլովութեանն* A
4.2.10 *տեսակն*] *տեսակ* A
4.2.10 *ամենայն*] *ամեն* A
4.2.11 *քանակին*] *քառակին* A
4.2.11 *որ*] *որք* A
4.2.11 *է*] omitted A
4.2.11 *տեղի*] *տեղ* A
4.2.12 *առընչին*] *առաջինն* A
4.2.12 *ունակութիւն*] *ունակութիւնք* A
4.2.14 *բատ*] omitted A
4.2.15 *ունելն*] *ունել* A
5.8.0 *ունայնի*] *առանձին* added A
5.8.1 *անբաւին*] *բաւին* A
5.8.2 *անբնական*] *անբնակ* A
5.9.4 *արարածոցն*] *արարածոյն* A
5.9.4 *մարդկան*] *եւ* added A
5.9.5 *այլ այս*] lacuna *յայս* A
5.9.7 *երեակք*] *որով* added A

These readings are quite sufficient to demonstrate that **BCD** have a common hyparchetype which is different from **A**.

Readings demonstrating the bifurcation **B** : **CD**

1.0.1 *պիտանացուք*] omitted CD
1.1.1 *բաժանի*] *բաժանին* CD
1.1.5 *է*] omitted CD
1.1.6 *է*] omitted CD
1.3.1 *եւ*] omitted CD
1.3.4 *ըստ*] omitted CD
1.3.4 *տարածմամբ*] *ի* added CD
1.3.5 *են*] omitted CD
1.3.5 *ըստ*] *եւս* CD
1.4.2 *կապոյտ*] *կարմիր* CD
1.4.2 *սաւս*] *դեղին* CD
1.4.3 *քառանկիւնի*] *երկայն* added CD
1.4.3 *այլ*] omitted CD
1.4.4 *ընտրեցան*] *եւ* added CD
1.4.6 *ըստ Հարաւոյ*] omitted CD
1.4.7 *եւ մարդոյն*] omitted CD
1.4.7 *բաբելացիոց*] *բաբելացիք* CD
1.4.7 *եկաւորին*] *եկաւորն* CD
1.4.7 *են*] *է* CD
1.4.7 *Հայոց*] *Հայք* CD
1.4.10 *ծունկքն*] *ծունքն* CD
1.4.10 *թաթք*] *թաթ* CD
1.5.4 *շարատնութեան*] *շարախատնութեան* CD
1.5.4 *ոչ*] *է* added CD
1.5.5 *ունկերք*] *ունկր* CD
1.5.6 *գանագանութիւն*] *գանագանութիւնք* CD
1.5.7 *պէս*] *լինին* added CD
1.5.10 *խորՀուրդք*] *խորՀուրդ* CD
1.5.10 *շնորՀս*] *շնորՀ* CD
1.6.1 *եւ են*] *են եւ են* CD
1.6.4 *գանագանի*] *գանագանին* CD
1.6.5 *ծննդեանց*] *ծնելոց* CD
1.6.6 *զբնականութիւն*] *զբնակութիւն* CD

In a single instance **CD** are accepted into the text against the reading of **AB**. This is, however, a phonetic phenomenon which has been discussed in the Textual Notes:

1.1.5 *բնդունակք*] *բնդունակ* AB

Instances of **AB** : **CD** with the article *-ն*, etc.

1.1.1 *առաջին*] *առաջինն* CD
1.1.3 *կիզողութեանն*] *կիզողութեան* CD
1.3.5 *տանցն*] *տանց* CD
1.4.2 *գոյն*] *գոյնն* CD
1.4.3 *սերիցն*] *սերից* CD
1.4.3 *տեսակացն*] *տեսակաց* CD
1.4.11 *խեցգետի*] *խեցգետին* CD
1.5.10 *մարտիցն*] *մարտից* CD
1.6.5 *անհատն*] *անհատ* CD
1.6.5 *տեսակն*] *տեսակ* CD
1.6.5 *յանհունան*] *յանհունա* CD
1.6.9 *գործնական*] *գործնականն* CD
1.6.9 *բանական*] *բանականն* CD

This stemma would be contradicted by readings **AC** : **BD** or **AD** : **BC**. A few such exist, but they are of no substantive text-critical weight. After discounting orthographic variation and instances of addition or omission of the article *-ն* the following cases remain.

AC : **BD**
1.5.6 *եւ*] omitted AC
1.5.12 *աւդն*] *աւդք* AC
1.5.5 *յիզական*] *իզական* BD
1.5.6 *չէ*] *կամ* added BD
AD : **BC**
1.5.11 *որդայթից*] *եւ* added BC
1.5.13 *սոցին*] *սոցայ* BC
1.6.3 *իմատնացուցիչք*] *իմատացուցիչք* AD
Thus it may be asserted confidently that the stemma has been proved and certainly reflects the relationship between the four manuscripts.

9. *The Text and Translation*

The text of the edition is a critical one. Cases in which variant readings exist were decided, if possible, by text-critical criteria. In cases where no decision could be reached, the reading of manuscript **A** has usually been preferred. Since the stemma is bifurcate, however, there are occasions where **B** and **C D** or combinations of these witnesses have been judged to preserve the preferable reading. Orthography has been standardized, *aw* is always written and not ō. All abbreviations have been resolved and only certain, very unusual ones have been noted above in these preliminary remarks. Punctuation has also been normalized.

Two apparatuses have been prepared. One of them shows all the variants between the manuscripts, including orthographic variants. The other apparatus, below the main one, is a record of scribal peculiarities, corrections *prima manu* in the manuscripts, and similar readings.

In the Textual Commentary, which is printed following the text and translation, we have included a discussion of all the instances in which the *variae lectiones* were of interest. Certain scribal phenomena have been discussed. An index of the main textual phenomena discussed in the Textual Commentary has been prepared.

BIBLIOGRAPHICAL ABBREVIATIONS

Abel Cain	=	*History of Abel and Cain* in W.L. Lipscomb, *The Armenian Apocryphal Adam Literature* (University of Pennsylvania Armenian Texts and Studies, 8) Atlanta, 1990
Arevšatyan	=	S.S. Arevšatyan, "Zeno Stoic's Treatise "On Nature" and its Ancient Armenian Translation," *Banber Matenadarani* 3 (1956) 315-342 (in Russian)
Armenian Apocrypha Relating to Adam and Eve	=	M.E. Stone, *Armenian Apocrypha: Relating to Adam and Eve* (Studia in Veteris Testamenti Pseudepigrapha, 14) Leiden, 1996
Armenian Text Commentary	=	M.E. Stone, *A Textual Commentary on the Armenian Version of IV Ezra* (Septuagint and Cognate Studies, 34) Atlanta, 1990
De Virtutibus et Vitiis	=	Critical edition under preparation by M.E. Shirinian
4 Ezra	=	M.E. Stone, *The Armenian Version of IV Ezra* (University of Pennsylvania Armenian Texts and Studies, 1) Missoula, 1979
Good Tidings	=	*Concerning the Good Tidings of Seth* in W. L. Lipscomb, *The Armenian Apocryphal Adam Literature* (University of Pennsylvania Armenian Texts and Studies, 8) Atlanta, 1990
NBH	=	G. Awetikʻan, X. Siwrmēlian and M. Awkʻerian, Նոր բառգիրք Հայկազեան լեզուի (New Dictionary of the Armenian Language) Venice, 1837
Schmidt	=	Ernst Günther Schmidt, "Die altarmenische 'Zenon'-Schrift," *Abhandlungen der deutschen Akademie der Wissenschaften zu Berlin: Klasse für Sprachen, Literatur und Kunst,* Jahrgang 1960, Nr. 2 (1961) 5-50
Testament of Levi	=	M.E. Stone, *The Testament of Levi: A First Study of the Armenian Manuscripts of the Testaments of the Twelve Patriarchs in the Convent of St. James, Jerusalem.* Jerusalem, 1969
Testament of Reuben, Testament of Simeon	=	Critical editions under preparation by M.E. Stone

Xač'ikyan = L. Xač'ikyan, "The Armenian Translation of Zeno's *Concerning Nature*," *Gitakan Niwt'eri Žołovacu* 2 (1950) 65-98 (in Armenian)

Zuckerman = Constantine Zuckerman, *A Repertory of Published Armenian Translations of Classical Texts*, Jerusalem, 1995

SIGLA AND TECHNICAL ABBREVIATIONS

The abbreviations for biblical books, philosophical works and the like follow usual scholarly practice. The following may not be self-evident.

( )	editors' additions or glosses in the translation
*	following a sigil, indicates the text first written by the scribe
°	following a sigil, indicates a correction by the original scribe.
2°, 3°, etc.	second, third, etc. occurrence of letter in word or word in section.
add	adds
fg.	fragment
fol.	folio
fols.	folios
ln.	line
M+ number	Matenadaran manuscript number
om	omits
r	recto
v	verso

PART TWO

TEXT AND CRITICAL APPARATUSES
TEXTUAL COMMENTARY

0.0.0   *ՃԵՆՈՆԻ ԻՄԱՍՏԱՍԻՐԻ*

1.0.0   *ՅԱՂԱԳՍ ՊԻՏԱՆԱՑՈՒ ՍԵՌԻՑ*

1.0.1 *Արդ, են սեռք պիտանացուք վեց՝ դիրք, կարգք, շրջանք, չափք, գաւրութիւնք, ազդմունք:*

1.1.0 *Յաղագս դրից*

1.1.1 *Արդ, դիրք ի տեսակս վեց բաժանի: Առաջին է ունայնին անգոյութիւն պարունակեալ յանքաւէն, եւ ի մէջս իւր կառուցմամբ բարձեալ ունի գրոյորն ի նոյն տրամագծին եւ փոփոխեալ շարժմամբ:*

1.1.2 *երկրորդ է, որ յանկրական Հրոյ եւ լուսոյ երկին բաղկացեալ յունայնէ եւ նիւթ եւ բնութին անմարմին կենդանեաց:*

1.1.3 *երրորդ՝ Հաստատութիւն շրայարկին պարունակեալ ընդ վերնովն վասն յաւէտ կիզողութեանն արգելման, եւ դարձեալ՝ պարփակող արտադատութեան եւ Հոսման զգալեացս:*

0.0.0 missing BC | *ղենոնի իմաստասիրի*] *այլ բան* A

1.0.0 missing C | *յաղագս*] add *դիտութեան* B | *սեռից*] add *աւգնեալ Հոգի սուրբ աստուած* D

1.0.1 *են սեռք պիտանացուք*] *պիտանացու սեռք* C *պիտացու սեռք* D | *կարգք*] *կարք* B | *գաւրութիւնք*] *գործութիւնք* BD

1.1.0 missing ABCD

1.1.1 *ի*] *եւ* D | *բաժանի*] *բաժանին* CD | *առաջին*] *առաջինն* CD | *ունայնին*] *ունայն* B | *անգոյութիւն*] *անգոււթիւն* A *դիտութիւն* B *անբաււթիւն* C *անգիտութիւն* D | *ունի*] om C | *տրամագծին*] *տրամագծի* A *տրամգծին* B | *եւ փոփոխեալ*] *անփոփոխ եւ* A | *փոփոխեալ*] *փոփոխման* C | *շարժմամբ*] *շարժմամբ* B *շարժմամբ* D

1.1.2 *է*] om D | *յանկրական*] *անկրական* D | *Հրոյ*] *Հրո* A | *լուսոյ*] *լուսո* A | *բաղկացեալ*] *պաղկացեալ* D add *պարփակեալ* A | *յունայնէ*] *յայնցանէ* C | *անմարմին*] *մարմին* B

1.1.3 *յաւէտ*] *յաւետ* D | *յաւէտ կիզողութեանն*] *յաւետակիզողութեան* B | *կիզողութեանն*] *կիզողութեան* CD | *արգելման*] *արդելման* B om C | *պարփակող*] *պարփակող* B *պարփակաւղ* C | *արտադատութեան*] *արտադատողութեան* B

1.0.1 *արդ*] coloured *Ա* omitted C

1.1.1 *անգոյութիւն*] in margin C* *անբաււթիւն* C* | *փոփոխեալ*] *փոփոխմամբ* C*

1.1.4 Չորրորդ՝ դիրք ծովուն, որ յաւդոցն հաստատեալ կայ առանց ծորման եզերիցն եւ փակեալ ընդ հաստատնովն, բաղկացուցիչ եւ բնակարան գետնոց եւ կիտիցն մեծամեծացն, եւ շուրջ զերկրաս՝ տալ զաւրութիւն ախտաժետութեանց եւ առողջութիւն մարմնական կենդանեացս, ի ձեռն հողմոցն բերման ի զգայութիւնս իւրաքանչիւր:

1.1.5 Հինգերորդ է երկրիս շարադրութիւն, որ թանձրութեամբ՝ լերամբք եւ բլրաւք, դաշտաւք եւ ձորովք, հաստատեալ ի կողմանց, ի խիստ եւ ի հող աղոց, եւ յոյորս ջրովք ծովուն փակեալ կայ չորեքանկիւնի ձեւով: Եւ ընդ սիրտ երկրիս գետք հրալիցք աղոց եւ ջրոց խաղացեալ լինին ընդ ամենայն երակս, ուստի աղբերք եւ հոսմք վերագնացեալ շարժմամբք. եւ այսպէս ծովուց եւ գետոց ընդունակք, եւ որ ի ջուրս, եւ որ ի ցամաքի են ծննդականք՝ ամենեցուն գոյացուցիչ եւ պաշարող կենաց գոյ:

1.1.6 Վեցերորդ է միջոցք աշխարհիս, որ յաւդոց բնադատեալ ուռուցմամբ ի ներքս արգելման, ի փորուածս մեկնութեան երից հաստադիմակայիցն, զաւղ եւ կապուած աշխարհիս բաղկանալ, որ է պատճառ կենդանութեան եւ է բնակութիւն:

1.1.4 չորրորդ] երրորդ C | ծովուն] ծովու D | որ] om B | յաւդոցն] յօդոցն BCD | կայ] կա A կալ D | հաստատնովն] հաստատովն BD | բաղկացուցիչ եւ] եւ բաղկացուցիչ եւ A | գետնոց] զերնոց D | կիտիցն] կիտացն B կիտաց CD | մեծամեծացն] մեծամեծ B մեծամեծաց CD | զերկրաս] զերկրեաս D | զաւրութիւն] զօրութիւն BD զաւր C | ախտաժետութեանց] ախտաժետութենէս B | առողջութիւն] առողջութին B | մարմնական] մարմնոյ BCD | կենդանեացս] կենդանեաց A | հողմոցն] հողմոյն B | զգայութիւնս] զգայութիւն A add իւր B

1.1.5 հինգերորդ] հինգերրորդ B հինկերորդ C | է] om CD | երկրիս] երկիրս AD երկրի B | շարադրութիւն] շարադրութիւնս BC շարոց դրութիւնս D | լերամբք] լերամբ B | բլրաւք] բլերօք B բլրօք CD | դաշտաւք] դաշտօք BCD | ձորովք] ձորօք BD | հաստատեալ] հաստատեալք A | ի հող] հող B | աղոց] օղոց BCD | յոյորս] հոյորս B յոյրդս D | կայ] կա A | չորեքանկիւնի] չորիքանկիւնի A | սիրտ] սիրրտս B | երկրիս] երկիրս D | հրալիցք] հրաշից BCD | աղոց] աղից B օղից CD | աղբերք] աղբիւրք ABC | հոսմք] հոսմունք B | վերագնացեալ] վերագնացեալք A | շարժմամբք] շարժմունք B | եւ այսպէս] եւսն C | ընդունակք] ընդունակ AB | ծննդականք] ծնընդականք A ծնունդք C | ամենեցուն] ամենիցուն AB | պաշարող] պատճով B

1.1.6 վեցերորդ] վեցերրորդ C | է] են B om CD | յաւդոց] ի յաւդոց A ի յօրոց B յօրոց CD | ներքս] ներք C | փորուածս] փորուած A | հաստադիմակայիցն] հաստադիմակաիցն A հաստադիմակայից B հաստա դիմա դիմակայիցն D | զաւղ] զօղ BCD | կապուած] կապուածս A | բաղկանալ] բաղկանա B | բնակութիւն] բնակութիւնք BCD

1.1.4 եզերիցն] երիցն D* եզ in margin D° | գետնոց] վերնոց D* | ախտաժետութեանց] ախտաժետաց C* following dittography erased C

1.1.6 վեցերորդ] written as վեց .Զ. A | արգելման] արգելմամբ C*

1.1.7 Եւ սահմանք աստեղատանցն ի մէջս իւր, ընդ Հաստատունովն, զի ի վարմանէ աղոցն ըստ իրաքանչիւր տանցն անսխալ շրջագային աստեղքն, յորս կարգեալ են ըստ ժամանակի եւ ըստ տեղեացն սահմանի:

1.2.0 Յաղագս կարգաց

1.2.1 Կարգք ըստ երից բաժանի. ըստ առաքինութեան, ըստ արրինի եւ ըստ բնականութեան:

1.2.2 Զի ըստ առաքինութեան եւ ըստ արրինի են Հրեշտակք եւ մարդիկ՝ զուգեալք ի տնաւրէնութեան իմացս: Իսկ ըստ բնականութեան՝ ամենայն, որ յաշխարհիս բնաւրեցան գոլ լիրաքանչիւր բնական սահմանս:

1.2.3 Արդ՝ որք ըստ առաքինութեան եւ ըստ արրինի ոչ վարեալք՝ անկարգութիւնք եւ կործանմունք Հանդիպին եւ Հետեւին նորին կենացն: Եւ որ ըստ բնականն արտաքս եղեալ փոխի՝ իսկապէս քակտումն եւ եղծումն լինի բնութեանն:

1.2.4 Իսկ աստեղատունքն կարգեալ են ի պարունակս աղոց եւ ի շաւեղս աղավարութեանն, ոչ զմիմեամբք եղանեն, եւ ոչ փոխին լիրաքանչիւրոցն:

1.1.7 աստեղատանցն] աստեղացն A աստեղատեացն C | Հաստատունովն] Հաստատովն D | աղոցն] աղոյն A օղոցն B օղոյն CD | ըստ] ընդ C | իրաքանչիւր] երկաքանչիւր C | շրջագային] շրջագային A շրջակային D | տեղեացն] տեղացն BD

1.2.0 missing C

1.2.1 կարգք] արդ BC կարգ D | արրինի] օրինի BCD | բնականութեան] բնակութեան BCD

1.2.2 առաքինութեան] առաքինութեանն C | արրինի] օրինի BCD | Հրեշտակք] Հրշտակք A Հրեշտակ BD | ի] om B | տնաւրէնութեան] տնօրէնութեան BCD | իմացս] իմաg A | բնականութեան] բնակութեան BD բնակութեանն C | ամենայն] ամենեքեան B | որ] որք D | բնաւրեցան] բնօրեցան B | բնական] իւր C

1.2.3 արրինի] արրինին AC օրինի D | կործանմունք] կործմանք B add անդի B | Հանդիպին եւ Հետեւին նորին] Հետեւին A | ըստ բնականն] զբնականն CD | փոխի] փոխի B | իսկապէս] իսկապես B | քակտումն] քատկում B | եւ եղծումն] follows բնութեանն BCD

1.2.4 աստեղատունքն] աստեղատունք A աստեղունքն C | աղոց] օղոց C յօղոց D | ի շաւեղս] շաւիդս C ի շաւիդս D | աղավարութեանն] աղավարութեան B օղավարութեանն C օղավարութեան D | զմիմեամբք] զմիմեամբ B | եղանեն] եղանել D | լիրաքանչիւրոցն] իրաքանչիւրոց D

1.2.1 կարգք] coloured կ omitted BC

1.2.4 եղանեն] եղանել C*

1.3.0 *Յաղագս շրջանաց*

1.3.1 *Շրջանք բոլորին ըստ երից յեղմանց բաղկանայ, որ է՝ տպաւորութիւն, բացերեւութիւն, մշտակացութիւն, զի տպաւրեալ աշխարՀս յանբաւին եւ բացերեւեալ ի ձեռն ունայնին՝ ի գոյն եւ ի ձեւ եւ ի տեսակս սերի:*

1.3.2 *Եւ ի նոյն դարձեալ մշտակային ըստ տպաւորութեան, ուստի բացերեւեցաւն անշարժելի բնութեամբ. քանզի ի նոյն անդրէն զկատարումն առնու բոլորն Համանգամայն գանագանութեամբ:*

1.3.3 *Իսկ երկնիցն շրջանս իմանալի է գպարունակս աւդոցն ասել, եւ ոչ գՀաստատութիւն ջրայարկին, որ ընտրողականն է, եւ ոչ գերրորդ երկին, այլ որ ընդ Հաստատնովս են աւդք պարունակեալ, ըստ եւթն բաժանման ընդ միմեամբք կարգեալ.*

1.3.4 *բոլորութեամբ շուրջ գոլով գանդնդովք, Հարթ ըստ չորեցունց կողմանց աշխարՀիս, յորս աստեղատունքն բաժանեալ եւ յամենայն վայրա աւդոցն ցրուեալ տարածմամբ յերկուս կիսագունդան անդադար շրջագայութեամբ, դիմաւք յարեւելից յարեւմուտս, որք ընդ նոյն շաւեղս վարին:*

1.3.0 missing C | *շրջանաց*] *շրջանացն* AD

1.3.1 *շրջանք*] *շրջան* B *րջանք* C add *գ* A | *յեղմանց*] *յեղման* B | *բաղկանայ*] *բաղկանա* A | *յանբաւին*] *անբաւին* B | *եւ բացերեւեալ*] *բացերեւեալ* CD | *ունայնին*] *ունայնի* A | *եւ ի ձեւ*] *ի ձեւ* B | *տեսակս*] *տեսակ* A | *սերի*] *էր* B

1.3.2 *եւ ի*] add *եւ ի* B | *մշտակային*] *մշտակաին* A | *ըստ*] *ըս* B | *բացերեւեցաւն*] *բացերեւեցան* BCD | *անշարժելի*] *անշարելի* D | *ի*] om BCD | *բոլորն*] *բոլորին* D

1.3.3 *երկնիցն*] *երկնից* A | *գպարունակս*] *գպարունակ* C | *աւդոցն*] *օղոցն* BCD | *գՀաստատութիւն*] *Հաստատութիւն* D | *ջրայարկին*] *ջրարկին* D | *որ*] *գորս* BD *գոր* C | *ընտրողականն*] *ընդրողականն* B | *է*] om BCD | *գերրորդ*] *գերրորդն* D | *երկին*] *երկինս* CD | *Հաստատնովս*] *Հաստատնովքս* C *Հաստատովքս* D | *աւդք*] *օղք* BCD

1.3.4 *բոլորութեամբ*] *բոլորութիւն* B | *գանդնդովք*] *գանդրնդովք* ABD | *ըստ չորեցունց*] *գչորեցունց* C *չորեցունց* D | *յորս*] *յոր* A | *աստեղատունքն*] *աստեղատունք* B *աստեղքն* D | *աւդոցն*] *օղոցն* B *օդիցն* CD | *ցրուեալ*] *ցրեալ* B | *յերկուս*] *ի յերկուս* CD | *կիսագունդան*] *կիսագունդս* BC | *շրջագայութեամբ*] *շրջագաւթեամբ* A | *դիմաւք*] *դիմօք* BCD | *յարեւելից*] *յարեւելս* B add *եւ* B | *նոյն շաւեղս*] *նոյն շաւիղս* BC *շաւիղս* D

1.3.1 *շրջանք*] ornamental Շ omitted C

1.3.2 *եւ*] *դարձեալ* erased D

1.3.3 *կարգեալ*] *ար* barely legible A

1.3.5 Իսկ մոլորակք են եւթն, բաժանեալ ըստ եւթն սահմանս աղդոցն, որք են այտոքիկ՝ երեւակն, լունթագն, Հրատն, արեգակն, լուսաբերն, փայլածուն, լուսինն. քանզի սոքա ինքնաշարժ դիմաւք յարեւմտից յարեւելս շրջագային եւ ըստ իւրաքանչիւր տանցն զժամանակս գոյացուցանեն ի շրջանս իւրեանց:

1.4.0 Յաղագս չափուց

1.4.1 Չափք աշխարհիս ըստ չորից բաժանի՝ ըստ տեղւոյ եւ ըստ գունոյ, ըստ ձեւոյ եւ ըստ թուականութեան:

1.4.2 Քանզի տեղին է երակաբար՝ վերին, ստորին, միջին. եւ զանազանի ըստ կողմանց վերինն եւ այլն եւս: Իսկ գոյն քառակի ասի՝ սպիտակ, կապոյտ, սեաւ, սաս: Եւ ի սոցանէ բաղկանան երանգք, երփունք, փայլմունք, պաղպաջմունք եւ այլ զանազանեալք ի միում ենթակայումն:

1.3.5 մոլորակք] մոլորականք B | են] om CD | աղդոցն] օդոցն B օդոց CD | որք] որ D | այտոքիկ երեւակն լունթագն] om A | լունթագն] լունթագ B | Հրատն] Հրատ AB | լուսաբերն փայլածուն լուսինն] եւ այլքն A | լուսինն] լուսին B | դիմաւք] դիմօք BD | յարեւելս] յարեւեալս A | շրջագային] շրջագահն A | ըստ] եւ CD | տանցն] տանց CD | գոյացուցանեն] գոացուցանեն A

1.4.0 missing C | չափուց] չափոց B

1.4.1 չափք] ափք BC | տեղւոյ] տեղոյ ACD ամենային տեղս B | եւ] om A | գունոյ] գունո A add եւ C | ձեւոյ] ձեւ A | թուականութեան] թւականութեան AB

1.4.2 քանզի] անզի C | երակաբար] երակարոյր B | միջին եւ] եւ միջին եւ CD | այլն] այլ D | իսկ] եւ A | գոյն] գոյնն CD | կապոյտ] կարմիր CD | սեաւ] սեւ B սեաւն D | սաս] դեղին BCD | սոցանէ] սոցանէն B | երանգք] երանք B երանգն C երագն D | պաղպաջմունք] պաղպաճմունք D om C | զանազանեալք] զանազանեալ A | ենթակայումն] ենթակառումն AC ենթակառում B

1.3.5 երեւակն] erasure of line and next word in margin C*

1.4.1 չափք] coloured Չ omitted B coloured Չ omitted C

1.4.2 քանզի] coloured Ք omitted C | երանգք] երկինք B* | զանազանեալք] displaced fol commences here B

1.4.3 Իսկ ձեւ երակաբար ասի՝ երանկինի, քառանկինի, եւ բոլորակ. եւ ի սոցանէ ըստ այլ տեսակս գանագանի ձեւ: Իսկ թիւ երակի բաժանի. զի է որ դար ասի՝ ըստ Հանգիտութեան Հատած ի սերիգն, եւ է որ կռճատ՝ ըստ անգուգութեան անՀարթ տեսակացն, եւ դարձեալ՝ որ յանՀատիգն բաղկանայ. իսկ որ ըստ այսոցիկ ոչ են՝ անբաւք եւ անչափք ասին:

1.4.4 Իսկ սաՀմանք աստեղատանցն ի ձեռն ժամանակի մոլորակացն չափի. թուով շրջագայիցն: Քանգի ընտրեցան աստեղատունք ամսոց երկոտասան երակի՝ ըստ չորեցունց կողմանց աշխարՀիս, ըստ նիւթոյ եւ ըստ յեղման Հասարակաց, ըստ երկրիս մասանց, եւ ըստ անդամոց մարդոյն, եւ ըստ ձննդականութեան, որք անուանադրեն՝

1.4.5 Խոյ, Ցուլ, Երկաւորի՝ ըստ արեւելից, որ է աւդ եւ գարնանային Հասարակածիր. Խեցգետի, Առիծ, Կոյս՝ ըստ Հիւսիսոյ, որ է Հուրն եւ ամառնային յեղանակ.

1.4.3 երակաբար] երակաբոլոր B քառակաբար C քառակի D | երանկինի] երանգինի AB | քառանկինի] քառանգինի ABC add երկայն CD | բոլորակ] բոլոր BCD | ի] om D | ըստ] om B | այլ] om CD | գանագանի] գանագան ի D | ձեւ] ձեւս BCD | իսկ] սկ C | Հանգիտութեան] Հանգիստութեան D | Հատած ի] Հասակիցն B Հատանի ի D | սերիգն] երիգն B սերից CD | անգուգութեան] անգդուգուգութեան B | անՀարթ] Հարթ B | տեսակացն] տեսակաց CD | որ] որպէս D om C | յանՀատիգն] անՀատիգն D | բաղկանայ] բաղկանա AB | որ] որք C | ոչ են] կոչեն C | անբաւք] նոքա B

1.4.4 սաՀմանք] սաՀմանքս B | աստեղատանցն] տեղացն B աստեղացն C | մոլորակացն] բոլորակացն B | չափի] add վաժտուն A | շրջագայիցն] շրջագայիցն A շրջանիցն B | քանգի] add եւ B | ընտրեցան] ընդրեցան BD add եւ CD | աստեղատունք] աստեղտունք B | երկոտասան] բաժանել B | ըստ չորեցունց] գչորեցունց C | նիւթոյ] նիւթո A անիւթոյ B թուոյ C | Հասարակաց] Հասարակացն AD | երկրիս] երիս B | մարդոյն] մարդոյս BCD | ձննդականութեան] ձնրնդականութեանն CD | անուանադրեն] անուանդրեն B անուանադրենն C անուանագրենն D

1.4.5 ցուլ] ցուլն D | երկաւորի] երկաւոր C երկաւորն D | արեւելից] յարեւելից D | աւդ] օդ BCD | գարնանային] գարնանաին A գարնան C գարնանայն D | Հասարակածիր] Հասարակածք A Հասարակածիրն B add իսկ A | խեցգետի] խեցգետին BCD | Հիւսիսոյ] Հիւսիւտ A Հիւսոյ B Հիւսիսոյ C | ամառնային] ամառնաին AB ամառային D | յեղանակ] յեղանակն B

1.4.3 իսկ] coloured Ի omitted C | Հանգիտութեան] Հանգիստութիւն D* | յանՀատիգն] սոյն Հատիգն B* | ոչ] ոչ omitted B* above line B°

1.4.4 շրջագայիցն] շրջանիցն with ն 1° above line B° | անուանադրեն] անդրեն B*

1.4.5 Հասարակածիր] Հասարածք A*

1.4.6 Կշեռ, Կարիճ, Աղեղնաւոր՝ ըստ արեւմտից, որ է Հող եւ աշնանային Հասարակածիր, Այծեղջիւր, Ջրհոս, Ձուկն՝ ըստ Հարաւոյ, որ է ջուր եւ ձմեռնային յեղանակ:

1.4.7 Իսկ ըստ երկրի ցատակից լինել եւ ըստ մասանց մարդոյն՝ խոյն Պարսից, որ է գլուխն. Ցուլն Բաբելացող, որ է պարանոցն. Եկաւորին Գամրաց, որ են ուսքն. Խեցգետինն Հայոց, որ է յանչքն.

1.4.8 Առիւծն Ասխացիք . \ BCD որ է կողքն \ A աջ ձեռն \. Կոյսն Ելլադացող եւ Յունաց, եւ \ BCD են ձեռքն. \ A ձախ ձեռն \

1.4.9 Կշերն \ BCD Արաբացող \ A Կիւլիկեցիք \ եւ են կոթունքն. Կարիճն Իտալացող, եւ են սրունքն. Աղեղնաւորն Կրետացող, եւ են երանքն.

1.4.6 Կշեռ] Կշիռ BCD | Կարիճ] Կարիճն B | արեւմտից] արմտից D | Հող] Հողմ A Հողն BCD | աշնանային] աշնանին A աշնան C | Հասարակածիր] Հասարակածք A Հասարակած D | Այծեղջիւր] Այծեղջ B Այծեղջուր D | Ջրհոս] ջրհո B ջրուհոս D | Ձուկն] ձուկ B | ըստ Հարաւոյ] om CD | Հարաւոյ] Հարաւտ A Հարեւտ B | ջուր] Հարաւ ջրոյ C Հարաւ D | ձմեռնային] ձմեռնաին AB

1.4.7 ցատակից] ցատակիցն A | լինել եւ ըստ մասանց մարդոյն] լինին CD | մարդոյն] մարդոյս B | խոյն] ոյն C | պարսից] պարսիկք C | որ է] եւ A | գլուխն] գլուխ C | բաբելացող] բաբելացոց A բաբել B բաբելացիք C բաբիլացիք D | որ է] եւ A | եկաւորին] եկորին B եկաւորն CD | որ են] եւ A | են] է CD | ուսքն] յուսքն B | խեցգետինն] խեցգետին A խեցգետ B | Հայոց] Հաոց A Հայք CD | որ է] եւ A | է] են B | յանչքն] յանչք D

1.4.8 առիւծն] առիւծ BD | ասխացիք] ասորոց B ասխացոց C | որ է կողքն] om A | է] են B | կողքն] կողք D | աջ ձեռն] om BCD | կոյսն] կոյս B կոյսրն D | ելլադացող] ելլադացիք A ելլադացոց BC ելադացող D | յունաց եւ են ձեռքն] om A | եւ] որ D | ձախ ձեռն] om BCD

1.4.9 Կշերն] Կշեր AB Կշիրն CD | արաբացող] om A արաբացոց BC | Կիւլիկեցիք] om BCD | եւ են կոթունքն] Կշ A | Կարիճն իտալացող եւ են սրունքն] Կարիճ լիտալացոց եւ աւան A | կոթունքն] կռունթքն C | իտալացող] իտալացոց BC իլատացող D | եւ] որ D | աղեղնաւորն] աղեղնաւոր A աղեղն B աղեղնաւորն կրետացող եւ են երանքն] om D | կրետացող] կրետացոց AC կրետացիքն B | են] om A

1.4.6 Կշեռ] Կշիռ dittography of Կշիռ erased C | աղեղնաւոր] աղեղնաւոր - Հասարակածիր omitted B* above line B°

1.4.7 ըստ 1°] ըստ above line B° | ըստ 2°] omitted B* | մասանց] g mostly lost in lacuna A | խոյն] coloured խ omitted | բաբելացող] լ mostly lost in lacuna A | ուսքն] յոյնքն B*

1.4.10 Այծեղջիւրն Ասորոց, որ են բարձքն. Չրհուն եգիպտացւոց եւ են ծունկքն. Չուկն Հնդկաց եւ Կարմիր ծովուն, եւ են թաթք ուռիցն:

1.4.11 Իսկ ըստ ծննդաբաշխութեան՝ արականք են վեց՝ Խոյ, Եկաւրի, Առիծ, Կշեռ, Աղեղնաւոր, Չրհոս. իսկ իգականք՝ Ցուլ, Խեցգետի, Կոյս, Կարիճ, Այծեղջիւր, Չուկն:

1.5.0 Յաղագս զաւրութեանց

1.5.1 Զաւրութեանց չորք են տեսակք՝ արտաբերութիւնք, արտահոսութիւնք, արտադատութիւնք, արտադրութիւնք, ուստի ծննդաբաշխականն եւ բժշկականն բաղկանայ:

1.5.2 Զի ծննդաբաշխութիւնն բաժանի ի տեսակս երիս՝ ի խոնաւային, ի ցամաքային, յերկակենցաղս. ըստ ժամանակի, ըստ նիւթոյ եւ ըստ կողման արտաբերի:

1.4.10 այծեղջիւրն] այծեղ2 B այծեղջուրն D | ասորոց] ասորց ABCD | որ] եւ ACD | են] om A | չրհուն] չրհոս B | եգիպտացւոց] եգիպտացող AC եգիպտացիքն B եկիպտացող D | եւ] որ D | եւ են ծունկքն] սրունքն A | ծունկքն] ծունկն B ծունքն CD | կարմիր] կարմար A | կարմիր ծովուն եւ] om BCD | եւ] որ A | թաթք] թաթ CD | ուռիցն] ուռին A

1.4.11 ըստ] om C | ծննդաբաշխութեան] ծնրնդաբաշխութեան AB ծննրնդաբաշխութեան D | արականք] արուականք B | եկաւրի] [ ]աւր B եկաւր CD | կշեռ] կշիռ BC կշիռն D | աղեղնաւոր] աղեղ B | իգականք] իգ[ ] B | ցուլ] ցուլն D | խեցգետի] խեծ B խեցգետին CD | կոյս] կոյսն D | կարիճ] կարիճն D | այծեղջիւր] այծ B om D

1.5.0 missing C | յաղագս] եւ վասն B | զաւրութեանց] զորութեանն D

1.5.1 զաւրութեանց] զորութեանց BD | չորք] երեք D | արտադատութիւնք] արտադատորութին B արտդատութինք C արտադասութինք D | արտադրութիւնք] արտատրութինք B արտատութինք C | ծննդաբաշխականն] ծնրնդաբաշխականն A ծնդաբաշխականն B ծննդաբաշխութինն C ծննրնդաբաշխականն D | բժշկականն] բժշկական B | բաղկանայ] բաղկանա AB

1.5.2 ծննդաբաշխութիւնն] ծնրնդաբաշխութիւնն A ծնդաբաշխութեանք B ծնդաբաշխութինն C ծննրնդաբաշխութինն D | տեսակս] տեսեսակս B | խոնաւային] խոնաւաինս A խոնաւին C add եւ D | ցամաքային] ցամաքաինս A ցամաքին C add ի C add եւ D | յերկակենցաղս] երկակենցաղս D | նիւթոյ] նիւթո A | եւ] om A

1.4.10 ուռիցն] ցն badly rubbed B

1.4.11 արականք] ու in the bottom margin B° | ցուլ] only tails of g and լ visible B

1.5.1 զաւրութեանց] coloured Զ omitted C

1.5.2 ծննդաբաշխութիւնն] ծնդաբաշխութեանք B* | տեսակս] տեսեսակս B* ս above line B°

1.5.3 Իսկ Հոգւոյ եղումն անյեղլի, կամ Հատումն անպակասաբար, կամ ստեղծումն արտաքոյ, կամ լինելութիւն ըստ նիւթի խառնակցութեանցն անմարմնաբար, այլ ոչ ըստ ժամանակի եւ ըստ կողման եւ ըստ թանձրութեան նիւթոյ ի Հոմանէ բաղկացումն ընութեան, եւ ոչ այլայլակ առնի, այլ որ գանագանի ըստ մարմնոյ կրից կամ խառնից:

1.5.4 Իսկ որ ոչն արտաքերի ըստ մարմնոյ շարաունութեան՝ ոչ այսպէս գոյացումն ընութեանն, այլ այլ իմն վերագոյն աճումն ընութեան եւ անյեղլի, առանց ձննդեան, յանկրական Հրոյ եւ լուսոյ՝ անմարմին եւ անմահ կենդանութեամբ, եւ կամ թէ Համանգամայն ի միոջէ նիւթոյ գլինելութիւն առեալ՝ անթուելի բազմութեամբ:

1.5.5 Իսկ բժշկականութիւն է ըստ մգան եւ ըստ ուղղոյ, ըստ արեան եւ ըստ մաղձոյ, եւ յորմէ նեարդք եւ ջիլք եւ ոսկերք եւ երակք եւ միսք եւ մորթք բաղկանան. զի բաժանի յաղդուածն եւ խառնուածն յարական եւ լիգական մասունս:

1.5.3 Հոգւոյ] Հոգոյն A Հոգո B Հոգոյ C | ելումն] բերումն D | լինելութիւն] լինելութեան B | խառնակցութեանցն] խառնակցութեան C խառնակցութեանց D | նիւթոյ ի] նիւթի A | նիւթոյ ի Հոմանէ] նիւթ յայնմանէ B | Հոմանէ] Հոմման A | ընութեան] ընութեանն B | առնի] առնէ B | մարմնոյ] մարմնոյն A մարմնո B | կրից կամ խառնից] խառնից կամ կրից A | կամ] կայ C

1.5.4 շարաունութեան] շարախաունութիւն B շարախաունութեան CD | ոչ] add է CD | գոյացումն] գոացումն A | ընութեանն] ընութեան D | այլ այլ] այլ A այլ յայլ B | վերագոյն աճումն ընութեան] աճումն ընութեան ի վերայ գոյ ընութեանն B | ընութեան] ընութեանն C om A | ձննդեան] ձնընդեան A ձնընդեն B ձննընդեան D | լուսոյ] լուստ A | միոջէ] միոշոյ B | նիւթոյ] նիւթո A | գլինելութիւն] գլինելութիւնն C լինելութիւն D | անթուելի] անմնդելի A

1.5.5 իսկ] սկ C | բժշկականութիւն] բժշկականութիւնն B բժշկանութիւն C | մգան] բագմական B | ուղղոյ] ըղղոյ C | մաղձոյ] մաղձի B | եւ] om A | յորմէ նեարդք] յարենէն օրք B | նեարդք] են օրք C են յօրք D | ոսկերք] ոսկր ACD | եւ] om A | երակք եւ միսք] միսք B | զի] add եւ B | բաժանի] բաժանին D | յաղդուածն] յօղուծն B յօղուածն C յատւածն D | յարական] յարուական B | լիգական] իգական BD

1.5.3 անպակասաբար] սա above line B° պ over another letter C° | արտաքոյ] over another word B° | անմարմնաբար] ան above line B° | ոչ 1°] over ինչ B° | գանագանի] ա above erased letter B°

1.5.4 շարաունութեան] ըստ շարաունութիւն between lines B°; այլ erased B | ընութեանն] abbreviation mark omitted B | եւ 4°] է over կ B°

1.5.5 իսկ] coloured ի omitted C | բժշկականութիւն] ն 2° above line B°

1.5.6 Իսկ զանազանութիւն խառնուածոյն յերիս զանազանի. ըստ մարմնոյն՝ վտիտ եւ գոզոր. եւ ըստ գունոյն շէկ, թուխ, խարտեաշ, պղնձուտ. եւ ըստ մազոյն՝ գռուզ, ձաղկ, գանգուր եւ նուրբ կամ ստուար. եւ ըստ ամռքացն եւ Հոտոցն՝ դառն, քաղցր, թթու եւ կճու:

1.5.7 Իսկ մաղձն եւ արիւնն են բարձրութիւն նիւթիցն եւ Հաստատութիւն յեղմանցն, եւ զանազանին ըստ ժամանակի յեղանակացն: Եւ ի սոցանէ լինին առողջութիւնք եւ Հիւանդութիւնք դժուարինք. զի ըստ գոյզ եւ ըստ կշեռ բարեխառնութեան լինի առողջութիւն, իսկ ըստ առաւելութեան՝ պէս պէս Հիւանդութիւնք:

1.5.8 Քանզի ի սեւամաղձութենէն՝ լուսնոտք, եւ ի միտաւտարենէն՝ ուրկութիւնք, եւ ի խատութենէն արգանդի արեանն՝ ամլութիւնք, եւ ի գրտոյ թիկանց՝ արուին անարութիւնք:

1.5.9 Այլք ըստ առաւելութեանցն բաղկանան:

1.5.6 իսկ] սկ C | զանազանութիւն] զանազանութեամբ B զանազանութիւնք CD | յերիս] om D | վտիտ] վատիտ A առոյգ C | գոզոր] գոզր A | եւ] om A | գունոյն] գունոցն D | շէկ] add կամ BCD | խարտեաշ] խարտէշ B | պղնձուտ] պղրնձուտ AB պղնձուր C պղրնձուր D | գռուզ] գռուտ D | ձաղկ] om C | կամ ստուար եւ ըստ ամռքացն եւ Հոտոցն դառն] om D | կամ] եւ կամ B | ամռքացն] ստամռքացն A | Հոտոցն քաղցր] լինդիցն [ ]առնաքաղցի B | թթու] թրթու D | եւ] եւ կամ B om ACD

1.5.7 մաղձն] մաղձ A | արիւնն] արիւն A ար[ ] B | են բարձրութիւն նիւթիցն եւ Հաստատութիւն] om D | Հաստատութիւն] Հոտոտութիւն B | զանազանին] զանազանի C | զանազանին ըստ ժամանակի յեղանակացն] զանազ[ ] [ ]եղանակացն B | զանազանին ըստ ժամանակի յեղանակացն եւ] om D | լինին] լինեն B լինի C | Հիւանդութիւնք] Հիւ[ ]ութիւնք B | կշեռ] կշիռ BCD | բարեխառնութեան] բարիխառնութիւնք B բարէխառնութեան C | լինի] լինին B om A | առողջութիւն] առողջութիւնք B | առաւելութեան] առօելութեան B | պէս պէս] պէս պէս լինին CD

1.5.8 սեւամաղձութենէն] սեւամաղձութենէն A սեւայմաղձութենէն B սեւմաղձութենէն C սեւամամաղձութենէ են D | լուսնոտք] լուսնոտքն C լուտոտք D | միտաւտարենէն] միտատարենէն A միտօտարենէն C միտատտարէն են D | ուրկութիւնք] ուրկութիւն B ուրկութիւնն C ունակութիւնք D | եւ ի խատութենէն] om B | խատութենէն] խատութենէ A խատութենէ D | արգանդի] արգանդին BCD | արեանն] արեան B | ամլութիւնք] ամլութիւնն C ամլութին D | ի] om B | գրտոյ] գրոյ A | արուին] om C | անարութիւնք] անտրութիւնք C անարութին D

1.5.9 missing BCD

1.5.6 իսկ] coloured ի omitted C | մազոյն] մաղձոյն B* մազոյն B°

1.5.7 իսկ] coloured ի omitted C | առողջութիւնք] abbreviation mark omitted B

1.5.8 սեւամաղձութենէն] ե 1° above line D°

1.5.10 Իսկ վարք կենացն ի բնութենէն պատժելով Հարկաբար պնդի, ուստի նախանձ եւ փառասիրութիւն եւ ցանկութիւն, զպարավիգն լինել, յորմէ պատերագմունք մարտից բաղկանան. եւ խորհուրդք միշտ ի շնորհս անձին իւրում ընկալեալ ծնանի գիմացուածս բանի եւ ներգործութեան, զի է, որ ըստ մարմնոյ եւ է, որ ըստ Հոգւոյ ապտի:

1.5.11 Իսկ մահ է լուծումն զգայութեանց եւ քակտումն եւ որոշումն նիւթոցն, զի է, որ պատահմամբ՝ ըստ խառնիցն եւ է, որ բնական՝ ըստ կրիցն: Եւ լինի պատահումն ըստ ժամանակի ի պատերագմի, կամ յայլ որոգայթից, կամ յախտից Հիւանդութենէ ի մէջս կենացն ծախիլ:

1.5.12 Իսկ բնականն է ըստ գաւրութեան մինչեւ ի պակասել չերմութեան ուժոյն, եւ գիտելի է ի ծնելութենէն ըստ ժամանակի, ի շրջագայէ մոլորակացն, իսկ ըստ գաւրութեան նիւթոյ լեղանակացն այլ է պատճառ զգայական մարմնոյ եւ աղն, զի ըստ բարեխառնութեանն եւ յառոյց սերմանեաց երկրին, յորմէ շաւշափի եւ կերակրի՝ առողջութիւնք եւ աճմունք բաղկանան:

1.5.10 Իսկ] սկ C | վարք] վարքն A | բնութենէն] բնութեան են A բնակութենէն D | պատժելով] պարժելով B վարժելով C | Հարկաբար] Հարկատրատբար BCD | պնդի] պնտի BC | փառասիրութին] փառասիրութիւնն D | ցանկութիւն] ցանգութիւն B ցանկութիւնն C add եւ C | զպարավիգն] զօրաւիքն B զօրաւիգն D | մարտից] մարտից CD | խորհուրդք] խորհուրդ CD | շնորՀս] շնորՀ CD | ընկալեալ] վկայել B վկայեալ C վկաեալ D | բանի] բանից B | եւ է որ] եւ C | Հոգւոյ] Հոգոյ ABC | ապտի] օգտի CD

1.5.11 Իսկ] սկ C | զգայութեանց] զգայութեանցն A զգութեանց B | քակտումն] քօկտումն B | որոշումն] յորոշումն B | նիւթոցն] նիւթիցն A | զի է] զէ D | ըստ] եւ ըստ C | խառնիցն] խռնաիցն B խառն C | պատահումն] պատաՀումն B | պատերագմի] պատերագմի եւ C պատերագմին եւ D | կամ] om D | յայլ] այլ D | որոգայթից] որոգաթից D add եւ BC | Հիւանդութենէ] Հիւանդութեան B | մէջս] մէջ B | կենացն] կենաց BCD

1.5.12 Իսկ բնականն է] ի սկզբանէ D | բնականն] բնական BC | է] om B | գաւրութեան] գօրութեան BD | չերմութեան] չերմութեան D | ուժոյն] ուոյն D | ի շրջագայէ ... լեղանակացն] շրջագայի մոլորակաց B | շրջագայէ] շրջագայութենէ C շրջագային D | մոլորակացն] մոլարացն A | գաւրութեան] գօրութեանն C գօրութեանց D | լեղանակացն] եղանակացն A | աղն] աղք A օղն B օղք C յօղք D | ըստ] om B | բարեխառնութեանն] բարիխառնութեան B բարէխառնութեանն C | յառոյց] առոյց B յառոյցք D | սերմանեաց] սերմանութեանցն C | շաւշափի] շաւշափի A շօշափի BCD | աճմունք] աճումն B | բաղկանան] բաղկան B բաղկանայ D

1.5.10 Իսկ] coloured Ի omitted C

1.5.11 Իսկ 1°] coloured Ի omitted C | ժամանակի] erase one line C°

1.5.12 մինչեւ] մինչչեւ D* չ 2° erased D°

1.5.13 *Իսկ սոցին Հակառակն պէսպէս ցաւոց եւ խառն՝ մահուան լինել պատճառ, որ ըստ շարժման աւդոյն դառնութեան, ի ժամանակս եկամտացն, ըստ նիւթոյ յեղմանցն եւ ըստ խառնուածոյ մարմնոյն, պատահիլ ազդմամբք ի սիրտն բարձումն կենդանութեան լինել:*

1.5.14 *Արդ, որ ըստ ժամանակի եւ ըստ գաւրութեան ոչ են՝ անեղին են սքանչելագործութիւնք եւ ոչ բնութեան նիւթականացն:*

1.6.0 *Յաղագս ազդմանց*

1.6.1 *Ազդումն բնութեանց եռակի բաժանի. գի են, որ սնուցիչք են եւ են, որ իմաստնացուցիչք եւ են, որ մակացելիք:*

1.6.2 *Արդ՝ սնուցչացն երկու են տեսակք՝ նիւթ եւ ժամանակ. գի քառակի ըստ Հանգիտութեան Հանդիպմանցն ոռոգանել գսերմանս տնկոց եւ բուսոց գանագանութեանց:*

1.5.13 *սոցին*] *սոցայ* BC | *Հակառակն*] *Հակառակքն* B | *ցաւոց*] *ցoing* B | *խառն մահուան*] *խառնման* B | *շարժման*] *շարժմանք* B | *աւդոյն*] *օդոյն* BC *յօդոյն* D | *դառնութեան*] *դառնութիւն* B | *ի*] om B | *նիւթոյ*] *նիւթի* ABD | *յեղմանցն*] *յեղմացն* B | *խառնուածոյ*] *խառնուածո* A *խառնուածոյ* B *խառնուածու* D | *մարմնոյն*] *մարմնոյ* B | *ազդմամբք*] *ասդմամբ* B | *բարձումն*] *բարձու* B add *ի* D | *կենդանութեան*] *կենդանութեանն* A | *լինել*] *լինի* A

1.5.14 *ըստ*] om A add *ամենայն* B | *գաւրութեան*] *գործութեան* B | *անեղին*] *անեղի* A | *են*] om B | *բնութեան*] *ի բնութեան* B *բնութեանն* C | *նիւթականացն*] *նիւթականք* B *նիւթականաց* D add *աց* B

1.6.0 missing C

1.6.1 *ազդումն*] *գդումն* C | *որ*] *որք* B | *սնուցիչք*] *սնուցիչ* C | *են որ*] *որք* A | *իմաստնացուցիչք*] *իմաստացուցիչք* D | *եւ են*] *են եւ* B *են եւ են* CD | *որ*] *որք* A

1.6.2 *տեսակք*] *տեսակ* C | *ժամանակ*] *ժամանակք* A | *ոռոգանել*] *ոռոգա[ ]ել* B | *գսերմանս*] *սերմանս* D | *տնկոց*] *տնկոցն* BD *բուսոց* C | *բուսոց*] *բուսոցն* B *տնկոց* C

1.6.1 *ազդումն*] coloured *Ա* omitted C

1.6.2 *Հանդիպմանցն*] *պ* written over *մ* B° | *գսերմանս*] right stroke of *ս* elongated B° | *բուսոց*] *ս* over *ղ* D°

1.6.3 Իսկ իմատնացուցիչք երկակի բաժանին՝ ըստ տեսանելեաց եւ ըստ ձայնից: Եւ տեսանելին երակի բաժանի՝ ի գոյն, ի ձեւ եւ ի կերպարան: Իսկ գոյն ըստ չորից բաժանի՝ սեաւ, սպիտակ, կապոյտ եւ սաւս, իսկ խառնուածքն ի սոցանէ բաղկանան ի զանազան տեսիլս գունոց:

1.6.4 Նոյնպէս եւ ձեւքն քառակի զանազանի՝ ըստ կրի բաժանականին, որ է եռանկիւնի եւ քառանկիւնի, երկարն եւ բոլորակ: Իսկ ի ձեւի կատարեալ է բոլորակն ըստ ձեւոյ եւ ըստ շարժման աշխարհիս ի նոյն անդրէն դառնալ:

1.6.5 Իսկ կերպարան է ի դէմս, եւ դէմք՝ յանհատի, եւ անհատն՝ ի տեսակի, իսկ տեսակն՝ ի սեռի: Եւ է կերպարան իսկապէս ի վերայ ծննդեանց եւ եղմանց եւ ստեղծմանց, որ յանհունն արտաբերեալ զանազանին՝ նմանք եւ աննմանք, ի ձեռն անգոյզ ժամանակի եւ շարժման:

1.6.3 իսկ] սկ C | իմատնացուցիչք] իմատացուցիչք AD | բաժանին] բաժանի B | տեսանելեաց] տեսանելեացն C | ձայնից] ձայնիցն C | տեսանելին] տես[ ] B | երակի բաժանի] եր[ ] [ ]նի A | ի 2°] եւ ի A | եւ] om C | կերպարան] կրպարան D | իսկ] սկ C | իսկ գոյն ըստ] [ ] A | գոյն] գոյնն C | սեաւ սպիտակ կապոյտ] սեաւ սպիտակ [ ] A ի սպիտակ կապոյտ սեաւ B սպիտակ կարմիր սեաւ C սպիտակն կարմիր եւ սեաւ D | եւ] [ ] A | եւ սաւս] դեղին D | սաւս] [ ]ս A դեղին BC | խառնուածքն] խառնակութիւնքն B խառնուածք CD | բաղկանան] բաժանի B | բաղկանան ի] [ ] [ ] A | տեսիլս] om C | գունոց] գունոցն B գունից C

1.6.4 Նոյնպէս եւ ձեւքն] նոյն[ ] [ ] [ ] A | եւ] om C | ձեւքն] ձեւք CD add ըստ BCD | քառակի] քառից D | զանազանի] զանազանին CD | կրի] կարի B կապի C | բաժանականին] [ ]կանին A բաժանականի D | եռանկիւնի] եռանգիւնի ABC | եւ] om D | քառանկիւնի] քառանգիւնի ABC | երկարն] եւ երկարն A երկայն BD եւ երկայն C | բոլորակ] բոլոր B | ի] om BCD | ձեւի] ձեւ BCD | շարժման] շարման D

1.6.5 իսկ] սկ C | կերպարան] կրպարան D | դէմս] դէմք C դեմի D | դէմք] դեմսն B դեմ D | յանհատի] հանդիպ B անհատի D | անհատն] անհատ CD | տեսակն] տեսակ CD | վերայ] վերա AB | ծննդեանց] ծնընդեանց A ծնընդոց B ծնելոց CD | յանհունն] յանհունս CD | արտաբերեալ] տարաբերեալ C | շարժման] շարման D

1.6.3 իսկ] coloured ի omitted C | բաժանի] ըստ – բաժանի omitted B* in upper margin B | իսկ 2°] coloured ի omitted C

1.6.5 իսկ] coloured ի omitted C | դէմք] ն above line B° | յանհատի] տ above դ by another hand B°

1.6.6 Իսկ պիտակաբար, որ ոչ ընդունի զբնականութիւն, որպէս ի վերայ չորեցունցն երեքի ախտատտացականից եւ ստորնոց եւ վերադասականաց, եւ ի վերայ գերագունին սահմանի, զի արտաբերեալ զանազանին ըստ լինելութեան նիւթոյ: Եւ ի սոցանէ են, որ կամաւ եւ են, որ ակամայ եւ, որ ոչ կամաւ եւ ոչ ակամայ՝ բռնադատութիւն, զի ոչ յումեքէ հարկի:

1.6.7 Իսկ ձայն է տարրական, բաժանեալ ի տեսակս չորս՝ անկենդանական, զգայական, բանական եւ պիտակաբար բանական: Զի անկենդանականն, միջնորդաւ ուռուցմանց, նշանակք են մարմնոց եւ բախման նիւթոց: Իսկ զգայականն՝ նշանակք են առ միմեանս սակս ծանաւթութեան տեսակացն: Եւ բանականին գծածք ձայնից են նշանակք եւ ձայնք իմացմանց, իսկ իմացուածն իրին եւ իրն անիրին:

1.6.8 Բայց բաղկանայ իմացուածն ի տեսլենէն եւ ի ձայնէն ի մարդս բնաւրեալ, ըստ շարադրութեան եւ առժամայն իմացմանց: Իսկ աստուածայնոցն ոչ այսպ բաղկացեալ իսկապէս, այլ երբեմն պիտակաբար ելով:

1.6.6 որ] om C | զբնականութիւն] զբնութիւն B զբնակութիւն CD | ի վերայ] om BCD | վերայ] վերա A | չորեցունցն] չորեցունց C | ախտատտացականից] ախտատտացականի BCD | եւ] om D | վերադասականաց] վերնադասականաց B վերոյ դասականաց D | ի] om C | վերայ] վերա AB | գերագունին] գերագունի A | սահմանի] om B | լինելութեան] om C | նիւթոյ] նիւթոյն C | կամաւ] կամo B | եւ են որ ակամայ] են եւ են որ ակամայ են C | եւ որ ոչ] եւ է որ ոչ A | ակամայ] ակամա A | յումեքէ] յումէքէ D

1.6.7 իսկ] սկ C | է] որ է BD է որ է C | տարրական] տարական B | անկենդանական] անկենդանականն B | զգայական] սգայական B | բանական] բնական A | բանական] բնական A | ուռուցմանց] ուռուցմանցն D | մարմնոց] մարմնոյ B | եւ] եւս D | բախման] բաբախման BC բատախման D | նիւթոց] նիւթից A | զգայականն] զգատականն A սգատականն B | ծանաւթութեան] ծանoթութեան BD | բանականին] բանականէն B բանականի C | իմացուածն] իմացւածն B

1.6.8 բաղկանայ] բաղկանա ABC | իմացուածն] իմացիծն B | տեսլենէն] տեսլենէ C add են A | շարադրութեան] շարադրութեանն C | առժամայն] առժաման D | աստուածայնոցն] աստուածայնոյն B add աստուածայնոցն B | այսպ] այս B | պիտակաբար ելով] պիտակաբերելով D

1.6.6 բռնադատութիւն] ո over ի C*

1.6.7 իսկ] coloured ի omitted C | մարմնոց] between lines above erasure of առ միմեանս B°

1.6.8 իմացմանց] ց over ն B°

1.6.9 Իսկ մակացելին է արհեստ եւ բաժանի ի տեսակս չորս՝ ի գործնական եւ ի բանական, ի տեսական եւ յիմացական։ Եւ գործնականն՝ ի տնաւրինական, ի բարոյական եւ ի քաղաքական։ Եւ բանականն՝ յապացուցական, ի տրամաբանական, յիմաստական, ի բաժանական, ի վերլուծական, ի սահմանական։

1.6.10 Եւ տեսականն, ի ձեռն որոյ խնդրականն՝ ի դիտաւորականն, յանմեկնելի որոշումն, ի ստորոգութիւնս էակացն, յանդէմ կացադրութիւնս, ի պատճառ մակագրութեան, ընդ որով՝ մասամբ վերաբերութին, յեղանակ վարդապետականին։

1.6.11 Իմացականին՝ չար եւ բարի, ժամանակ, կատարելութին, սկիզբն եւ կատարած, բնութին՝ սահմանական եւ արարչական, էականութին, նիւթ եւ շարժումն, ունայն, անբաւ։ Չի եւ սահմանաւ բաժանեալ առանձնանան։

1.6.9 տեսակս] om C | գործնական] գործական A գործնականն CD | եւ] om C | բանական] բանականն CD | տեսական] տեսականն C տնտեսականն D | յիմացական] յիմացականն C իմացականն D | գործնականն] գործական A | տնաւրինական] տնօրինականն BCD | ի բարոյական] [ ] [ ]արական A | բարոյական] բարոյականն BD բարուական C | ի] om D | քաղաքական] քաղաքականն BCD | յապացուցական] յապացուցականն BCD | տրամաբանական] տրամաբանականն BCD | յիմաստական] յիմաստականն BD յիմաստաիրականն C | ի] om A | բաժանական] բժշկանն B բժշկականն C բժշկական D | ի] om AD | վերլուծական] վերլուծականն BC | ի] om AD | սահմանական] սահմանականն BC

1.6.10 տեսականն ի] ի տեսականն ի B | որոյ] որո A | խնդրականն] manuscript ends here C | դիտաւրականն] դիտաւրականաւ D | ստորոգութիւնս] ստորոգութեան B | յանդէմ] add եւ B | յանդէմ կացադրութիւնս] յանդէմակացադրութեան B | կացադրութիւնս] կացադրութին A բացադրութիւնս D | ի] add եւ B | վերաբերութին] վերբերութին A վերաբերութեան B | յեղանակ] եղանակ D

1.6.11 missing C | իմացականին] om B | չար] չարոյ BD | բարի] բարո B բարոյ D | կատարելութին] կատարելութեան BD | սկիզբն] սկիսբն D | կատարած] կատարածն D | բնութին] բնութեան BD | եւ] om D | արարչական] արրչան B | էականութին] էականութեան BD add ի D | շարժումն] յոյժ իմն B | եւ] om B | բաժանեալ] բաժանել B | առանձնանան] առանձնականք B

1.6.9 է] omitted C* above line C°

1.6.10 յանդէմ] ակ above line B°

1.6.12 Քանզի սահմանք գործնականին են՝ կամք, յաւժարութիւն, ընտրողութիւն, բարկութիւն, ցանկութիւն: Եւ բանականին՝ անուն եւ բայ, բան եւ բացերեւական բան, ստորասութիւն եւ բացասութիւն:

1.6.13 Իսկ տեսականին՝ զգայութիւն, երեւակայութիւն, կարծիք, տրամախոհութիւն, միտք: Եւ իմացականին՝ որոշմունք մտաց, իմաստք եւ խորհուրդք, գիտութիւն եւ յառաջտեսութիւն:

1.6.14 Իսկ կալմունք արհեստից է բնութիւն անխնդրելի, անհատ ի ժողովմանն, որ ասի մարդ, յորս ամենայնքն երեւեալք բաժանին՝ բաղկացելիք եւ անբաղկացելիք եւ մակացելիք:

1.6.15 Իսկ բաղկացելիքն եւ անբաղկացելիքն ընդ միմեամբք՝ դասիւ եւ ստորադասիւ երկմասնաբար: Եւ մակացելիքն ի բաղկացելիսն եւ յանբաղկացելիսն. տրամանկիւնիք բաղկանան. ուստի կատարեալ լինի վեցեակն:

1.6.16 Քանզի են երկու բաղկացելիք ընդ միմեամբք եւ մի տրամանկիւնի: Եւ դարձեալ բաժանի մարդն ըստ բնութեան եւ ըստ ախտի, ըստ Հաւատոյ եւ ըստ յուսոյ եւ ըստ սիրոյ:

1.6.12 missing C | *քանզի*] *զի* B | *սահմանք*] *սահման* AD | *գործնականին*] *գործականին* A | *յաւժարութիւն*] *յօժարութիւն* B om D | *ընտրողութիւն*] *ընդրողութիւն* B | *բարկութիւն*] *ցանկութիւն* B *յօժարութիւն* D | *ցանկութիւն*] *բարկութիւն* B add *բարկութիւն* D | *եւ բայ*] *բա* B | *բացերեւական*] *բացերեւակաբան* B *բացերեւականն* D | *բան ստորասութիւն*] *ստորոգութեան* B | *բացասութիւն*] *բացասութեան* B

1.6.13 missing C | *զգայութիւն*] *զգաութիւն* A *զգայութեան* B | *երեւակայութիւն*] *երեւակացութիւն* A *երեւակութեան* B | *միտք*] *մի*[ ] A | *մտաց*] *մտացականին որոշմունք մտացն* D | *իմաստք*] *իմացուացք* B | *յառաջտեսութիւն*] *յառաջատեսութիւն* B

1.6.14 missing C | *անհատ*] *յանհատ* B | *ամենայնքն*] *ամենայնք* B *ամենեքեան* D | *երեւեալք*] *երեւեալ* BD | *բաղկացելիք*] *բաղկացելիքն* B | *եւ մակացելիք*] *է* B

1.6.15 missing C | *իսկ բաղկացելիքն եւ անբաղկացելիքն*] om B | *դասիւ*] *դասի* B | *ստորադասիւ*] *ստորադասի* B | *եւ մակացելիքն*] *մակացելիքն* D | *եւ յանբաղկացելիսն*] om D | *տրամանկիւնիք*] *տրամանգիւնիք* A *տրամանգինիւք* D

1.6.16 missing C | *բաղկացելիք*] *բաղկացելիքն* B | *տրամանկիւնի*] *տրամանգիւնի* AD | *ըստ բնութեան*] *ընդ բնութեան* B | *Հաւատոյ*] *Հաւատո* A | *եւ*] om B | *յուսոյ եւ ըստ*] om D | *սիրոյ*] *սիրո* A

1.6.15 *տրամանկիւնիք*] *տրամանգիւնք* A*

1.6.16 *քանզի*] *քան* B* *զի* above line B°

1.6.17 *Արդ՝ յաղագս պիտանացու սերիցն այսքան ասացեալ, որ ի վերայ ժամանակի արտադրեցան՝ դիրք, կարգք, շրջանք, չափք, գաւրութինք, աղդմունք: Վասն գասՀմանս բնութեանն ամանակի Հաստատուն ունել գշարժմունս շրջագայ մոլրակացն, որ են գոյացուցիշք ժամանակի:*

1.6.18 *Իսկ անմոլարքն՝ նշանակք տեղեաց, ընթացից եւ որոշմանց ժամուց, եւ ի պատաՀմունս առ ի շեղ շրջագայիցն ընդ նմին շալիղ տալ գազդումն գիտութեան իմաստասիրին: Այսք են սաՀմանք բանի առաջնոյ երրեկին, որ է Աստուծոյ բանաւորութին, գոր եւ մասնական գոլ ասացին:*

2.0.0 *ՅԱՂԱԳՍ ԳՈՐԾՆԱԿԱՆԻՆ գոր ի վերայ կատարելութեան բանի առադրեցին*

2.0.1 *Իր է՝ տնաւրինական, բարոյական, քաղաքական:*

2.1.0 *Յաղագս տնաւրինականին*

1.6.17 missing C | *յաղագս*] *բստ* B | *պիտանացու*] *պիտացու* D | *սերիցն*] *սերից* D | *վերայ*] *վերա* AB | *դիրք*] *գիրք* D | *կարգք*] *կարգ* BD | *գաւրութինք*] *գօրութինք* BD | *գասՀմանս*] *սաՀմանս* B *գի սաՀմանս* D | *բնութեանն*] *բնութ[ ] ի* B *բնութեան ի* D | *ամանակի*] *ժամանակի* BD | *Հաստատուն*] *Հասստատ* D | *գշարժմունս*] *ի շարժմունս* A | *շրջագայ*] *շրջագա* A *շրջակայի* D | *մոլրակացն*] *մոլրութեանց[ ]* B

1.6.18 missing C | *նշանակք*] *նշանակ* B | *տեղեաց*] *տեղ[ ]* B *տեղեացն* D | *որոշմանց*] *որոշման* A | *ժամուց*] *ժամուցն* A *ժամունց* B | *շեղ*] *[ ]* B | *շրջագայիցն*] *շրջագաիցն* A | *գազդումն*] *գասդումն* B *գագտումն* D | *առաջնոյ*] *առաջնո* A | *երրեկին*] *յերրեկին* B | *եւ մասնական*] *իմաստնականն* B *իմաստնական* D

2.0.0 missing C | *յաղագս*] *իսկ* D | *գործնականին*] *գործականին* A | *վերայ*] *վերա* A | *կատարելութեան*] *կատարեալ* B

2.0.1 missing C | *տնաւրինական*] *տնօրինական* BD | *բարոյական*] *բարոական* B add *ի* B | *քաղաքական*] *քաղական* B

2.1.0 missing ABCD

1.6.18 *շրջագայիցն*] *g* over *ն* D° | *այսք*] *ք* below line A°

2.1.1 Արդ, բաժանի տնաւրինականն՝ ի Համեստական, ի պատշաճական, ի տնտեսական: Զի Համեստականն է արգելուլ ըստ վեհագունին, պատշաճականն է չափաւորելն ըստ ճոխութեան, իսկ տնտեսականն է պաճարելն ըստ յաջողութեան: Եւ ասի տնաւրինականն Հոգացողութիւն Կազթեանց:

2.2.0 Յաղագս բարոյականին

2.2.1 Բարոյականն է շարադրութեամբ աւրինակեալ առ ի վարս առաքինութեան կամ չարութեան:

2.2.2 Եւ առադրի սողնոցն ըստ բնութեան, եւ գազանացն եւ անասնոցն՝ ըստ աննդեան, եւ թռչնոցն եւ լուղակացն՝ ըստ սովորութեան:

2.2.3 Եւ ասի բարոյականն խաւսք բարուց զգայուն կենդանեաց: Իսկ բարառնականն է, որ ըստ ժամանակի շարադրի, զի ի բուսոց կամ ի տնկոց առադրեալ աւրինակի:

2.3.0 Յաղագս քաղաքականին

2.1.1 missing C | տնաւրինականն] տնաւրինական A տնօրինական B տնօրինականն D | Համեստական] Համեստականն D | Համեստականն] Համեստ[ ]անն A Համետրականն D | պատշաճականն] պատշաճ[ ]կանն A պատշաճական D | է] ըստ B om D | չափաւորելն] չափաւորին B չափաւորել D | ըստ] om BD | ճոխութեան] ճոխութեանն A | տնտեսականն] տն[ ]եսականն A | է] om D | տնաւրինականն] տնօրին B տնտօրինականն D | Հոգացողութիւն] Հոգցուղղութիւն B Հոգւոց ուղղութիւն D | կազթեանց] om BD

2.2.0 missing C | բարոյականին] բարուականին B

2.2.1 missing C | բարոյականն] բարռականն A բարուականն B | աւրինակեալ] օրինակեալ BD

2.2.2 missing C | սողնոցն] սողնոց B | գազանացն] գազանաց BD | անասնոցն] անասնոց B | աննդեան] անընդեանն AD անընդեան B | թռչնոցն] թռչնոց B | լուղակացն] լօղակացն B լօղականաց D | սովրութեան] սովրութեանն A

2.2.3 missing C | բարոյականն] բարռականն A բարուականն B | խաւսք] խօսք BD | զգայուն] զգաուն A սգայուն B | կենդանեաց] կենդանեացն A կենդեաց D | բարառնականն] բարառնական AB | աւրինակի] օրինակի BD

2.3.0 missing C | քաղաքականին] քաղաքականի B քաղաքականնին D

2.1.1 չափաւորելն] ել above line D°

2.2.2 սողնոցն] ն above line A°

2.3.1 Քաղաքականացն նախադրի քերականութիւն։ Եւ է քերականութեանն երեք տեսակք՝ Հմտութիւն, քերթութիւն, քերթողութիւն։ Եւ ասի Հմտութիւն մասնական իրաց։

2.3.2 Եւ մասունք են վեց՝ վերծանութիւն ներկուռ ըստ առոգանութեան, գրուցատրութիւն ներգոյս ըստ քերթողական լեղանակս, լեղուաց եւ Հնագէտ պատմութեանց առձեռն բացատրութիւն, ստուգաբանութեան գիտ, Համեմատութեան տեղեկութիւն, դատումն քերթածացն։

2.3.3 Եւ քերթութիւն ասի առապելավարժութիւն՝ ըստ ընտրութեան տառից, ըստ վանգից եւ ըստ փաղատութեանց, ըստ բառից եւ ըստ շարադրութեան, ըստ պարգութեան ուտիցն վարման։

2.3.4 Եւ քերթողութիւն է ըստ մասանց բանի։
Եւ են մասունք բանի ութ՝ անուն, բայ, ընդունելութիւն, յաւդ, դերանուն, նախադրութիւն, մակբայ, շաղկապ։ Իսկ անուն եւ բայ կատարեալք են Հոլովմամբ եւ շարադրութեամբ եւ ըստ յառաջադասութեան։

2.3.1 missing C | *նախադրի*] *նախատադրի* A | *քերականութիւն*] *քերականութիւնք* B | *քերականութեանն*] *քերականութեան* B *քերակութեան* D | *տեսակք*] *տեսակ* BD | *Հմտութիւն*] *Հմտութեան* B *Հպմտութիւն* D | *քերթութիւն*] *քերղութիւն* A *քերթութեան* B | *քերթողութիւն*] *քերղողութիւն* A *քերթողութեան* B | *Հմտութիւն*] *Հմաութիւն* B

2.3.2 missing C | *վեց*] add *առաջին* B | *վերծանութիւն*] *վերծանութիւնն* B | *ներկուռ ըստ*] *ըստ ներկուռ* D | *առոգանութեան*] *ոռոգանութիւն* D add *երկրորդ* B | *գրուցատրութիւն*] *գրուցատրութեան* B | *ներգոյս ըստ*] *ըստ ներգոյս* BD | *բացատրութիւն*] *բացատրութեանց* B add *չորրորդ* B | *ստուգաբանութեան*] *ստուգաբանութեանցն* D | *գիտ*] add *Հինգերորդ* B | *Համեմատութեան*] *Համեմատութեանցն* B *Համեմատութեանց* D | *տեղեկութիւն*] add *վեցերորդ* B add *եւ* D | *քերթածացն*] *քերղածացն* A *քերթածաց* D

2.3.3 missing C | *քերթութիւն*] *քերղութիւն* A *քերթութեան* B | *առապելավարժութիւն*] *առապելավարժութեան* B *առապէլավարժութիւն* D | *ըստ*] add *տառից* BD | *ըստ ընտրութեան տառից ըստ*] om D | *ընտրութեան տառից ըստ*] om B | *ըստ փաղատութեանց*] *փաղատութեանց* A | *ըստ շարադրութեան*] *շարադրութեան* A | *շարադրութեան*] *շարադրութեանց* B | *ուտիցն*] *տառից* B *ուտից* D | *վարման*] *նման* D om B

2.3.4 missing C | *քերթողութիւն*] *քերղողութիւն* A *քերթողութեան* B | *եւ են մասունք բանի*] om B | *ութ*] om D | *բայ*] *եւ բայ* A *բա* B | *ընդունելութիւն*] *ընդունելութեան* B | *յաւդ*] *յօդ* BD | *նախադրութիւն*] *նախադրութեան* B | *մակբայ*] *մակբա* AB | *բայ*] *բա* B | *Հոլովմամբ*] *Հոլովմամբք* B | *յառաջադասութեան*] *առաջադրութեան* B

2.3.2 *գիտ*] add *ե էր* two dots over *ի* B | *տեղեկութիւն*] add *Ձ էր* two dots over *ի* B

2.3.3 *տառից*] *ից* badly rubbed, perhaps effaced A

2.3.5 Իսկ այլքն են որ ընդունելութիւն են, եւ որ յաւդ են ըստ բայի, եւ են, որ նախդիր են, եւ որ փոխանակ են ըստ անուանն, եւ են, որ մակազդ են եւ որ կապ են։ Եւ նաւավարի բանն Հանդերձ իրաւք ի ձեռն ձայնի ի վերայ աւդոյ։

2.3.6 Իսկ քաղաքավարականն շարադրի ըստ նախերգութեան, ըստ կազմութեան եւ ըստ յորդորման։

2.3.7 Եւ բաժանին գլուխք մասանցն ի բաղխոճականն, ի յատենականն, ի կացրդականն։ Զի բաղխոճականն պատմութիւն է ըստ ժամանակի եւ ատենականն է տեղի ըստ տեսլարանի, իսկ կացրդականն է գրվել կամ պարսաւել։

2.4.0 Յաղագս միմուսութեան

2.4.1 Միմուսութիւն է կերպարանումն պիտակաբար առ ի խաբէութիւն. եւ լինի ըստ այտոցիկ՝ ի խամուսթենէ եւ ի տկարութենէ միտք եւ գիտութիւնք այլոցն քննեալ չափին.

2.4.2 Եւ ի խռովութենէ եւ ի գուարթութենէ՝ կարծիք այլոցն երկբայացեալ լինին։ Եւ ըստ գովին եւ ըստ դիւրացուցանելոյն խախտումն եւ շրջումն իմաստիցն լինի. եւ է ըստ քաղաքական վարուց։

2.3.5 missing C | *որ ընդունելութիւն*] *ներընդունելութեան* B | *ընդունելութիւն*] *ընդունելութեանն* D add *է* D | *են եւ*] *եւ են* BD | *յաւդ*] *օդ* B *յօդ* D | *ըստ*] add *ամենայն* B | *բայի*] *բաի* AB | *նախդիր են*] *նախադրեն* AD *նախդրեն* B | *որ*] *են որ* BD | *ըստ* 2°] add *ամենայն* B | *անուանն*] *անուան* BD | *որ*] om B | *մակազդ*] *մակազք* B *մակազղ* D | *որ*] *են որ* B | *բանն*] *բան* A | *իրաւք*] *իւրովքն* B *իւրով* D | *վերայ*] *վերա* B | *աւդոյ*] *ուդա* A *օդոյ* B *օդոյն* D

2.3.6 missing C | *քաղաքավարականն*] *քաղաքավարական* A

2.3.7 missing C | *բաժանին*] *բաժանեն* A *բաժանի* B | *գլուխք*] *գլուխն* B | *բաղխոճականն*] *բախոճականն* A *բան* B | *յատենականն*] *յատենական* A *յաղենականն* D | *կացրդականն*] *կացրդական* A *կացրդկանն* B *կացրդականն* D | *բաղխոճականն*] *բախոճական* A *բաղՀստական* B | *պատմութիւն*] *պատմութեան* B | *ատենականն*] *աղենական* D | *տեսլարանի*] *ամենայն տեսական* B *տեսարանի* D | *կացրդականն*] *կացրդական* A *կացդուր* B *կացրդականն* D | *գրվել*] *գրվեալ* B | *կամ*] *եւ* B | *պարսաւել*] *պատուեալ* B *պարասաւել* D

2.4.0 missing C

2.4.1 missing BCD | *պիտակաբար*] *պիտակարար* A | *խաբէութիւն*] *խաբեութիւն* A

2.4.2 missing BCD | *երկբայացեալ*] *երկբաացեալ* A

2.3.7 *բաղխոճականն*] add erasure of one letter-space B

2.5.0 *Յաղագս բովանդակութեան*

2.5.1 *Զբովանդակութիւն յորժամ լսիցես զՀամար առ շիր, տես զիարդ խառնեալ են երկինքն եւ երկիր զուգակցութեամբ յերկնից առեալ Հրաման զաւդս ընդ Հող խառնեալ:*

2.5.2 *Արդ՝ Հմտացիս զաւրութեամբ, որ ի մէջ երկնի եւ երկրի, զաւրութիւն չրոյ եւ յայտնութիւն Հողմոց է, տեւս զիարդ ժողովեաց, մածոյց զիւրովին եւ արգել իւր կանգնեաց:*

2.5.3 *Արդ՝ երեք ինչս պարտ է ասել չուր, եւ որ իցեն ասացուք շտեմարան, զաւրութիւն, բուրումն: Արդ՝ յայտնապէս ասացուք շտեմարան է ի չուրս, յորմէ աւդք ելանեն ի դուրս՝ Հռասափն եւ քարսափն, սարսափն եւ նագատն: Եւ ելք սոցա ի ծովէ են, եւ զնացք ընդ երկինս, զշտեմարանս նոցա եւ զնացս նոցա անցեալ յայտ արարից:*

2.5.4 *Չուր է լայնանիստ շտեմարանափակ, աւդք անՀանգիստ, ելք նոցա արտաքին ծովէ է, եւ զնաց նոցա յարտաքին չուրան: Թանձի ծով, որ ծածուկ ոչ ունի՝ արտաքին է, իսկ յորոյ վերայ երկինք է՝ ներքին է, եւ ընդ մէջ չրոց եւ երկրի աւդք են եւ բացում անգամ վնաս եւ շարժմունս առնեն, եւ բացում աւգուտ յաղբերս եւ յերակս չուրց, եւ երկինք Հաստեալ են ի վերայ երկրի:*

2.5.0 missing ABCD | *յաղագս*] om B | *բովանդակութեան*] *բովանդակութիւն* B *արՀեստի յայլ գրոց* B

2.5.1 missing AC | *զբովանդակութիւն*] *բովանդակութիւն* D | *երկինքն*] *երկինք* B | *առեալ*] *տուեալ* B | *զաւդս*] *զօդս* BD

2.5.2 missing AC | *Հմտացիս*] *Հմա[ ]ցիս* B | *որ*] add *է* B | *զաւրութեամբ*] *զօրութեամբ* BD | *զաւրութիւն*] *զօրութեամբ* B *զօրութին* D | *յայտնութիւն*] *յայտնութեան* B | *տեւս*] *տես* B | *կանգնեաց*] *կարգեաց* D

2.5.3 missing AC | *իցեն*] *ինչ են* D | *զաւրութիւն*] *զօրութին* BD | *չուրս*] *չուրցս* D | *աւդք*] *օդք* B *օդ* D | *եւ*] om B | *զնացք*] *զնացք սոցա* D | *ընդ երկինս*] *յերկինս* D | *անցեալ*] *անցել* B | *յայտ արարից*] *յայտարարից* B

2.5.4 missing AC | *աւդք*] *օդք* D | *աւդք անՀանգիստ*] *օդք Հանգիստք* B | *նոցա*] *նոցայ* B | *արտաքին*] *յարտաքին* B | *զնաց*] *զնացք* B | *նոցա*] *ն[ ]* B | *ոչ ունի*] *ո[ ]* B | *վերայ*] *վերա* B | *ներքին*] *արտաքին* B | *չրոց*] *չուրց* B | *աւդք*] *օդք* BD | *վնաս*] *վնասք* D | *շարժմունս*] *շարմունս* B *շարժմունք* D | *աւգուտ*] *անգամ* B *օգուտ* D | *յերակս*] *երակս* D | *չուրց*] *չրոց* B | *եւ*] om B | *երկրի*] *երկր[ ]* B

2.5.1 *երկինքն*] written over another word B° | *երկիր*] *եւ երկիր* above line B°

2.5.4 *չուր*] *չրային* B* *չուր* B° | *նոցա*] *եւ զնաց* B* *ելք նոցայ* B°

2.5.5 *Այտոքիկ բովանդակութիւնք, զոր ասեմ քեզ բովանդակութիւն նոցա ամենեցուն, եւ տէր բանն աստուծոյ է:*

3.0.0 *ՅԱՂԱԳՍ ...*

3.1.0 *Յաղագս սահմանաց եւ բաժանմանց գոր ի վերայ բնութեան առադրեցին*

3.1.1 *Արդ, քանզի պարտ է նախ բաժանման գոլ եւ ապա սահմանին: Զի է բաժանումն երակի՝ ստորական եւ վերական եւ ... : Եւ ի տեսակս չորս բաժանի՝ տեսական եւ մասնական, ի նման եւ յաննման եւ դիմադրական կրկին միաւորութիւն, որ է առանձնական:*

3.1.2 *Իսկ սահմանականն բաժանի ի տեսակս չորս տրամաբանութեամբ, այսպէս, թէ՛ գի՞նչ է, եւ ուստի՞ է, եւ որպիսի՞ են, եւ վասն է՞ր է:*

3.1.3 *Իսկ Հատածք աւրինակի գանագանութեամբ մասանցն, ըստ սոցա բաժանի այսպէս: Առաջին, գի՞նչ է սահման բաժանեալ յանկին ի սեռէ եւ ի բաղկացուցիչ գանագանութեանց, ի՞ւ գանագանի ստորադրականն, որ ի պատահիցն պարագայի.*

3.1.4 *երկրորդ, ուստի՞ յայտ է սահման՝ յագարակայնոցն ցուցմանէ, յորմէ՞ առնու յենթակայէ եւ ի կատարմանէ, ո՞ր է կատարեալ սահման եւ ո՞ր անկատար. կատարեալ է, որ զբնականն ընդունի, ըստ Հոլովմանցն՝ անուանցն եւ բայից. նաւավարիլ աո ի լրութիւն ինչ իրաց գոլ: Եւ անկատարն է, որ ի պարագայիցն պարագայի, որ նշանակ է անուան կամ բայի:*

2.5.5 missing AC | *բովանդակութիւնք*] *բովանդակութին* BD | *բովանդակութին*] *բովանդակութիւնք* B | *նոցա*] om B

3.0.0 missing ABCD

3.1.0 missing BCD | *վերայ*] *վերա* A

3.1.1 missing BCD | *... եւ*] om A | *դիմադրական*] vacat follows A

3.1.2 missing BCD

3.1.3 missing BCD | *պարագայի*] *պարագաի* A

3.1.4 missing BCD | *յենթակայէ*] *յենթակաէ* A | *բայից*] *բաից* A | *պարագայիցն*] *պարագայիցն* A | *պարագայի*] *պարագաի* A | *կամ*] *կա* A | *բայի*] *բաի* A

3.1.3 *աւրինակի*] *ինակի* A* *աւր* above line A°

3.1.4 *յագարակայնոցն*] *գկ* with *գ* surmounted by two dots A* | *կամ*] *մ* badly rubbed A*

3.1.5 Քանզի են սահմանք իմաստասիրութեան՝ գիտութին էակացս, գիտութին աստուածայնոց եւ մարդկայնոց, խոկումն մահու, նմանութին աստուծոյ, արհեստ արհեստից եւ մակացութին մակացութեանց, իմաստասիրութին՝ սիրելութին իմաստութեան, որք են վեց:

3.1.6 Եւ դարձեալ, ըստ քառակին բաժանի՝ Հուպ ենթակայ՝ անդունդ եւ Հուպ կատարումն՝ լուութին, Հեռի ենթակայ՝ միտք եւ Հեռի կատարումն՝ ճշմարտութին: Եւ ըստ առաւելութեան՝ բան եւ կեանք, եւ ըստ ստուգաբանութեանն՝ մարդ եւ ժողովումն, գոր պիթագորեանքն պատուեն. քանզի էակն ի չորից բաղկանայ, չորս շարժմամբ:

3.1.7 Վասն է՞ր սահմանք իմաստասիրութեան վեց: Առաջին՝ է վասն էակացն, քանզի է, որ ասի եւ ոչ է, եւ է, որ ոչ ասի եւ է. եւ երկրորդ՝ վասն Թուականութեանն, քանզի վեց կատարեալ է երկմասամբ եւ երրեկով եւ կիսով երկուտասանեկին:

3.1.8 Եւ քառակն է դար, յորմէ գլուխք կոճատադարուցն բաղկանան, ըստ արհեստիս:

3.1.9 Եւ են տառանեակք՝ Դ. Ժ. Ճ. Ռ. Ա. Դ. Գ. Բ. Ա.: Եւ ասի մասնական ի տեսակս իմացականին: Իսկ եռակն է կոճատ եւ նշանակ դարկոճատացն գոլ, եւ ըստ արհեստիս կատարեալ է ի տեսակացն եւ ի ճատելոցն:

3.1.10 Եւ դարձեալ սահմանի թիւ եռակի ըստ արհեստիս, դար է լեզն գԱստուծոյ եւ կոճատ է խաւսելն ընդ Աստուծոյ, իսկ յերկրոցունց է քննելն գԱստուած որ է առաջին եւ որ վերջին:

3.1.5 missing BCD | *արհեստ*] *արհ*[ ]*տ* A

3.1.6 missing BCD | *ենթակայ*] *ենթակա* A | *ենթակայ*] *ենթակա* A | *բաղկանայ*] *բաղկանա* A

3.1.7 missing BCD | *Թուականութեանն*] *Թւականութեանն* A

3.1.8 missing BCD

3.1.9 missing BCD

3.1.10 missing BCD

3.1.5 *են*] omitted A∗ above line A°

3.1.7 *քանզի*] *քան* A∗ *զի* above line A° | *երկմասամբ*] *ա*2 ° lost in lacuna, *մբ* partly preserved A

3.1.10 *քննելն*] *ն* 3° above line A°

3.1.11 Առաջին է գիտութիւն էական, որք շուրջ են զգայութեամբք, եւ գիտութիւն աստուածայնոց եւ մարդկայնոցն դրութեանց. քանզի ոչ ամենայն աստուած պաշտաւն եւ ամենայն մարդ պաշտաւնեայ:

3.1.12 Երկրորդ է խզումն մարդկան ախտի կենաց եւ ըմբռնիլ ի պարգն եւ յանախտական, եւ նմանութիւն Աստուծոյ կարին եւ գիտնականաւն եւ բարեաւն. գնման ըստ մարդկային բնութեանս է, եւ ոչ Ճշմարիտ Աստուած գոլ.

3.1.13 քանզի Աստուծոյ կարեին եւ գիտեին եւ բարերարեին յանբաւս է, իսկ մարդկայինս` ընդ բաւականաւ, զի միայն կամեին եւ յաւժարեին եւ ընտրեին առ ի նմանութիւն Աստուծոյ բաղկանալ է:

3.1.14 երրորդ է արՀեստ արՀեստից եւ մակացութիւն մակացութեանց: Արդ, արՀեստիցն է գործականն, իսկ արՀեստ` բանականն, եւ մակացութեանցն է տեսականն, իսկ մակացութիւն` իմացականն, եւ այսպէս` իբրու թագաւոր թագաւորաց եւ աստուած աստուծոց:

3.1.15 եւ իմաստասիրութիւն` սիրել գիմաստութիւն, ստուգաբանութեամբ: Քանզի ամենայն իմաստասիրութիւն եռակի բաժանի` ի լեւ իբրեւ գԱստուծոյ, եւ խաւսել իբր ընդ Աստուծոյ, եւ քննել իբրեւ գԱստուած:

3.1.16 իսկ գիտ սաՀմանացն է ըստ բանական արՀեստիցն եւ պատՃառ է Հնարական միտք աշխարՀս, որ է Աստուած:

3.2.0 Յաղագս ապացուցի եւ տրամաբանութեան

3.1.11 missing BCD | զգայութեամբք] զգաութեամբք A | պաշտաւնեայ] պաշտաւնեա A

3.1.12 missing BCD | յանախտական] յանախտկաան A | մարդկային] մարդկաին A

3.1.13 missing BCD | մարդկայինս] մարդկաինս A

3.1.14 missing BCD | մակացութեանց] մակացո[ ]g A

3.1.15 missing BCD | եւ իմաստասիրութիւն] եւ իմաստութիւն A

3.1.16 missing BCD

3.2.0 missing BCD

3.1.11 մարդկայնոցն] Ա 2° above line A°

3.2.1 Ապացուցականն ի շարաբանութենէ բաղկանայ, իսկ շարաբանութիւն ի նախադասութենէ եւ ի ստորադասութենէ, իսկ նախադասութիւն եւ ստորադասութիւն՝ յենթակայէ եւ ի ստորոգելոյ, եւ ենթակայն՝ եւ ի ներքոյկացեաց դիմաց, իսկ ստորոգեալն է գայլմեգն, որ ի վերոյն անցեալ լինի շարասութիւն:

3.2.2 Իսկ տրամաբանականն տարբերի Հարցմամբ եւ պատասխանեաւ՝ Հակադարձաբար: Եւ գանագանի Հարցական ձայնիւ եւ կարճաբառութեամբ, եւ ասի քննական, տեղական, ուսումնական:

3.2.3 Իսկ պատասխանականն գանագանի ներածութեամբ եւ շարաբառութեամբ, եւ ասի՝ ցուցական եւ Հատուցական եւ Հաւանական, եւ դարձեալ՝ ըստ ստորասութեան եւ ըստ բացասութեան, եւ ասի Հաստանական՝ Հակադրութեամբ ճառեցելովք:

3.3.0 Յաղագս իմաստակութեան եւ վերլուծութեան

3.3.1 Իմաստակութիւն է ըստ Հոմանուն եւ ըստ փաղանուն, ըստ այլ եւ ըստ այլ թուոյ, ըստ այլում եւ ըստ այլում եւ ժամանակի եւ գաւրութեան, ըստ այլապէս եւ ըստ այլապէս շարժման եւ տեղւոյ:

3.3.2 Իսկ վերլուծական է քակտումն եւ որոշումն Հիւթից եւ մասանց եւ ձայնից:
Այսք են բանական արՀեստին տեսակք, որք ի բնութեան կարգեցան:

4.0.0 ՅԱՂԱԳՍ ...

4.1.0 Յաղագս ի ձեռն խնդրականի գոր ի տեսականէն առաղրեցին:

3.2.1 missing BCD | *բաղկանայ*] *բաղկանա* A | *յենթակայէ*] *յենթակաէ* A

3.2.2 missing BCD | *ուսումնական*] *ուսմնական* A

3.2.3 missing BCD | *ըստ ստորասութեան*] *ստորասութեան* A

3.3.0 missing BCD

3.3.1 missing BCD | *թուոյ*] *թւոյ* A | *տեղւոյ*] *տեղոյ* A

3.3.2 missing BCD | *կարգեցան*] *կարգեցաւ* A

4.0.0 missing ABCD

4.1.0 missing BCD

3.2.3 *Հաւանական*] *Հաւական* A* *ան* above line A°

4.1.1 Խնդրականին չորք են տեսակք։ Զի է որ ձայն մի եւ իրն գանագանեալ, եւ է որ իրն մի եւ ձայնն, եւ է, դարձեալ, որ Հասարակ՝ ի ձայնն եւ իրն, եւ է որ յարակցեալ վանգիւ մի մի կամ փաղառութեամբ:

4.1.2 Եւ ասի սեռ եւ տեսակ, զի սեռ է ըստ ենթիւ գանագանութեան իրին եւ ձայնին, եւ տեսակ է ըստ Հասարակ ձայնին եւ իրին. իսկ թիւ՝ ըստ յարակցութեան վանգին կամ փաղառութեան:

4.1.3 Իսկ դիտաւտրականն բաղկանայ լիրէ եւ յիմացուածէ եւ ի ձայնէ եւ ի գրեցելոյ:
Քանգի իրն է անիրին նշանակ, եւ իմացուածն՝ իրին, իսկ ձայնն՝ իմացուածին, եւ գրեցեալքն՝ ձայնից են նշանակք: Եւ ասի պարգ եւ շարադրեալ, զի է, որ իմացուածն եւ ձայնն, եւ է, որ ձայնն շարադրեալ եւ իմացուածն:

4.2.0 Յաղագս անմեկնելի որոշման եւ ստորոգութեան էակացս

4.2.1 Անմեկնելի որոշման երկու են տեսակք՝ գոյացութին եւ պատահումն. քանգի ուր գոյացութին՝ եւ պատահումն, եւ ուր պատահումն՝ եւ գոյացութին:

4.2.2 Այլ ըստ նախկնի եւ ըստ բարձմանն որոշի գոյացութին ի պատահմանէ. եւ դարձեալ, է որ ըստ քառակին գանագանի, զի է, որ գենթակայէ ասի եւ է, որ յենթակայում է. եւ է, որ ոչ յենթակայում է եւ ոչ գենթակայէ ասի, ըստ առաջին գոյացութեանն:

4.1.1 missing BCD

4.1.2 missing BCD

4.1.3 missing BCD | բաղկանայ] բաղկանա A | իմացուածն] իմացու vacat ծն A

4.2.0 missing C | եւ] ի D om A | եւ ստորոգութեան էակացս] սղուե B | ստորոգութեան] ստորոգութիւնն D | էակացս] om D

4.2.1 missing C | անմեկնելի] անմեկնել D | գոյացութին] գոացութին A | պատահումն] պատահմունք B | քանգի] գի B եւ D | գոյացութին] գոացութին A add է B | գոյացութին … պատահումն 2°] պատահումն է D | ուր] որ B | պատահումն] add է B | գոյացութին] գոացութին A գոյութին D

4.2.2 missing C | նախկնի] նախ[ ] տեսակն է B | բարձմանն] բաժանմանն B | որոշի] որոշէ B | գոյացութին] գոացութին A | որ] om D | քառակին] քանակին D | գենթակայէ] գենթակաէ A | ասի] ասէ BD | որ] որով D add ոչ A | յենթակայում] յենթակատում AB | է որ ոչ յենթակայում է եւ] om AD | յենթակայում] ենթակատում B | գենթակայէ] գենթակաէ A | ասի] ասէ B | առաջին] յառաջին D | գոյացութեանն] գոացութեանն B գոյացութեան D

4.2.2 ասի] ի above line A°

4.2.3 Իսկ ստորոգութիւն էակացս առաջինն ի չորս բաժանի՝ ի սեռ եւ ի տեսակ, ի տարբերութիւն եւ ի յատուկ:

4.2.4 Եւ սեռ երակի ասի՝ ըստ սերման գոյացութեան. եւ ըստ յոլովման ազգի, որ ի միոյ ցուցանի աճումն. եւ ըստ ինքեան բաժանի ի տեսակս Հինգ՝ երակաբար, որք ասին տեսակագոյնք եւ սեռականագոյնք, որ է գոյացութիւն, մարմին եւ անմարմին, կենդանի եւ անկենդանի, զգայուն եւ անզգայուն, բանական եւ անբան, տեսակ եւ անՀատ:

4.2.5 Եւ տեսակն բաժանի քառակաբար. գի է, որ ի ներքոյ սեռի դասի, եւ է, որ սաՀմանաւ ունի գսեռն եւ սեռն գնմանէ իբրեւ գենթակայէ ասի: Եւ դարձեալ, սաՀմանի տեսակն եւ սեռն ի գինչէումն եւ ըստ գոյգ յոլովմանն, եւ է, որ ի վերնագոյնան տեսակականայ եւ ի ներքինան սերանայ:

4.2.6 Իսկ տարբերութիւն երակի բաժանի՝ ի գոյացութիւն եւ ի պատաՀումն, անչատական եւ անանչատական. է, որ անեղծանելի եւ է, որ դժուարաշարժելի. եւ Հաստակաբար ասին վասն ընդդիմակացն:

<hr>

4.2.3 missing C | *ստորոգութիւն*] *ստորոգութեան* B | *էակացս*] *ակացս* B | *առաջինն*] *առաջին* B | *եւ ի տեսակ*] *ի տեսակ* D

4.2.4 missing C | *ըստ*] add *ամենայն* B | *գոյացութեան*] *գոյութեանն* A | *յոլովման*] *ոլովման* D | *որ ի միոյ*] *յորմէ* B | *ի*] om D | *ինքեան*] *ինքեանց* A | *որք*] *որ* D | *տեսակագոյնք*] *տեսագոյնք* A | *եւ սեռականագոյնք*] om D | *սեռականագոյնք*] *երականագոյնք* A | *գոյացութիւն*] *գոյացութիւնք* B | *անկենդանի*] *անկենդան* D | *զգայուն*] *գոգայուն* B | *անզգայուն*] *անզգաուն* A *անագայուն* B | *տեսակ եւ*] *տեսակ* AB add *է* B

4.2.5 missing C | *եւ* 1°] *եւ եւ* B | *ի*] om AB | *ներքոյ*] *ներքո* A | *դասի*] *դասէ* B | *սաՀմանաւ ունի*] *սաՀմանիին ի* A *սաՀման անուանի* B *ի սաՀմանաւ* D | *սեռն*] *գսեռն* B | *իբրեւ*] *իբր* A | *գենթակայէ*] *գենթակաէ* A | *եւ*] *է* B | *սաՀմանի*] *սաՀման է* A | *սեռն*] *սեռ* D | *վերնագոյնան*] *վերնագոյնումն* B *վերագոյան* D | *տեսակականայ*] *տեսականա* A | *սերանայ*] *սերանա* A

4.2.6 missing C | *տարբերութիւն*] *տարբերութեան* B | *գոյացութիւն*] *գոյութիւն* A | *եւ*] om D | *անչատական*] *անչատականն* D | *անանչատական*] *անանչատականն* AD | *եւ է*] *է եւ է* B | *դժուարաշարժելի*] *դժորարաշարժելի* B | *Հաստակաբար*] *Հաստակաբարին* D | *ասին*] om D | *ընդդիմակացն*] *դիմակաց* B

<hr>

4.2.3 *ստորոգութիւն*] *ստորութեան* B∗

4.2.5 *գսեռն*] *սեռն* A∗ *գ* above line A° | *ասի*] *ասէ* B∗ *ասի* B° | *վերնագոյնան*] add *յոլ* A∗ erased A°

4.2.7 Իսկ յատուկն քաղաքաբար ասի, զի է որ միայնում եւ է, որ ամենին եւ դարձեալ է, որ միայնում եւ ամենին, եւ է, որ Հակադարձին, ըստ կատարելութեան յատկի:

4.2.8 Իսկ երկրորդ ստորոգութեանցն ի տասն բաժանի՝ ի սեռս, որ է գոյացութիւն, որակ, քանակ, առինչ, ուր, երբ, կալ, ունել, առնել, կրել:

4.2.9 Եւ են մասնականք, որ ըստ շարամանութեան կատարին, զի լինի ստորասութիւն կամ բացասութիւն եւ արդար կամ սուտ, եւ ասին Հատարակաբար եւ յատկապէս:

4.2.10 Արդ, երրորդն՝ իսկագոյն եւ տիրագոյն, նախկին եւ կատարեալ ըստ ամենայնի, իսկ այլքն՝ ամենայն պատահք ասին: Եւ բաժանի յերկուս՝ առաջինն է անճատ եւ առաջին թուեալ, եւ երկրորդ չորս է՝ տեսակն եւ սեռն, ըստ գոյգ յոլովութեան, եւ յատուկ է ըստ միայնումն:

4.2.11 Եւ քանակին է, որ տարորոշ է, եւ է, որ շարունակ, եւ այնք, որ դիր ունին. եւ տարորոշ է բան եւ թիւ, շարունակ է գիծ, մակերեւութին, մակարդակ, տեղի, իսկ ժամանակ՝ եւ է, որ դիրն ունին գիծ մակարդակ տեղի մակերեւութին եւ ժամանակ, բան եւ թիւ յաւէտ դաս ինչ ունել, եւ յատուկ է ըստ ամենայնին:

4.2.7 missing C | յատուկն] յատ[ ]կն B | ամենին] ամենայնի BD | եւ] om D | դարձեալ] om B | միայնում եւ ամենին եւ է որ Հակադարձին] [ ]ակադարձին B | ամենին] ամենայնին D | յատկի] յատկին BD

4.2.8 missing C | ի սեռս] սեռ B ի սեռ D | գոյացութիւն] գրացութիւն A գոյութիւն B | ունել] ուն B

4.2.9 missing C | կատարին] կատանին D | բացասութիւն] բացութիւն D | արդար կամ սուտ եւ] արդ պատկանաւոր B

4.2.10 missing C | երրորդն] երեք են BD | տիրագոյն] տիրակագոյն D | ամենայն] ամեն A | պատահք] պատահմուն B | առաջինն] առաջին B | առաջին թուեալ] անաչ իմն թւել B | երկրորդ] երկորդ B երկրորդն D | չորս] չորրորդ B om D | տեսակն] տեսակս A տեսակ B | յոլովութեան] յոլովութեանն AB

4.2.11 missing C | քանակին] քառակին AB քառակի D | որ տարորոշ] որ տարոշ D | է 3°] om B | եւ 3°] է եւ D | այնք] այն B | որ դիր] որք դիր A | թիւ] add եւ ABD | գիծ] գիծն D | մակերեւութին] մակերեւույթ եւ B մակերեւույթ D | մակարդակ] մակաղրակ D | իսկ] եւ AD | իսկ ժամանակ] om B | դիրն] դիր B | մակարդակ] մակաղրակ D | տեղի] տեղ A | եւ] իսկ ABD | թիւ] թիւն D | ամենայնին] ամենայնի D

4.2.11 ունին] ուն above line B° | տեղի] B* omits from ժամանակ 1°– 2° and has ժամանակ 1° – տեղի in lower margin and remaining words written over the extant text B°

4.2.12 Եւ առնչին չորք են տեսակք՝ ունակութին, զգայութին, մակացութին, դրութին:

4.2.13 Իսկ նիստ եւ ընդկողմանումն եւ ընդկայութին՝ յարանունաբար ի գրոցն ասին եւ ի յատկէ ըստ Հակադարձին:

4.2.14 Եւ որակն քառակի ասի՝ ըստ ունակութեան եւ ըստ տրամադրութեան, ըստ գաւրութեան եւ ըստ ախտի, ըստ դառնութեան եւ ըստ քաղցրութեան, ըստ ձեւոյ եւ ըստ կերպի: Եւ յատուկ է ըստ միայնումն եւ ըստ ամենայնին:

4.2.15 Իսկ ուրն եւ երբն՝ ըստ քանակին ասին, իսկ կայն եւ ունելն՝ ըստ առինչունակին, եւ առնելն եւ կրելն՝ ըստ որակին:

4.3.0 Յաղագս զանազանութեան

4.3.1 Ընդդիմակայքն քառակաբար ասին: Զի է որ առինչունակապէս, եւ է որ ներհակաբար, եւ է որ ունակաւրէն եւ պակասաբար, եւ է որ ստորասութեամբ եւ բացասութեամբ. եւ մին առանց նախկնի ընդդէմ միմեանց: Իսկ պատճառ մակադրութեան նախերգութեամբ դասի:

4.2.12 missing C | *առնչին*] *առաջինն* A *առաջին* BD | *չորք են*] *չորեքին* B | *են*] om D | *տեսակք*] *տեսակ* B | *ունակութին*] *ունակութինք* A *ունակութեան* B | *զգայութին*] *զգաութինք* A | *մակացութին*] *մակացութեան* B | *դրութին*] *դրութեան* B

4.2.13 missing C | *ընդկողմանումն*] *ընկողմանումն* BD | *ընդկայութին*] *ընդկայութեան* B | *յարանունաբար ի*] *յարանուն եւ բարի* BD | *գրոցն*] *դրոցն* B | *Հակադարձին*] om B

4.2.14 missing C | *եւ որակն քառակի ասի*] *տրամատրութեան* B | *ունակութեան*] *գործութեան* B | *եւ*] om B | *տրամադրութեան*] *տրամատութեան* D | *տրամադրութեան ըստ*] om B | *գաւրութեան*] *գործութեան* BD | *ձեւոյ*] *ձեւտ* A | *կերպի*] *կրպի* D | *յատուկ է*] *յատկէ* D | *ըստ*] om A | *միայնումն*] *միայնում* BD | *ամենայնին*] *ամենայնում* B *ամենայնումն* D

4.2.15 missing C | *եւ*] om B | *քանակին*] *քանակի* D | *ունելն*] *ունել* A | *առինչունակին*] add *ասին* B

4.3.0 missing BCD

4.3.1 missing BCD

4.2.12 *առրնչին չորք*] *առինչ որ էք* B* | *ունակութին*] *ունակութինք* two dots over *ք* as erasure marks A | *զգայութին*] *զգայութինք* two dots over *ք* as erasure marks A

4.2.13 *եւ* 2°] *եւ* mostly rubbed A

4.3.2 Զի է ըստ ժամանակի, որ Ճնագոյն եւ վաղագոյն ասի քան զնորն, եւ միտք նախկին քան զիմացմունս, եւ տեսութիւնք քան զտեսուածս, եւ տառք քան զվաղադատութիւնս, եւ մին քան զերկուս, եւ ասի առանց Հակադրութեան:

4.3.3 Իսկ մասնական վերաբերութիւն՝ առանց Հակադրութեան եւ առանց Հոլովման ժամանակի, այլ ըստ միում մասին ժամանակի լինելութիւնքն վերաբերին, ըստ Հոլովման անուան տեսակի ածանցիցն, ըստ յեղանակ վարդապետութեան:

4.3.4 Ըստ շարժման բաժանի ի տեսակս վեց, որ է՝ լինելութիւն, ապականութիւն, աճելութիւն, նուազութիւն, այլայլութիւն, ըստ տեղւոյ փոփոխութիւն: Եւ ասի ըստ դիմակայութեան եւ ըստ մակադրութեան, եւ ըստ մասնական վերաբերութեան:

4.3.5 Արդ, են զանազանիչք սոքա առաջին եւ երկրորդ ստորոգութեանցն՝ սեռի եւ տեսակի, տարբերութեան եւ յատկի, գոյացութեան եւ քանակի, առինչունակի եւ որակութեան: Այլք են տեսական արՃեստին տեսակք, որ լեականութեանն կարգեցաւ: Կատարեցաւ երկրորդ մասն արՃեստիս, որ ասի աստուածխաւսութիւն:

5.0.0 ՅԱՂԱԳՍ ...

5.1.0 Յաղագս ...

5.1.1 ... Եւ դարձեալ զանազանի նախխասութեամբ ըստ սկզբանն բարին եւ ըստ կատարածին չարն: Իսկ որ ընդ մէջ ի բաղկանաց ըստ չորս իմն տեսակս տարբերի՝ ըստ ներածութեանց եւ ըստ ձայնից եւ ըստ ներգործութեանց, որ ասի մեղք կամ արդարութիւն:

4.3.2 missing BCD | *տառք*] *տաղք* A

4.3.3 missing BCD | *վերաբերութիւն*] *բերաբերութիւն* A

4.3.4 missing BCD | *տեղւոյ*] *տեղո* A | *դիմակայութեան*] *դիմակաութեան* A | *վերաբերութեան*] *վերբերութեան* A

4.3.5 missing BCD

5.0.0 missing ABCD

5.1.0 missing ABCD

5.1.2 Չորրորդ, վասն զի է, որ բնութեամբ է բարի եւ չար եւ է, որ պիտակաբար: Բնութեամբ է, որ զբնակութիւնն անեղծանելի եւ դժուարափոխ, զի թէեւ գփոփոխումն առնու, անդրէն ի նոյն՝ ի բնական սահմանն հաստատի:

5.1.3 Իսկ պիտակաբար է, որ ոչ բաղկանայ բնականութին սահմանի, եւ դարձեալ դիւրաշարժ ի պատահմունս ենթակային:

5.1.4 Արդ՝ բնաւորեցաւ բարին բնութեամբ, իսկ չարն առանց բնութեան եւ սահմանի: Զի բարին, թէ ի չարն յեղաւ, ոչ միայն չար կայ, այլ ի նոյն դարձեալ փոփոխի բնութեամբ: Իսկ չարին գփոփոխումն առնուլ բարի՝ միանգամայն բաղկացաւ բնութեամբ:

5.1.5 Հինգերորդ, զի ըստ տեսակին բաժանման՝ բարին ի գոյացութենէ եւ չարն ի պատահմանէ ստորոգեցաւ: Եւ դարձեալ ի չորս տրամատեալ լինի. զի է, որ բարի, եւ է, որ չար, եւ է, որ չար եւ բարի, եւ է, որ ոչ չար եւ ոչ բարի:

5.1.6 Արդ, զի են ի սոցանէ, որ կրին ի ներքուստ եւ վարին արտաքուստ: Քանզի բարւոյն եւ չարին իմանալի է ի շարժմանէ եւ ի նիւթոյ առնուլ զբաղկացութիւն:
Եւ որոշեալ զանագանի նախկնութեամբ շարժումն ի նիւթոյ, որ բարւոյն է գոյացուցիչ, իսկ նիւթ յետոյ քան զշարժումն՝ չարին է բաղկացուցիչ:

5.1.7 Իսկ գոյացութիւն ըստ չորից իմն է խառնից՝ ի Հրամանէ եւ ի վարմանէ եւ ի ստուերէ եւ յերեւմանէ: Այսոքիկ սահմանեալ երկակի որոշմամբ. Հրաման է պատճառ վարման՝ յորմէ բարի ասի, իսկ ստուերն պատճառ երեւման՝ յորմէ չար ասի:

5.1.8 Եւ դարձեալ Հրամանն յատուկ եւ անխառն ի միջի նոցա եւ յանսահման մնայով, իսկ վարմանն տեղիանալ ի ստուերէն, եւ երեւմանն ի ստուերէն գործոշումն առնուլ.

5.1.2 missing BCD | դժուարափոխ] դժուարափոփ A

5.1.3 missing BCD | բաղկանայ] բաղկանա A | ենթակային] ենթակաին A

5.1.4 missing BCD | կայ] կա A

5.1.5 missing BCD | գոյացութենէ] գոացութենէ A

5.1.6 missing BCD | բարւոյն] բարոյն A | նիւթոյ] նիւթո A | զբաղկացութիւն] զբաղկացու[ ]ն A | բարւոյն] բարոյն A | յետոյ] յետո A

5.1.7 missing BCD

5.1.8 missing BCD | նոցա] նոցա

5.1.9 ի նոյն սահման էակին դբաղկացութիւնն առնլով՝ սեռիք եւ տեսակաւք եւ ելիւք եւ ծննդիւք եւ ձեւաւք եւ գունովք:

5.1.10 Արդ. յայտնեցաւ չարն եղծանելի եւ որոշիչ բարւոյն. իսկ բարին համայն անապական եւ ընդունակ լեղման չարին:

5.2.0 Յաղագս կատարեալ գիտութեան բանի

5.2.1 Կատարեալ բան է ի մասանց եւ յանհատից եւ ի տեսակաց եւ ի սեռից եւ ի թուոց: Բանդի իւրաքանչիւր ոք սոցա դկատարելութիւն առնուն. իսկ համանգամայն սոքա կատարելագոյն ասին: Իսկ որ ի միմեանց բաղկանան. անկատարք գոն եւ ոչ կատարեալ բան:

5.2.2 Առաջին. իսկ ըստ այլոցն խնդրոց. ի ժամանակի ըստ շրջագայութեան մասանցն՝ Ա. Բ. Գ. Ե. Գ. ԺԲ. ԻԴ. Ե. Է. ԺԱ. ԻԱ. ՅԿԵ. ՕԲ. ԺԲ. Գ. ԺԵ. ԺԹ. ԻՀ. Ժ. առնուն դկատարումն իւրաքանչիւր սահմանքս:

5.2.3 Իսկ համանգամայն սոքա. ի վերագոյն հատածն կատարելագոյնք ասին եւ դանդրէն դասութիւնն առնուն, որ ՇԼԲ. Գ...ակ. որ ի միմեանցն գոյանան. ըստ Հոլովման բանիցն եւ անուան Հատիցն անկատարք ստորոգին:

5.2.4 Երկրորդ. դանագանի եւ ըստ սկզբան եւ կատարածի կատարելական բանն: Բանդի ըստ կատարածին կատարեալք ասին ամենայն լինելոցքս եւ եղեալքս: Եւ ոչ ըստ Հոլովմանցն կատարիք, այլ յիւրաքանչիւր սահմանս. որ ինչ եղելոցն էր՝ կատարեցաւ. եւ որ ինչ լինել Հարկի՝ դկատարումն առնու:

5.1.9 missing BCD | *ծննդիւք*] *ծնրնդիւք* A

5.1.10 missing BCD | *բարւոյն*] *բարոյն* A

5.2.0 missing BCD

5.2.1 missing BCD

5.2.2 missing BCD | *ի*] *գի* A | *շրջագայութեան*] *շրջագատութեան* A

5.2.3 missing BCD | *ասին եւ*] *աս*[ ] [ ] A | *գ*] *գ*[ ] A

5.2.4 missing BCD

5.2.5 Այլ է ընդ մէջ եւ ամանակ ըստ ներկայումն։ Արդ, ըստ վերատեսութեան երկակի սոքա զկատարելագոյն բաղկացուցանեն բան։ Իսկ ըստ ակզբանն ոչ է կատարեալ, զի որ ներածեն, կամ ասեն, կամ ներգործեն ի մէջս բաղկանաց եւ կամ ոչ է իսկ մարտուցեալ։

5.2.6 Երրորդ. արդ, ըստ բնութեան սահմանական յենթակայէ եւ ի կատարմանէ, ըստ Հուպ եւ ըստ զանազանութեան քառակին իւրաքանչիւրովքն կատարեալք ասին, իսկ ընթանուր Հատածքն՝ իննակի սահմանացն զերակատար ելով։

5.2.7 Եւ ըստ արարչականին է, որ միայն գտեսակն գոյացուցանէ անկատար գոլով եւ ոչ կատարեալ բան։ Քանզի ըստ էակին է ի նախադասութիւնան լեակնացն բաժանումն ի ստորոգութիւն, իսկ լիւրաքանչիւրան կատարեալ եւ յամենայնէն կատարելագոյնն։

5.2.8 Չորրորդ. իսկ ըստ բաժանման պատահմանգն վասն ստոյգ պատահին եւ յենթակայումն գոլ, անկատար ելով եւ ոչ կատարեալ։

5.2.9 Հինգերորդ. իսկ ըստ վեհագոյն եւ ըստ ներարՀեստուս է քառակն, յորմէ ամենայնքն զբաղկացութիւն առեալ սաՀմանեցան. լիւրաքանչիւրան սոքա կատարեալք ասին։

5.2.10 Իսկ ըստ անբաւին անխառնութիւն գերագանցեալ ասի։ Եւ դարձեալ յերիցն եւս, որք ի քակտումն եւ յեղծումն դիմեալ միշտ անկատար եւ ոչ կատարեալ բան։

5.2.11 Արդ, երեւեցաւ կատարելութիւն բանի եւակի տեսութեամբ ըստ մասանց, որ լիւրաքանչիւրան սաՀմանին. իսկ Համանգամայնքն կատարելագոյնք, եւ որք ի միմեանց իմանին գոյացութիւնքն, անկատար գոլ եւ ոչ կատարեալ բան։

5.2.5 missing BCD | *ներկայումն*] *ներկատումն* A

5.2.6 missing BCD | *յենթակայէ*] *ի յենթակաէ* A

5.2.7 missing BCD | *կատարեալ*] [ ]*ատարեալ* A | *բան*] add Գ A | *նախադասութիւնան*] *նախադ*[ ]*ու*[ ]*ան* A

5.2.8 missing BCD | *յենթակայումն*] *յենթակատումն* A

5.2.9 missing BCD

5.2.10 missing BCD

5.2.11 missing BCD | *գոյացութիւնքն*] *գոացութիւնքն* A

5.2.5 *եւ* 2°] *եւ* badly rubbed A

5.2.12 Քանգի գերագանցեալն ի կատարմանն բաղկանայ եւ ոչ յանկատարէն, զի անկատարքն կատարելականին են մասունք, որ շարագրինն:

Այսքան է կատարեալ գիտութեան բան:

5.3.0 Յաղագս ժամանակի առանձին

5.3.1 Ժամանակ է ոլորումն ըստ ամենայն մասանց, եռակի եւ աորնդդեմ խաղացումն տրամադրութեամբ, չափք բերմանց իւրաքանչիւրոցն եւ ըստ յեղման շրջագայիցն, յորս թիւքն բաղկացեալ յանգին, որ է Ե. Լ. ԺԲ. ԻԴ. Ե. Է. ԺԲ. ՂԱ. ՅՕԴ. ԺԱ. ԺԲ. Գ. Ե. Լ. Ժե. ԺԹ. ԻԼ. Ժ. ՁՂ. ՆՕՉ. ՇԼԲ. ԺԴ. ՉԴ.

5.3.2 այսչափի են թիւք շրջագայիցն, որ կարգաւք ցուցեալ լինին՝ մասունք, ժամք, աւուրք, շաբաթք, ամիսք, յեղանակք, ամք, շրջանք, դարք, կատարմունք ժամանակաց: Իսկ ըստ նոցա եւ թիւք պատշաճին, քանգի են, որք ի միմեանց բաղկանան, եւ են, որք սկսանին, եւ այլք զկատարումն առնուն:

5.3.3 Եւ դարձեալ որք կատարինն այլոցն մէջ բաղկանան կամ ոլորտք: Իսկ իննեստասաներեակն քանութիւք կատարեալ Համանգամայն տեսակաւքն, որք են շրջանակք. ԺԴ. եւ ՉԴ. ամք եկամուտ, որ ոչ դասի ի զգալիս կենցաղական վարուց աշխարհիս:

5.3.4 Այլ ըստ կատարման երեքտասանիցն՝ լրումն եւ քակումն բաղկանայ Հռոմանուտ եւ գանագան տեսակի բոլորիս, եւ յանՀռոմանուտ եւ յանգանագան տեսակն չլինել Հարկի, որ է անժամանակ:

5.3.5 Առաջին. իսկ ըստ այլոցն բաժանի ժամանակ ի տեսակս Հինգ, որ է սկիզբն բոլորին եւ կատարած ընութեանց եւ գաւրութինք յեղմանց եւ չափք միջոցացն եւ ...մանցն Հատած
: Արդ, որք Հետեւին այսմ՝ անժամանակ ասի:

5.2.12 missing BCD | *բաղկանայ*] *բաղկանա* A

5.3.0 missing BCD

5.3.1 missing BCD | *ոլորումն*] *ոլրումն* A | *շրջագայիցն*] *շրջագաիցն* A | *ՉԴ*] *ՉԴ* A

5.3.2 missing BCD | *շրջագայիցն*] *շրջագաիցն* A

5.3.3 missing BCD | *իննեստասաներեակն*] *իննեստասանեակն* A | *զգալիս*] *սգալիս* A

5.3.4 missing BCD | *բաղկանայ*] *բաղկանա* A

5.3.5 missing BCD | *գաւրութինք*] *զ[ ]ւթինք* A | *մանցն*] [ ]*մանցն* A

5.3.2 *որք*] *որ* A* *ք* above line A°

5.3.6 Երկրորդ. իսկ ի բնութեան ըստ արարչին չորիւք զանազանի տեսակաւք, որ են ամանցականք յիւրաքանչիւրոցն ենթակայիցն, որք ասին Համանգամայնք: Եւ ոչ նախկին կամ վերջին ժամանակ ինչ բաղկանայ: Այլ իւրաքանչիւր սահմանքն զգայութեանցն ժամանակաւ յայտնին ըստ գաւրութեանց խառնից կամ կրից: Չի լուծումն զգայութեանցն յերկուսին բաղկանայ: Չի եւ որ ըստ այսոցիկ ոչ է՝ անժամանակ ասի:

5.3.7 Երրորդ. իսկ ըստ էականին ի բաժանմունս պատահից բնաւորեցաւ գոլ, ըստ շարունակութեան առկայ դրից եւ դասաւորութեան: Չի շարունակ է ըստ ինքեան, ի վերայ պատահից եւ գոյացութեանցն:

Իսկ վերագոյնքն քան գտտա անժամանակ ասին:

5.3.8 Չորրորդ. իսկ բաղկացութիւն ժամանակի ըստ քառակին է՝ ի նիւթից եւ շարժմանէ ի սահմանս ունայնին վարիլ կառուցմամբ, ի Հրամանէ անեղին բնութեան:

5.3.9 Արդ, երեւեցաւ ժամանակ եռակի տեսութեամբ ըստ բոլորին, զի է որ ըստ յերկարման առեալ վասն ծննդից անՀատիցն բազմութեանց եւ գաւորութեանց վարման պատաՀից: Իսկ յառաջ քան զբոլորն եւ զկնի՝ անժամանակք ասին եւ ոչ այսք բաղկանան:

5.4.0 Յաղագս աստուածխաւսութեան սկզբան եւ կատարածի առանձին

5.3.6 missing BCD | ենթակայիցն] ենթակաիցն A | բաղկանայ] բաղկանա A | զգայութեանցն] զգաութեանցն A | զգայութեանցն] զգաութեանցն A | բաղկանայ] բաղկանա A

5.3.7 missing BCD | առկայ] առկա A | վերայ] վերա A | գոյացութեանցն] գոացութեանցն A

5.3.8 missing BCD

5.3.9 missing BCD | ծննդից] ծնրնդից A

5.4.0 missing BCD

5.3.6 զգայութեանցն] add յերկուսին բաղկանա surmounted by erasure dots differing from those elsewhere in the manuscript A*

5.4.1 Քանզի է սկիզբն եւ կատարած՝ նիւթական, տեսական, հիմնական, գործական: Եւ բաժանի ըստ արարչութեանն եւ ժամանակի: Քանզի սկիզբն, ըստ արարչութեանն եւ կատարած ըստ ժամանակի: Չի է սկիզբն, որ կատարած է, եւ է կատարած, որ սկիզբն, եւ է սկիզբն, որ ոչ կատարած է, եւ է՝ որ ոչ կատարած եւ ոչ սկիզբն:

5.4.2 Իսկ ըստ այլոցն է խնդրոց. զի ի բնութեան ըստ քառակին գանագանի, զի է, որ Հուպ սկիզբն եւ Հուպ կատարումն, եւ է, որ Հեռի սկիզբն եւ Հեռի կատարած: Եւ բաժանի սկիզբն ըստ առաւելութեան եւ կատարած ըստ ստուգաբանութեան:

5.4.3 Առաջին, իսկ լեականութեանն գանագանի սկիզբն ըստ գոյացութեան եւ կատարածն ըստ պատաՀման:

5.4.4 Երկրորդ. եւ դարձեալ ընթանուր եւ մասնական գոլով, զի է, որ սկիզբն է, եւ է, որ կատարած յենթակայումն, եւ է, որ սկիզբն եւ ի նմին կատարած, եւ է, որ ոչ սկիզբն եւ ոչ կատարած:

5.4.5 Երրորդ. գանագանի եւ ըստ շարժման եւ ըստ նիւթոյ: Քանզի սկիզբն ըստ շարժման նախ էին գոլով, իսկ կատարած ըստ նիւթի վերջին գոլ:

5.4.6 Քանզի գոյանայ բոլորն ըստ քառակին երկդիմի բաժանմամբ՝ ի նիւթոյ եւ ի շարժմանէ եւ յունայնէ, որ է սկիզբն եւ կատարած, եւ ընդ մէջան՝ յեղումն ըստ շարժման եւ ըստ նիւթի: Եւ ամանակ եռակի տեսութեամբ՝ յարաձգական, գերակատար, անորիշ, որ է ըստ ունայնի Հոլովման չափուցն:

5.4.1 missing BCD | ո_չ] om A

5.4.2 missing BCD

5.4.3 missing BCD

5.4.4 missing BCD | երկրորդ] om A | յենթակայումն] յենթակատումն A

5.4.5 missing BCD | նիւթոյ] նիւթո A

5.4.6 missing BCD | գոյանայ] գոանա A

5.4.1 արարչութեանն] one letter space rubbed between ր and ու A

5.4.6 եռակի] ի above line A° | գերակատար] vacat of one letter-space between ա and կ with slight signs of erased letters visible A

5.4.7 Իսկ ըստ անբաւին եակ անսկիզբն, անկատարած, անչեղլի, անամանակ, աննԵրկայ, անանցեալ, անապառնի. եւ է դարձեալ գոյացուցիչ սկզբան եւ կատարածի եւ որ ընդ մԵջն են բաղկացութիւնք:

5.4.8 Արդ, երեւեցաւ սկիզբն եւ կատարած եռակի իմացութեամբ՝ զի է, որ անսկիզբն է. եւ է, որ անկատարած: Իսկ սկիզբն եւ կատարած ընդ մԵջան բաղկացան յոքնակի Տատուածիւք:

5.5.0 Յաղագս ընութԵան առանձին

5.5.1 Բնութիւն է սաՏմանական եւ արարչական: ՍաՏմանական է բնական եւ Տատուատուն, իսկ արարչականն է անբնական եւ անՏատտատ: Քանգի բնականն ի սեռԵ եւ ի բաղկացուցիչ գանագանութԵանց, եւ անբնականն է շարժումն տեսակացն եւ յեղումն նմանից եւ աննմանից: Եւ թիւքն ՏանգԵտ ի պարգապար անՏատտն բաղկանայ:

5.5.2 Իսկ դարձեալ. է բնական, որ սաՏմանի ի սեռԵ եւ ի բաղկացուցիչ գանագանութԵանց. եւ է, որ սաՏմանադրի անուամբ, եւ է, որ առաւելու ըստ նուագութԵան բառիցն եւ պակասի ըստ յոլովման:

5.5.3 Առաջին. իսկ ըստ Եակին գանագանի սաՏմանականն ըստ գոյացութԵան եւ արարչականն ըստ պատաՏման: Եւ դարձեալ. է, որ սաՏմանական է. եւ է, որ արարչական, որ յենթակայում, եւ է, որ սաՏմանական եւ ի նմին արարչական, եւ է դարձեալ, որ ոչ սաՏմանական եւ ոչ արարչական:

5.5.4 Իսկ բաղկացութիւն ընութԵան է ըստ քառակին: Քանգի անբառն է պարգ եւ անշարադրԵլի, եւ նիլթ եւ շարժումն՝ խառն եւ խուռն շարադրութԵամբ, իսկ ունայնն՝ ընդ մԵջան, պատՃառ որոշման գոլով:

5.4.7 missing BCD | *աննԵրկայ*] *աննԵրկա* A

5.4.8 missing BCD | *իսկ*] *ի* [ ]*կ* A | *բաղկացան*] *բաղկաց*[ ] A

5.5.0 missing BCD

5.5.1 missing BCD | *բաղկանայ*] *բաղկանա* A

5.5.2 missing BCD

5.5.3 missing BCD | *գոյացութԵան*] *գոացութԵան* A | *յենթակայում*] *յենթակատում* A

5.5.4 missing BCD | *ընութԵան*] *ընութիւն* A

5.5.1 *արարչական*] *չ* badly rubbed A | *բնական*] *բանական* A* *ա* erased A

5.5.3 *արարչականն*] *ն* 2° badly rubbed A

5.5.5 Արդ. է բնութիւն եռակի բաժանմամբ, զի է, որ պարզ է ըստ սահմանականին, եւ է, որ շարադրելի ըստ արարչականին, եւ դարձեալ. է որ ընդ մէջսն կցորդին: Զի շարադրելին ի պարզէն բաղկանայ, իսկ պարզն ի շարադրականէն զերեւումն առնու:

5.6.0 Յաղագս էականութեան առանձին

5.6.1 էականութեան երկու են տեսակք՝ զգալի եւ իմանալի: Զի ի զգալոյն անզգալին եւ յիմանալոյն անիմանալին:

Քանզի գոյացութիւն յանզգալոյն ասի, իսկ պատահումն յանիմանալոյն գոլ: Եւ է գոյացութիւն ընթանուր եւ պատահումն մասնական: Եւ դարձեալ. պատահումն է ընթանուրն իսկ գոյացութիւն մասնական:

5.6.2 Առաջին. եւ զանազանի ըստ քառակին: Քանզի անբաւ ընթանուր ասի ըստ գոյացութեան, եւ ունայն՝ մասնական ըստ պատահման, իսկ նիւթ՝ մասնական ըստ գոյացութեան, եւ շարժումն ընթանուր ասի ըստ պատահման:

5.6.3 Երկրորդ. իսկ գոյացութիւն էականութեան ըստ քառակի բաժանի: Քանզի անբաւն է ասի, առանց սկսման եւ դադարման եւ շարժումն եւ նիւթ էակ, ի ձեռն սկսման եւ կատարման: Իսկ ունայն ոչ է ասի ոչ էակ, այլ Հոլովի ըստ պիտանացուին անուամբ եւ բայիւ:

5.6.4 Արդ, երեւեցաւ էականութիւն եռակարար:
Զի է, որ Հատդական է ըստ զգալոյ եւ անիմանալոյ եւ է, դարձեալ, որ յերկոցունց՝ ըստ գոյացութեան եւ ըստ պատահման:

5.7.0 Յաղագս գոյացուցիչ եւ մշտաբուխ քառակին որ է աստուածաբանական շարժման եւ նիւթի առանձին

5.5.5 missing BCD | *բաղկանայ*] *բաղկանա* A

5.6.0 missing BCD

5.6.1 missing BCD | *են*] om A | *զգալոյն*] *սգալոյն* A | *գոյացութիւն*] *գոացութիւն* A | *ընթանուրն*] *ընթանուր* A

5.6.2 missing BCD | *գոյացութեան* 1°] *գոացութեան* A

5.6.3 missing BCD | *ասի*] add *եւ* A | *բայիւ*] *բաիւ* A

5.6.4 missing BCD | *զգալոյ*] *զգալո* A | *յերկոցունց*] *յերկուցունց* A

5.7.0 missing BCD

5.7.1 *Արդ, է ամենայն ինչ շարժումն ի շարժմունս նիւթ եւ, դարձեալ, ամենայն ինչ նիւթ եւ ի նիւթան շարժմունք: Այսոքիկ իրք եւ իմացեալք, տրամաբանեալք եւ ներգործեալք: Չի որ շարժումն է` եւ նիւթ, եւ որ նիւթ է` եւ շարժումն:*

5.7.2 *Քանզի գոյացուցիչք են միմեանց: Չի նիւթին կիզումն եւ ցրտումն եւ խոնաւումն եւ ցամաքումն ի շարժմանէ բաղկանայ, շորք, իսկ շարժմանն լինելն եւ ապականելն, աճելն եւ նուագելն, այլայլելն եւ փոփոխելն ի նիւթոյ բաղկանայ:*

5.7.3 *Առաջին. եւ զանազանի ի շարժումն յենթակայն ըստ նաւսրութեանն յունայնի: Իսկ նիւթին յենթականայն` ըստ թանձրութեանն շարժման, եւ յունայնէն գերեւումն առնու:*

5.7.4 *Երկրորդ. իսկ ըստ անբաւին է անշարժ եւ աննիւթ, զի անխառն ասի: Քանզի շարժումն եւ նիւթ յանշարժէն եւ յաննիւթէն բաղկանայ, իսկ դադարումն եւ ի նիւթէ եւ ի շարժմանէ, որ է առակապար ասացութեամբ:*

5.8.0 *Յաղագս ունայնի առանձին*

5.8.1 *Ունայն ասի անիր անիմացուածն` անբան եւ աններգործեալ, եւ է որոշումն մասնական եւ հանրական մտաց: Չի է ի խառնս ընդ նիւթի եւ ընդ շարժման: Իսկ արտաքոյ` անբաւ ասի ի բաւականէ բոլորին, իսկ ըստ անբաւին բաւականեալ, այսպէս երկակաբար ասի:*

5.7.1 missing BCD

5.7.2 missing BCD | *գոյացուցիչք*] *գոացուցիչք* A | *բաղկանայ*] *բաղկանա* A | *շորք*] *դ* A | *նիւթոյ*] *նիւթո* A | *բաղկանայ*] *բաղկան* A

5.7.3 missing BCD

5.7.4 missing BCD | *բաղկանայ*] *բաղկանա* A

5.8.0 missing BCD | *ունայնի*] *ունայնին* D add *առանձին* A

5.8.1 missing C | *ունայն*] *յունայն* D | *անիմացուածն*] *անիմացուած* BD | *աններգործեալ*] *աններգործ*[ ] B *աններգործել* D | *արտաքոյ*] *արտաքո* A | *բաւականէ*] *բա*[ ]*ական է* B | *բոլորին*] *բոլումն* B | *իսկ*] om D | *անբաւին*] *բաւին* A | *անբաւին բաւականեալ*] *անբաւականելով* B | *ասի*] add *առաջին* A add *առաջինն* BD

5.8.1 *ըստ*] omit A* above line A°

5.8.2 Իսկ բաղկացութիւն ունայնի է ըստ այտոցիկ՝ գի ի գոյէ եւ չիրէ անգոյ եւ անիր ասի. Եւ ի մշտակացութենէ եւ ի յափտենականէ անցական եւ անբնական: Այլ ոչ որպէս ումանք կարծեցին թէ իցէ ինչ. այլ է ոչինչ. քանզի եւ կարծեյն իսկ ընդունայն եւ անվայր ասի:

5.9.0 *Յաղագս անբաւի*

5.9.1 Անբաւ է, որ ամենայնիւ է անբաւ, որ ասի բոլոր, անմասն եւ անտեսակ: Եւ է միտք եւ խորհուրդք, իմաստք եւ գիտութիւնք եւ տեսութիւնք ընդհանուր եւ անչափի: Իսկ ըստ այլոցն է ըստ վեցեկին եւ ըստ չորրեկին: Քանզի անբաւ է ոչ բարի եւ ոչ չար, ոչ սկիզբն եւ ոչ կատարած, ոչ շարժումն եւ ոչ նիւթ:

5.9.2 Ըստ այտոցիկ անեղ ասի, գի ոչ յայլմէ եւ ոչ յինքենէ ունել զգոյութիւնս: Եւ դարձեալ, ըստ երկրորդին է անբաւ՝ գերազանցագոյն գերազանցագունիցն, անժամանակագոյն անժամանակագունիցն, բնականագոյն բնականագունիցն, էագոյն էագունից, ունայնագոյն ունայնագունից, անբաւագոյն անբաւագունից:

5.8.2 missing C | ունայնի] ունայնին D | այտոցիկ] ա[ ]ոցիկ B | մշտակացութենէ] մշտակցութ[ ] B | ի] om BD | յափտենականէ] յափտենականութենէ D | անցական] առանցական D | անբնական] անբնակ A բան բանական B add եւ [ ]ական B | իցէ] իցեն B | այլ է ոչինչ] om D | է] եւ B | ոչինչ] է ոչ ինչ B | քանզի եւ կարծեյն իսկ ընդունայն եւ անվայր] [most of line] վայր B | ընդունայն] ունայն D

5.9.0 missing C | անբաւի] om B

5.9.1 missing C | անբաւ է] անբաւին D | ասի] ասէ B | եւ] om B | իմաստք] իմաստ B | գիտութիւնք] գիտ[ ]թիւնք B | ընդհանուր] ընթհանուր B | անչափի] անչափք BD | այլոցն է ըստ] om B | է] om D | վեցեկին] վեցեկի BD | ըստ] om D | ըստ չորրեկին] չորեկի B | չորրեկին] չորսեկի D | ոչ] om B | ոչ] om B

5.9.2 missing C | անեղ] աղեղ D | յինքենէ] յինք[ ] B ինքնէ D | ունել] ունի B | զգոյութիւնս] զչգոյութիւնս B | եւ] om B | դարձեալ] manuscript D ends here | անբաւ] անբա[ ] B | գերազանցագունիցն] գերազանցագունին B | բնականագոյն] բնականագոյ[ ] B | բնակագունիցն] [ ]նականագունիցին B | էագոյն] էականագոյն B | բնականագունիցն … անբաւագոյն] անունայն ա[ ]ին B | ունայնագունից] անունայնագունից A | անբաւագունից] անբաւագուն B

5.8.2 ի 3°] ի omitted A* above line A° | ոչ] ոչ above line B°

5.9.2 ասի] ասս above line B°

5.9.2 անժամանակագունիցն] ն 3° with erasure dots A | բնականագոյն] բնակագոյն A* ան above line A°

5.9.3 Ըստ այսորիկ անհասապգոյն ասի չեակացս, զի սահման քննութեանցս յանհունն գանցեալ գտանի։ Զի ըստ այսորիկ ոչ գոյ հասումն բնութեան երկրորդ անբաւին։

5.9.4 Իսկ ըստ չորրեկին միայն ճանաւթութիւն արարածոյն գարարիչն, ի բանաւորութենէ Աստուծոյ առ ազգս Հրեշտակաց եւ մարդկան. եւ ի խաւսելոյ Աստուծոյ Հրեշտակաց եւ մարդկան։ Եւ աստուածաբանելն երիս աստուածս իւրաքանչիւր առանձնաւորութեամբ, զի է, որ ծնող ասի, եւ է, որ ծնունդ, եւ է, որ ելող։

5.9.5 Այլ այս ըստ մարդկային բնութեան երեւի, յաղագս գթութեան Հաւր եւ մարդասիրութեան որդւոյ եւ ողորմածութեան Հոգւոյն։ Քանզի երեք են՝ մի են բնութեամբ, կամաւք եւ արարչութեամբ։

5.9.6 Նոյնպէս եւ ըստ Հրեշտակաց փառաւորեալ երիս անձինս՝ գարարիչ, եւ գՀաստիչ, եւ գկազմիչ, որում ասեն սուրբ, սուրբ, սուրբ միանգամայն տէր գաւրութեանց։ Փառք եւ պատիւ եւ գոհութիւն անեղին եւ անՀասին եւ մշտնջենաւորին այժմ եւ յաւիտենից յաւիտեանս։

5.9.7 Կատարեցան վեցեակքն, որ ի միմեանց սահմանին, եւ չորրեակքն որովք Ճառքն գլխաւորին եւ երեակքն Ճարիցն մասնականք ասին, եւ գլրումն էառ երկուտասանեակն մասամբքն, եւ գերագանցեալ գտաւ յանՀատիցն, ըստ իւրաքանչիւր մասանցն տեսակաց եւ սեռից։

5.9.3 missing CD | *ըստ այսորիկ անհասապգոյն ասի*] *անհաս ի* B | *զի* 1°] add *ոչ* B
manuscript B ends here

5.9.4 missing BCD | *Հրեշտակաց*] *Հրշտակաց* A | *Հրեշտակաց*] *Հրշտակաց* A | *ծնող*]
ծնաւղ A

5.9.5 missing BCD | *այլ*] [ ]*յլ* A | *մարդկային*] *մարդկաին* A | *որդւոյ*] *որդո* A |
Հոգւոյն] *Հոգոյն* A

5.9.6 missing BCD | *Հրեշտակաց*] *Հրշտակաց* A | *մշտնջենաւորին*] *մշտրնջենաւորին* A

5.9.7 missing BCD | *երեակքն*] add *որով* A

5.9.4 *գարարիչն*] *արարչինն* A*

5.9.7 *որովք*] *ք* with two erasure dots A

5.9.8 *Բանգի է խորհուրդ ամենայն երակի եւ իմացմունք ընթանուր արհեստ փիլիսոփայական եւ սահմանք ուսմանց, եւ թողլով որ բստ աշխարհիս են տումիշք արհեստ անյաղթ փիլրսոփայից:*

6.1.1 *Աստուած, Աստուած, Աստուած, փարք քեզ այժմ եւ յաւիտեան:*

5.9.8 missing BCD | *փիլիսոփայական*] *փիլիսոփաակական* A | *փիլրսոփայից*] *փիլրսոփաից* A

6.1.1 missing C | *աստուած աստուած աստուած փարք քեզ այժմ եւ յաւիտեան*] *գյակոր դրիմեցի սպասաւոր բանի աղաչեմ յիշել ի տէր* C

TEXTUAL COMMENTARY

0.0.0   *զենոնի իմաստասիրի* 'Of Zeno the Philosopher': This phrase is extant only in D. It is not at all certain that this attribution is original in the Armenian tradition. Zeno the Stoic was known as the author of a work entitled Περὶ φύσεως. Pseudepigraphical attribution of philosophical works is not unknown in the Armenian tradition: cf., e.g., *De Virtutibus et Vitiis* and *De Mundo* attributed to Aristotle. Following this name, Xačʻikyan introduced a title for the treatise, *Յաղագս Բնութեան* 'Concerning Nature', without any manuscript basis.

Thus, Xačʻikyan's title is composed of two different phrases, one from D and one of his own. The second phrase was doubtless suggested to him by the attribution of the work to Zeno by D. This is the latest manuscript and the attribution is secondary, it appears, to the manuscript tradition. We prefer to designate the work as pseudo-Zeno, *Anonymous Philosophical Treatise.*

1.0.0   B reads 'Concerning the knowledge of … '.

1.0.1   *կարգք* 'ranks': The reading of B, omitting the *դ* is a common variant. See for such cases §§1.2.1, 1.2.2, 1.4.10, 1.5.13 (B), 1.6.2 (C), 1.6.17, 1.6.18, 2.3.1, 2.3.5; *Armenian Text Commentary* p. 11; *4 Ezra* 3:7B, 4:36, 5:9, 5:45, 6:1J, 6:24, 6:47, 8:50, 10:29, 10:60, cf. 6:54B, 11:29.

1.1.0   The only manuscript with this title is A. However, in an equivalent position, ABD have a similarly structured title in §1.2.0 and in §1.3.0, etc. So it seems reasonable to restore it here from A.

1.1.1   *բաժանի* 'is divided': CD offer the plural *բաժանին*. The singular might be regarded as later usage but is likely that some other process is going on, because the phenomenon occurs repeatedly in similar positions: cf. §§1.2.1, 1.3.1, 1.4.1, 1.4.3, 1.5.5, 1.6.1, 1.6.3bis, 1.6.4, 1.6.12, 2.3.7, etc. It apparently refers to the category under discussion as a singular entity.

առաջին 'the first': CD add the article *-ն*. However the words *երկրորդ* 'second' (§1.1.2), *երրորդ* 'third' (§1.1.3), *չորրորդ* 'fourth' (§1.1.4), *հինգերորդ* 'the fifth' (§1.1.5) and *վեցերորդ* 'the sixth' (1.1.6) do not have the article in this position.

ունայնին 'the void': This is the reading of ACD. B has *ունայն*, probably part of the same textual process that brought about the loss of the privative *ան-* immediately following. Alternatively, it might be part of B's tendency to omit final syllables, see §1.4.11 (commentary).

անգոյութիւն 'non-existence': Three readings are offered: (1) *անգոութիւն* A 'non-existence'; (2) *անգիտութիւն* (*գիտութիւն* B) BD 'ignorance'; and (3) *անբաւութիւն* C 'infinity'. If we regard C as secondary, contaminated by the following *անբաւէն*, we are left with A and BD. A seems more plausible on grounds of content.

ի նոյն տրամագծին եւ փոփոխեալ 'of equal diameter which has been modified': This reading, accepted by Xač'ikyan, is that of BD. A reads *տրամագծի անփոփոխ եւ*. Here the transposition of *անփոփոխ եւ* precedes the loss of *-եալ* so we may assume that an intermediate textual state existed, namely **տրամագծին փոփոխեալ եւ*. The *-ն* of *տրամագծին* was corrupted into *ան-* of *անփոփոխ* and *-եալ*, abbreviated as *-էլ*, was lost by dittography with the following *եւ*. The addition or omission of privative *ան-* is found elsewhere, see: §§1.4.3, 1.5.3, 2.5.4, 5.8.1, 5.9.2 and *4 Ezra* 3:30, 4:30, 4:39, 6:24, 6:54D, 7:52, 8:41B. The reading *փոփոխման* 'of change' of C makes no sense.

1.1.2   *բաղկացեալ յունայնէ* 'constituted ... (and) of the void': Here Xač'ikyan has included in his text: (1) *պարփակեալ* the reading only of A, might be a doublet variant of *բաղկացեալ*, which latter is present in ABCD. (2) *յայնցանէ*, the reading of C, which is a corruption of *յունայնէ* partly at least by *այ* > *յ** > *ց* and correction. (3) *է* which occurs in no manuscript whatsoever.

անմարմին 'incorporeal': B has *մարմին*. See above §1.1.1 on the addition or omission of privative *ան-*.

1.1.3   *արգելման* 'to prevent': B has the meaningless *արդելման* a graphic corruption of *գ* and *դ*. See other instances at §§1.1.4, 1.4.3, 1.4.4, 1.5.1, 1.6.17, 2.3.5.

պարփակող 'enclosing': BC offer the ending in *-աւղ*. *Non liquet*.

1.1.4   *չորրորդ* 'fourth': The reading *երրորդ* 'third' of C is corrupt by graphic confusion of the abbreviated forms *գ* and *դ*: see §1.1.3.

որ 'which': Omitted by B for no obvious reason.

հաստատնովն 'the firmament': The form *հաստատովն* in D is corrupt, since *հաստատ* is *-i-* declension and a shift from *-i-* to *-o-* is unlikely. See §1.5.8.

կիտիցն 'marine animals': This is the reading of A. B also has an article, but it has the declension *կիտացն*; CD have *կիտաց*. Both declensions are possible.

մեծամեծացն 'enormous': The undeclined form in B cannot be

explained. B frequently loses the last syllable of a word; see §1.4.11 (commentary).

զաւրութիւն 'health': Literally 'power'. C has the concrete noun *զաւր* 'force'; compare *սերմանեաց* / *սերմանութեանց* §1.5.12 and *մոլորակ* / *մոլորութիւն* §1.6.17. On such variants, see M.E. Stone, "Assessment of Variants in Armenian Manuscripts," *Armenian Texts, Tasks and Tools,* ed. H. Lehmann and J.J.S. Weitenberg (Acta Jutlandica LXIX:1, Humanities Series 68, Aarhus, 1993), 21-22. There is no reason to regard C as primary here.

ախտաժետութեանց 'infirmities': Observe that below, e.g. §1.5.7, we also find a plural *Հիւանդութիւնք* 'illnesses'. The singular in B probably arises from a graphic error in the abbreviated ending.

Հողմոցն 'winds': The singular *Հողմոյն* of B is due to graphic confusion of *յ* / *ց*. The variant is very common, see below §§1.1.7, 1.5.6, 1.6.7, 1.6.8.

1.1.5 *է* 'is': This word is omitted by CD. If we examine the cases in the present list which are syntactically similar to this instance, we observe:

§1.1.1	*է*	A		B		C		D
§1.1.2	*է*	ABC	omit				D	
§1.1.3	*է*		omit	A	B	C		D
§1.1.5	*է*	AB	omit			C		D
§1.1.6	*է*	A	*են* B	omit		C		D

This evidence is inconclusive, except that CD definitely tend to omit the word.

երկրիս շարադրութիւն 'the compound of the earth': B omits the *ս* of *երկրիս* and BCD add it to the next word. D is corrupt, reading *երկիրս* for *երկրիս*.

Հրալից 'fire-filled': This is the reading of A. BCD read *Հրաշից* 'of miracles, miraculous'. This can only be decided *ad rem.*

և այպէս 'and similarly': C has *եան* which probably goes back to an abbreviation.

ծննդականք 'the begotten things': This is the reading of ABD. C has *ծննդունք* 'births', presumably by misreading an abbreviation.

պատճառող 'cause': B has *պատճառով* presumably derived from *պատիճ* 'proboscis'.

1.1.6 *է* 'is': This, the reading of A, has been put in the text for the sake of stylistic consistency. There is no decisive argument for its inclusion or exclusion. See note on §1.1.5, above.

1.1.7 *աստեղատանցն* 'constellations': A has *աստեղացն* which is corrupt, perhaps from an abbreviation. C has *աստեղատեացն* which is also corrupt. Similar corruptions occur in §§1.2.4, 1.3.4, 1.4.4.

Հաստատունյն 'the firmament': The form *Հաստատույն* in D is not correct, see §1.3.3.

աղոցն 'the airs': ACD have the singular; B has the plural, probably by corruption of *յ* / *g*: see also §1.1.4. On the basis of the context, the editors' view is that *աղոցն* (plural) was the original reading and we have put this reading in the text. We regard the coincidental reading of B as a secondary (but excellent) scribal correction.

1.2.1 *կարգք* 'ranks': The reading (*կ*)*արգ* in BCD is of phonetic origin. Therefore, read the plural *կարգք*, against Xač'ikyan: cf. §1.0.1 (commentary).

բնականություան 'nature': This reading of A is correct. *բնակութեան* 'dwelling' in BCD is definitely secondary here, cf. §§1.5.10, 1.6.6, 5.1.2 and also *4 Ezra* 6:1L, 7: 89, *Testament of Reuben* 3:1, 3:3 which have the similar corruption *բնակութիւն* / *բնութիւն*. The same variant as here occurs in §§1.2.2, 1.6.6. All three variants occur in §1.6.6. The similar variant *բնական* / *բանական* occurs in §1.6.7.

1.2.2 *Հրեշտակք* 'angels': So A (with a spelling variant) and C. BD have *Հրեշտակ* in the singular, which is secondary. See §1.0.1.

բնականություան 'nature': So A, correctly. BCD have the corrupt reading *բնակութեան(ն)* 'dwelling', the same variant as §1.2.1.

բնական 'natural': C reads *իւր* as the result of scribal intervention. Perhaps it is caused by the earlier corruption of *բնականություան* to *բնութեան*.

1.2.3 *օրինի* 'law': The form without the article is to be preferred on stylistic grounds, cf. the preceding *առաքինություն*; so Xač'ikyan.

կործանմունք 'catastrophes': B has a corrupt variant, reading the word *կործմանք*. which does not exist.

Հանդիպին եւ 'encounter (them) and': A omits *Հանդիպին եւ* perhaps by homoeoteleuton of *Հ — Հ*. B is corrupt, with the word *անդի* added before *Հանդիպին*, perhaps a corrupt dittography.

նորին 'of that selfsame one': A omits and is easier to translate. Xač'ikyan includes this in his text..

ըստ բնականն 'against the natural': CD have *զբնականն*. In §§1.3.4, 1.4.4 we find a similar variation of *զ-* and *ըստ*, in both instances with the word *շրեցունց*. Because of the oblique case, in those instances *ըստ* must be the correct reading.

կորխի 'moves': *կորփի* of B is corrupt; see §5.1.2.

եւ եղծումն 'and corruption': BCD omit, perhaps by homoeoteleuton.

1.2.4 *աստեղատումբն* 'constellations': *աստեղումբն* of C is corrupt, cf. similar corruption in §1.1.7.

ելանեն 'proceed around': D has the infinitive. Variation between a present indicative and an infinitive also occurs elsewhere, e.g., §§1.4.7 (CD), 1.5.13 (A), 2.1.1 (B), 5.9.2 (B). Thus it occurs in all four manuscripts of pseudo-Zeno. One suspects that this is more than a random phenomenon. We have also noted it in *Abel Cain* 6, *Testament of Simeon* 4:8 and *De Virtutibus et Vitiis* 1250a 19, 1251a 36, 1251b 18, 1251b 21. We have found no explanation and the solution may lie in the hands of experts in the Armenian language.

1.3.0 C omits this title and a number of the following ones.

1.3.1 A has *Գ* at the beginning of this section. Perhaps it indicates that this deals with the third 'position'. No other such numbers are found in the other manuscripts of this section, but a similar phenomenon recurs in §5.2.3.

տեսակ սեռի 'species of kind': This has become *տեսակս էր* in BCD, by corruption.

1.3.2 *ըստ* 'according to': B has lost the *ը* of *ըստ* by haplography.

բացերեւեցան 'that which appeared': The singular of this verb (manuscript A) seems better than the plural of BCD, on grounds of sense. The 'world' remains the subject.

անշարժելի 'unmoving': D has *անշարելի*: see §1.5.12 for further instances of this variant.

*ի*2° 'in': Omitted by BCD through haplography.

բոլորն 'the sphere': The oblique case of D cannot be construed.

1.3.3 *ջրայարկին* 'of the watery vault': *ջրարկին* of D is corrupt.

որ 'which': Three readings are offered: *որ* A; *զորս* BD; *զոր* C. A is taken into our translation as a nominative. The other readings are definitely accusative. The same manuscripts BCD omit the verb *է* 'is' following *ընտրողականն* 'separating one'. This seems to mean much the same and here the *nota accusativi* is attracted from the preceding phrase.

Հաստատնովս 'the firmament': This is plural in CD (conjunctive reading); for the spelling in D, see above §1.1.7.

1.3.4 *բոլորութեամբ* 'in spherical fashion': B has a nominative case, apparently secondary.

ըստ 'according to': C has the preposition *զ-* and D has a lacuna. See §1.2.3 for other examples of this variant.

աստեղատունքն 'the constellations': For the reading *աստեղք* of D, see above §1.1.7.

յարեւելից 'from East': B reads *յարեւելս եւ* 'East and'.

1.3.5   *մոլորակք* 'planets': B reads *մոլորականք* which may also mean 'planets'.

են 'are': AB read thus, CD omit. The decision as to the text is stemmatic.

այսորիկ երեւակն լուսնթագն 'these, Saturn, Jupiter': These words are omitted by A for no clear reason.

ըստ 'according to': CD have *եւս*. The derivation of this reading cannot be discerned readily. The sense of the text of CD is unclear and it must be regarded as secondary. See §1.4.3 commentary.

1.4.1   *չափք* 'measures': The omission of the initial coloured letter by B and C is coincidental, as it is in §1.2.1.

տեղւոյ 'place': B has *ամենայն տեղ*. Armenian has two forms, *տեղ* with Classical genitive *տեղոյ* and *տեղի* with Classical genitive *տեղւոյ*. In medieval Armenian, endings like *-ւոյ* became *-ոյ*. This medieval form dominates in the manuscripts of pseudo-Zeno. Consequently it is impossible, in the specific case of *տեղոյ*, to know whether it is derived from *տեղ* or *տեղի*. We have chosen the latter option in normalizing the spelling of pseudo-Zeno. Additions of *ամենայն* are fully discussed in §2.3.5 (commentary).

1.4.2   *սաս* 'clear': BCD have *դեղին* 'yellow': see below §1.6.3 on this list.

երանգք 'shades': D has, corruptly, *երագն* 'quick'.

պադպաշմունք 'effulgences': Omitted by C through homoeoteleuton.

1.4.3   *երակարար* 'three-fold': Each manuscript has a different reading here:

(1) A has *երակարար*, a rare word, cited by *NBH* only from pseudo-Zeno. It apparently means 'three-fold'. This manuscript enumerates only three aspects of form.

(2) B has *երակարոյոր*, a word not found in the dictionaries. It is probably a corruption of a text like A. Thus, B also has three aspects of form.

(3) C has *քառակարար* 'four-fold' a formation comparable to that in A. It has four aspects of form.

(4) D has *բառակի* 'four-fold', in this respect resembling the reading of C. It, too has four elements.

Thus:

(1) The ancestors of AB / CD separated as a result of the confusion of *գ* '3' / *դ* '4' in an abbreviation: see also §§1.1.3 (commentary).

(2) One text has been expanded or the other shortened to fit the number so created.

(3) On stemmatic grounds CD form a sub-group, and so the hypearchetype of AB seems to be more original.

We have accepted A into the text, supported by B, thus differing substantially from Xač'ikyan. See also §1.6.4 where a similar list occurs and is discussed.

գոյն 'colour': For a discussion of this list, including the variants here, see below §1.6.3 (commentary).

բոլորակ 'circular': This is the reading of A. BCD have *բոլոր* which means 'round', but can also mean 'circle'.

* լստ*1° 'into': The preposition is not found in B here. Compare its omission from §§1.3.5 (CD), 1.4.6 (CD), 1.4.11 (C), 1.5.12 (B), 1.5.14 (A), 2.1.1 (BD), 3.2.3 (A), 4.2.14 (A). The spread of these readings across the manuscripts shows no significance.

այլ 'various': Omitted by CD.

Հատած ի սեռիցն 'divided by kinds': So A, cf. C. The text of B, *Հատակիցն երիցն* is corrupt from this. D seems to be a development of AC, but has maintained the general meaning of the phrase.

անՀարթ 'unequal': B has lost the privative, compare above §1.1.1.

այսոցիկ ոչ են 'those things which are not': The reading of C is a clear corruption of this.

անբաւր 'unbounded': The origin of the variant *նորա* 'they' in B remains unclear.

1.4.4 *աստեղատանցն* 'of the constellations': Two corruptions may be observed, B having *տեղացն* with -*ս* on the end of the preceding word. This goes back to **ստեղացն*, and that to *աստեղացն*, itself a corruption, which is found in C. The variant is discussed above, §1.1.7.

շրջագայիցն 'revolutions': A reads *վաթսուն շրջագայիցն* 'sixty revolutions'. *շրջայիցն* in B is corrupt. The number sixty is signaled by Philo, *Quaestiones in Genesin* 4.164 as related to the bodies of the Zodiac; cf. *Quaestiones in Exodum* 2.81. This might explain the introduction of "sixty" here, but pseudo-Zeno refers to the revolutions. Moreover, it is syntactically awkward. Thus, the Philonic text may explain why "sixty" is introduced, but does not demonstrate its originality.

երկոտասան 'twelve': B has *բաժանել* 'to divide', an incorrect reading of the numerical notation *Ւ* for *երկոտասան* 'twelve'.

անուանադրեն 'they call': D has *անուանագրենն* 'inscribe names'. This is due to confusion of *գ* / *դ*: see §1.1.3.

1.4.5 *Հասարակածիր* 'equinox': A has *Հասարակած իսկ* 'equator, but' and indeed less commonly *Հասարակած* may also mean 'equinox'. This reading probably derives from that of the other manuscripts, compare a similar corruption of A and D in §1.4.6.

1.4.6 *Հող* 'earth': A has *Հողմ* 'wind', clearly a corruption. See M.E. Stone, *Armenian Text Commentary*, 38 where it is discussed. Considering A here and the other items of this list, the emendation of Xačikyan to the indefinite form is accepted.

Հասարակածիր 'equinox': So B and C. The readings of A and D are comparable with that of A in §1.4.5. Since they differ, this cannot be regarded as a conjunctive error.

ջրՀոս 'Aquarius': B has lost the final *-ս*. D has *ջրուՀոս,* an unusual form of the variant orthography *ջրՀոս*.

ըստ Հարաւոյ 'to the South': This is the reading of A with regularized spelling. B has an even more deviant orthography than A. CD omit *ըստ* and place *Հարաւ* after *որ է* 'which is'. See §1.4.3 on this omission.

ջուր 'water': D omits this word.

1.4.7 *եւ ըստ մասանց մարդոյն* 'and with human limbs': This phrase is omitted by CD. There is no obvious explanation of this conjunctive error. The phrase is best regarded as original. *մարդոյն* (A) is preferable to *մարդոյս* (B) on stemmatic grounds.

բաբելացւոց 'of the Babylonians': This ethnonym is in the nominative in C and D. Similarly, subsequent names of nations are in the nominative in C (*յոյնք*, etc.) and are not discussed in the notes on the rest of this list. B has *Բաբել*. On its omission of final syllables, see §1.1.4.

են ուսքն 'are the shoulders': The plural verb occurs in B, but in that manuscript, the word *յուսքն* 'the shoulders' is written with a superfluous *յ-*. In CD the verb is singular, but compare below where the parts of the body are plural. A is differently corrupt, reading *եւ* 'and' for *են* 'are'.

խեցգետինն 'Cancer': So CD. The form with the article is preferred over A which is unarticulated, since the other elements of this list are articulated. B has lost the final syllable through some sort of abbreviation. Other instances may be observed in B: see above §1.1.4. Since B reads independently, it is stemmatically permissible to read with CD against A here.

1.4.8 *ասիացիք* 'the Asians': Two readings seem of note here. B has corrupted the text to 'Syrians'; but these occur in §1.4.10, corresponding to Capricorn. The genitive plural only occurs in C which thus preserves stylistic consistency. One wonders about its originality, however, since both A and D have the nominative plural. The individual manuscripts are quite haphazard in shifting between the nominative and genitive. See commentary on §1.6.11.

է կողրն 'is the thorax': A has, instead of this, *եւ աջ ձեռն* 'and the right arm'. The origin of this reading is unclear, but A also differs in some further instances of these equivalations. The reading has been included as an alternative in the text, though it does not fit the formulaic pattern exactly.

եւ յունաց 'and Greeks': This phrase is omitted from A. Since the list is quite formulaic, it might be regarded as a gloss. In *72 Nations* (Stone, *Armenian Apocrypha Relating to Adam and Eve*, 162-3) we find 'Greeks' (l. 37), 'Hellenes' (l. 57) and 'Helladians' (l. 72).

եւ են ձեռքն 'and they are the arms': A, continuing its reading above, has instead *եւ ձախ ձեռն* 'and the left arm'. B and C have 'and they are', and only D reads *որ են* 'which are': see §4.2.2.

1.4.9 *կշեռն* 'Libra': We have preferred the orthography of AB, but the article of CD on stylistic grounds. This reading is of no stemmatic significance, cf. *Հրատն* in §1.3.5.

արաբացւոց 'of the Arabians': So, basically, BCD, and D has the Classical Armenian ending *-ոց*. A reads *կիլիկեցիք* 'Cilicians' and this has been given as an alternative reading in the text.

եւ են կռթունքն 'and they are the fists': This is the reading of BC. This textual situation is also found in §1.4.8 *եւ են ձեռքն* 'and they are the arms'. A has omitted this phrase, but has the two letters *կշ*, the beginning of the preceding constellation *կշեռ* 'Libra'. We may assume a scribal error.

եւ են սրունքն 'and they are the legs': So BC. D reads *որ են* 'which are': see §4.2.2 (commentary). In A, the Italians are said to be *աւան* 'village'. This must be corrupt for a variant reading, perhaps **եւ են* 'and they are', but the underlying text would then be obscure.

աղեղնաւորն կրետացւոց 'Sagittarius of the Cretans': So AC, though A does not have the article. This reading is obliquely supported by B (*աղեղն*). D omits from *աղեղնաւորն* to the end of the section.

եւ են 'and they are': So D: ABC have *եւ են*. See below §4.2.2 (commentary).

1.4.10 *որ են*1° 'and they are': So B while A has simply *եւ* 'and'; CD have *եւ են* 'and they are'. See below §4.2.2 (commentary).

*եւ են*2° 'and they are': So BC, while A omits; D has *որ են* 'which are'. See below §4.2.2 (commentary).

ծունկրն 'the knees': A has *սրունքն* 'legs, shanks', which it did not have in §1.4.9 where it was found in the other manuscripts. The spelling is corrupt in BCD. B omits the *-ր* and CD omit the *-կ-*. See commentary on §1.0.1.

եւ կարմիր ծովուն 'and of the Red Sea': This phrase is omitted by BCD. The reading of the second word is unmistakably *կարմար* in A, but we have emended its text to *կարմիր* 'Red'. This is plausible in view of the connection with the Indians.

*եւ են*2° 'and they are': So BC; AD have *որ են* 'who are'; see §4.2.2 commentary. The reading of A, however, is connected with its unique addition preceding and is not genetically related to the apparently identical reading of D.

1.4.11 *աղեղնաւոր* 'Sagittarius': This is shortened to *աղեղ* 'bow' in B. The same may be observed above in §1.4.9. Similarly in this section, B gives *խեծ* for *խեգգեւորի* and *այծ* for *այծեղջիւր*. See also B in §§1.1.1, 1.1.4, 1.4.7, 1.5.7, 1.5.12, 1.5.13, 2.1.1, 2.3.7, 4.2.0 and other instances throughout.

այծեղջիւր 'Capricorn': D omits this word for no obvious reason.

1.5.1 *չորք* 'four': D has 'three', due to confusion of the notation for numerals. See above §1.1.3.

արտադրատութիւնք 'separatings forth': This is the reading of AC, the latter with an inconsequential orthographic variant. B has the cognate *արտադրատորութիւն* which does not appear in *NBH*, while D has *արտադրատութիւնք* by corruption.

1.5.2 *ծննդարաշխութեան* 'coming into being': The ending *-ութեան* in B, an oblique case, produces an impossible reading. Its origin may lie in a misread abbreviation. See commentary on §1.6.11.

1.5.3 *եյուն* 'coming out': D has *բերուն* 'bringing'.

լինելութիւն 'generation': In genitive in B, see §1.6.11 commentary.

անմարմնաբար 'in a bodiless way': The privative *ան-* is lost in B. We have remarked on this variant above, in the comment on §1.1.1.

նիւթոյ ի հոսմանէ 'of matter from the flux': The form *նիւթի* in A does exist, and a corruption of its ending and the following *հոսմանէ* produced *յայնմանէ* of B. The reading *հոսման* found in A would produce 'consistency of flux of matter'.

կրից կամ խառնից 'passibilities or mixtures': The words are transposed in A: C has *կայ* by corruption.

1.5.4 *շարատնութիւն* 'production': The form in B supports this reading, but is corrupt as it stands. We have given the form from which the reading of B must have derived. CD have *շարախառնութեան* 'compounding', which is graphically very similar.

այլ այլ 'but … other': So CD, with the support of B which reads *այլ յայլ*. One *այլ* has been lost by haplography in A.

վերագոյն 'higher': In B a complex textual development has taken place. Presumably in a *Vorlage*, *վերագոյն* fell out and was added subsequently above the line. This correction was misunderstood and produced a phrase in which *վերագոյն* > **վերա գոյ* > *ի վերայ գոյ*, to which a second occurrence of *բնութեանն* was added. Thus, in the final analysis, B witnesses a corruption of the same text as the other versions.

բնութեան 'of nature': This is the reading of BD, supported by C. The word does not occur in A.

անթուելի 'innumerable': A has *անթնդելի* which, although not in *NBH*, probably comes from the word *թնդեմ* 'throb, shake'.

1.5.5 *բժշկականութիւն* 'medicine': C has an orthographic error, *ժշկանութիւն*.

մզան 'urine': This rare word engendered the corruption *բազմազան* 'multi-varied' in B.

յորմէ 'from it': This is the reading of A. C and D add the word *են*. Their reading must lie behind the text of B *յարենէն* 'from the blood'.

նեարդք 'nerves': So A alone. This has been corrupted into *որդք* in CD and a further corruption has taken place in B.

ոսկերք եւ երակք 'bones and veins': A does not have *եւ* 'and'. Its text stands behind *ոսկերք* in B, which consequently does not read *երակք*. We have preferred the reading *ոսկերք*, regarding the uncertainty about the last syllable as the result of contamination with *երակք* 'veins'.

բաժանի 'is divided': Xač'ikyan emends to *բաժանեն*. The reason is unclear. For the singular, witnessed here by ABC, see the note on §1.1.1. *բաժանեն* does occur as a variant of *բաժանին* in A §2.3.7.

յիգական 'female': There seems to be no good reason for the omission of the initial *յ-* in B and D.

1.5.6 *զանազանութիւն* 'variety': This word is nominative singular in A and instrumental singular in B. That seems secondary.

վարիա 'thin': A has *վատիա* which is presumably a corruption and is not found in *NBH*. C has *առոյգ* which means 'young, brisk'.

գողտր 'delicate': A has *գոտր*, an orthographic variant.

գունոյն 'colour': D reads the plural *գունոցն* 'colours', due to the corruption of *յ / ց*: see §1.1.4 commentary.

պղնձուտ 'bronze': The variant *պղնծուր* of D is to be explained by the common shift of *ձ* to *ծ* in such environments, and a graphic error, reading *տ* as *ր*. The orthography has been normalized and happens to coincide with that of C.

կամ — դառն 'or — bitter': Omitted by D for no obvious reason. This textual process, however, may be related to the omission by D at the start of §1.5.7.

ամռպացն 'flavors': A has a strange orthography, *ամրպացն*.

Հոտոցն դառն քաղցր 'smells, bitter, sweet': B has variants, but they seem to make no sense. Corresponding to *Հոտոցն* 'smells', it reads *լինդիցն*, a non-existent word. Then a small lacuna intervenes, followed by]*առնապացqի*. This is a variation of the end of *դառն* and a corrupt form of *քաղցր* 'sweet'. No sense can be made of it.

1.5.7 *են բարձրութիւն — Հաստատութիւն* 'are the height — foundation': Omitted by D, through homoeoteleuton.

զանազանին — յեղանակացն եւ 'they are distinguished — of the changes and': This phrase is omitted by D, perhaps by homoeoteleuton *եւ — եւ*.

լինին 'arise': The form *լինեն* in B is odd. With the singular of C, compare §1.1.1 and below in the present section.

բարեխառնութեան 'balanced blending': The loss of the last syllable of B is an abbreviation, resembling its readings discussed in §1.4.11 (commentary).

պէս պէս 'various': CD add *լինին* 'come into being'. This is probably secondary.

1.5.8 *սեւամաղձութենէն* 'melancholy': D has *սեւամաղձութենէ են* which is a case of wrong division and correction. Compare also §1.6.8. AB and C have inconsequential orthographic variants.

լուսնոտք 'being moonstruck (somnambulating)': D has the orthography *լուսոտք* which is perhaps comparable with *Հաստատով* for *Հաստատնով* in §1.1.4. D has other orthographic peculiarities in the following lines, viz. *միստատարենէն* is written as *միստատարէն են* (cf. A in §1.5.10); *ունկութիւնք* is written as *ունակութիւնք*.

եւ ի խստութենէն 'and from severity': B omits these words, for no obvious reason.

արուին 'of the male': This word is omitted by C for no obvious reason.

1.5.9 BCD omit this short section.

1.5.10 *բնութենէն* 'by nature': D reads *բնակութենէ* 'from the dwelling'. See §1.2.1 where further examples of the variant *բնութիւն* / *բնակութիւն* and allied readings are cited. The reading of A *բնութեան են* is a simple corruption, cf. D in §1.5.8.

պատժելով 'having been punished': Here AD present *պատժելով* 'having been punished'; B has *պարժելով* 'punished' and C has *վարժելով* 'learned'. We accept the reading of AD for the following reasons.

1. It is the *lectio difficilior*. Why would *վարժելով* become *պատժելով*?

2. It is easier to assume *պատժելով* which developed independently into *պարժելով* and *վարժելով*.

3. It is strengthened by stemmatic considerations, in which AD:B:C implies that AD yield the original.

հարկաւար 'necessarily': BCD have *հարկաւորաբար* which is very similar in meaning and is more usual.

զաւրավիգն 'support': The alternative spelling of BD is also listed in *NBH*.

ընկալեալ 'having been accepted': BCD have *վկայեալ* 'having witnessed' (with orthographic variants). This is due to a graphic confusion of *ըն* with *վ*. The text of BCD is, in any case, corrupt.

1.5.12 *իսկ բնականն է* 'but the natural (death) is': The variant text of D is produced by abbreviation, wrong division and subsequent, minimal correction.

ուժոյն 'power': D has omitted the *ժ* by error; cf. §§1.3.2, 1.6.4, 1.6.5, 1.6.17, 2.5.4 where the same error has taken place. No explanation of it is evident.

ի շրջագայէ 'through the circling': BD *ի շրջագայի(ն)* would mean 'in the revolution'. C uses a different word-formation, basically identical with A in meaning. B perhaps omitted the words from *ի3°*— *յեղանակացն* 'through—the qualities' because of a certain graphic resemblance of *ժամանակի* 'time' and *յեղանակացն* 'qualities'.

բաղկանան 'are constituted': B has an apocopated form, see §1.4.11 commentary.

1.5.13 *խառն մահուան* 'the mortal mixture': B has corrupted this to *խառնման*.

բարձումն 'destruction': *բարձու* in B is the same sort of shortening that has been noted above, see §1.4.11.

1.5.14 *ըստ* 'according to': B adds *ամենայն* 'all'. The variant is found elsewhere, see below, commentary on, §2.3.5.

նիւթականացն 'material things': *նիւթականք այ* of B is a corruption of this.

1.6.1 *եւ են որ* 'and there are those which': In many cases with this phrasing, the verb *են* 'are' is omitted. In Armenian, the relative pronoun in the nominative plural may be either *որ* (like BCD) or *որք* (like A) twice here. B adds a superfluous *եւ* 'and' following *են* 'are'. This type of reading is discussed below, §4.2.3.

1.6.2 *տեսակք* 'species': For the singular of C, see §1.0.1. The same process affects A's reading of *ժամանակք* 'times'.

1.6.3 A has many lacunae in the first part of this section, due to poor physical preservation.

բաժանին 'are divided': B adds *ի* 'into', not required by the syntax, probably due to dittography of the last letter of *բաժանի*, its rendering of the verb here.

սպիտակ 'white': A is incomplete because of a lacuna, but it had a different order of the colours, *սեաւ. սպիտակ* [ ] 'black, white [ ]'. Moreover, the *-ս* following the lacuna indicates that the fourth member of the series was not *դեղին* 'yellow', like the other manuscripts. It was probably *սատ* 'clear'. The list of colours in the four manuscripts is:

A *սեաւ*	*սպիտակ*	[	*սատ]ս*
B *սպիտակ*	*կապոյտ*	*սեաւ*	*դեղին*
C *սպիտակ*	*կարմիր*	*սեաւ*	*դեղին*
D *բսպիտակ*	*կարմիր*	*սեաւ*	*դեղին*

In §1.4.2 there is another form of this list of four colours. In it, A has *սատ* where BCD have *դեղին*. Therefore, we restore the fourth member of the present list to *սատ*. In §1.4.2 AB have *կապոյտ* where CD have *կարմիր*, the same situation as here. In this instance we read with A, supplementing the lacuna with B. We chose the readings of AB, *սպիտակ. կապոյտ. սեաւ. սատ* 'white, blue, black, clear' which are also justified by the stemma.

Here and in §1.4.2 the problem is the choice between *կապոյտ* 'blue' and *կարմիր* 'red' and between *սատ* 'clear' and *դեղին* 'yellow'.

On intrinsic grounds it is difficult to say which member of the first pair was original, and both start with the letter կ-. The reading *կարմիր* 'red' is supported by Greek sources such as Empedocles, *Testimonia* fg. 19, ln. 8 λευκὸν, μέλαν, ἐρυθρὸν, and ὠχρόν. See also Democritus, *Testimonia*, fg. 125, ln. 5 and *idem*, fg. 135, ln. 5.

The second instance, *սասս* 'clear' and *դեղին* 'yellow', is easier to explain because *սասս* means 'of bright colour' and thus 'clear'. It is a very rare word and so it might easily have been replaced by a scribe with *դեղին* 'yellow'. The same contrast may be found in Greek between ὠχρὸν (in the sources cited above) and λαμπρὸς in Proclus, *Comm. on Plato's Republic*, 2.224 line 6.

խառնուածքն 'mixtures': B has secondarily *խառնակութիւնքն* 'disorders'.

տեսիլք 'appearances': Omitted by C, for no discernible reason.

1.6.4 *քառակի* 'into four': The *ըստ* of BCD is not necessary, see the construction with *երկակի* in the preceding paragraph and §§1.4.3, 1.6.1, 3.1.15, 4.2.6, though *ըստ* is to be found in such phrases in pseudo-Zeno, cf. §§3.1.6 and 5.6.3. It has begotten the shift to *քառից* in D, a form of *քառ*, which is an alternative for *չորք* 'four'. Pseudo-Zeno, however, uses *չորից*, see §1.6.3.

զանազանին 'are differentiated': The verb is singular in AB and plural in CD. AB should be accepted: see note on *բաժանի* in §1.1.1 where similar instances are discussed.

ըստ կրի 'according to the impact': This is the reading of AD, while B has *ըստ կարի* = κατὰ στένον. Manuscript C has corruptly *ըստ կապի* 'according to bond' which probably develops from the reading of B.

երկարն 'length': This element corresponds to one which was regarded as doubtful in §1.4.3 and relegated to the apparatus. Here A has *երկարն* 'length' and BCD have *երկայն* 'long'. The stemmatic consideration is not determinative here.

շարժման 'movement': D omits *ժ*, cf. the cases of the same variant assembled in §1.5.12.

1.6.5 *դէմս* 'countenance1°': This must be taken as a locative and the plural is preferable, so the reading of AB is accepted rather than the nominative plural of C and the locative singular of D.

դէմք 'countenance2°': Nominative plural is required, so this reading of AC is accepted. D has the nominative singular and B has the accusative/locative plural.

յանհատի 'in the individual': The variant *յանղիպ* of B (perhaps = *յանդէպ* 'unbecoming') must be corrupt.

108   TEXTUAL COMMENTARY

ծննդեանց 'births': This is the reading of AB (the latter has the variant *ծնրնդոց*), while CD have *ծնելոց*, a genitive of the aorist participle, to be translated in much the same way.

շարժման 'movement': The loss of *ձ* in D is a corruption; see §1.5.12 above.

1.6.6   *որ*1° 'that which': B omits corruptly through a haplography.

զբնականութիւն 'nature': Alternatively render 'naturalness'. This is the reading of A. B has *զբնութիւն* 'nature' and CD read (corruptly) *զբնակութիւն* 'dwelling'. Concerning these variants, see commentary on §1.2.1.

*ի վերայ*1° 'upon': This is the reading of A. BCD omit.

լինելութեան 'the generation': C omits for no obvious reason.

եւ են որ 'and ... there are those': The word *են* 'there are' is added before this phrase by C. This is apparently corrupt. There are various small variants in the occurrences of this or very similar expressions, see §4.2.2 (commentary).

1.6.7   *է* 'is': BD have *որ է* 'which is' and C adds a superfluous *է* 'is' before that; see §4.2.2 commentary. The decision between *է* 'is' and *է որ* 'is which' is stemmatic. Either reading is possible in context.

տարրական 'elemental': B has *տարակ* which does not exist in the dictionaries and must be an orthographic variant.

բանական 'reasonable': A has, corruptly, *բնական* 'natural'; see §1.2.1 on this and similar variants.

մարմնոց 'of bodies': B has the singular *մարմնոյ* 'of a body'. There seems to be no reason to regard this as significant and a graphic confusion *յ / ց* is rather widespread as is the orthography omitting the final *-յ*: see §1.1.4.

բախման 'knocking': BC offer *բաբախման* 'pulsation, irregular beating' and D reads a corruption of this. There is no basis upon which we can make a determination between the readings of A and of BC.

բանականին 'of the reasonable': B reads the ablative case 'from the reasonable'.

1.6.8   *տեսլենէն* 'of the visible': A adds the word *են* 'are' which is probably a corrupt dittography of the last two letters of *տեսլենէն* 'of the visible'. There are other instances of the addition or omission of the verb 'to be' in such contexts, following an ablative singular ending: see §1.5.8.

աստուածայնոցն 'of the divine': B has the singular form *աստուածայնոյն* preceding the plural *աստուածայնոցն* which it shares with the other manuscripts. This is the result of a dittography. The variation *յ* / *ց* is common: see §1.1.4. It also has *այս* 'this' for *այսք* 'these'.

պիտակաբար ելով 'used improperly': The reading of D, *պիտակաբերելով* is corrupt for this.

1.6.9 *տեսակս* 'species': C omits this word, for no obvious reason and is corrupt.

*գործնականն*1° 'practical1°': This is the reading of B, cf. CD. A has the synonymous *գործականն*. In the second instance in this section, A has *գործական* and BC have *գործնական(ն)*. C has a series of small variants in the following lines, such as the addition of the article *-ն*, the omission of *եւ* 'and', etc. They do not combine to form a systematic revision of the section.

յիմաստականն 'into the sophistical': Manuscript C has *յիմաստասիրականն* 'into the philosophical'.

բաժանական 'divisible': By context we may determine that this is correct and that *բժշկական(ն)* 'medical' of BCD is a corruption of it.

1.6.10 *խնդրականն* 'searchable': C ends here with a short colophon: *զյակոբ որիմեցի սպասաւոր բանի աղաչեմ յիշել ի տէր* 'I beg to remember Jacob of Crimea, servant of the Word, to the Lord'. Jacob is discussed in the Introduction.

դիտաւորականն 'intentional': This word is in the instrumental in D for no clear reason.

ստորոգութիւնս 'the categories': Manuscript B has the locative singular. This is to be regarded as secondary on both contextual and stemmatic grounds.

յանդէմ կացառդրութիւնս 'the opposites': These two words are omitted by B. D has *բացադրութիւն* 'setting outside, exclusion'.

վերաբերութիւն 'reference': This is the reading of AD (A has a slight orthographic variant). B has the genitive-dative singular. See commentary on §1.6.11.

1.6.11 *իմացականին* 'comprehensible': This word is omitted by B due to homoeoteleuton with *վարդապետականին* 'dogmatic', the preceding word.

չար եւ բարի 'evil and good': In the genitive in BD. See following.

կատարելութիւն 'perfection': So A reads, making this word a member of the list being enumerated. Manuscripts BD have the genitive case, that could be translated 'time of perfection'. A seems preferable on grounds of sense. The same variant occurs with the following words *բնութիւն* 'nature' and *էականութիւն* 'being'. See also §§1.4.8, 1.5.2, 1.5.3, 1.5.13, 1.6.10, 1.6.12, 1.6.13, 2.3.1, 2.3.2, 2.3.3, 2.3.4, 2.3.5, 2.3.7, 2.5.2, 5.5.4

շարժումն 'movement': This has been corrupted into *յոյժ իմն* by the scribe of manuscript B.

1.6.12 *սահմանք* 'divisions': B alone of all the witnesses has the plural. AD have the singular. The plural fits well into the context and seems to be the subject of the plural verb *են* 'are'. See the singular verb in §1.1.1 and the commentary there. Alternatively, the pluralizing *ք* has been lost in A and D, perhaps due to the influence of the following *գ*. The situation of the witnesses here contradicts the stemma. It could be explained by assuming B to be a correction of a corruption in A and D. Lacking further instances of such stemmatic problems, this reading cannot be given great weight.

ստորասութիւն եւ բացասութիւն 'affirmation and negation': So manuscripts AD. B has *ստորոգութեան* 'category'. Both words are in the genitive-dative case in B. See note on §1.6.11 above. There are variations of order in the different manuscript copies of this list.

1.6.13 *զգայութիւն երեւակայութիւն* 'sensibility, imagination': B varies orthographically but it also has the genitive-dative case, not the nominative; see note on §1.6.11 above.

մտաց 'mental': Literally 'of mind'. In D a dittography has been engendered by the *-աց* of *մտաց* 'of mind' and the latter part of *իմացականին* 'intelligible', and the following words have been added.

1.6.14 *ամենայնքն* 'all': D has *ամենեքեան*. The variant is not uncommon. Here it might well have arisen from an abbreviation to *ամքն* of the unusual form *ամենայնքն*.

եւ մակացելիքն — §1.6.15 *անբաղկացելիքն* 'and mathematical — §1.6.15 unconstitutable': The words are lost from B, perhaps by homoeoteleuton. B adds *է* 'is'.

1.6.15 *դասիւ եւ ստորադասիւ* 'by class and by subclass': This is the reading of AD. Both words are in the genitive case in B.

եւ յանբաղկացելիսն 'and the unconstitutable ones': Omitted by D through homoeoteleuton.

տրամանկիւնիք 'the diagonals': D has an instrumental case, which reading is accepted by Xač‘ikyan . There are two declensions listed in *NBH*: *տրամանկիւն, -կեան* and *տրամանկիւնի, -նոյ*. Neither would produce an instrumental ending *տրամանգիւնիւք* as in D. If the instrumental were correct, we might render, 'The mathematical are constituted of the constituable ones and the unconstitutable ones, through diagonals, whence ...'.

1.6.16 *յուսոյ եւ ըստ* 'hope, and according to': These words have fallen out of D through a case of homoeoteleuton.

1.6.17 *յաղագս* 'about': B has *ըստ* 'according to'.

դիրք 'positions': D has *գիրք* 'book', by graphic error of *գ* / *դ*: see above, §1.1.3.

կարգք 'ranks': BD have the singular *կարգ*. This error is created by phonetic confusion and has no probative value for stemmatics, see §1.0.1 where further examples are listed.

վասն 'for the sake of': D has the variant *վասն զի*.

զսահմանս 'the definitions': D has *զի սահմանս* a variant of *զ-* / *զի* which is found elsewhere, see *Testament of Levi* 16:1.

ամանակի 'time': BD have the graphically similar and largely semantically identical *ժամանակի*. Note that some omissions of *ժ* were discussed above in §1.5.12. In those instances, however, the omitted letter was not initial and, no doubt, the loss of *ժ* here is at a different linguistic level.

մոլորականն 'planets': B has *մոլորութեանց*[ ] 'wanderings'. Is this a case of the variation of abstract and concrete nouns noted above in the commentary to §1.1.4?

1.6.18 *նշանակք* 'symbols': The pluralizing *ք* has been lost from B: see comments on §1.0.1.

որոշմանց 'of distinctions': A has the singular *որոշման* 'distinction'. In fact, no decision seems possible between these two readings.

մասնական 'partial': This is the reading of A. BD have the graphically similar *իմաստնական*(*ն*) 'wise'.

2.0.0 *զոր — առադրեցին* 'to which — speech': Xač'ikyan omits these words for no evident reason.

կատարելութեան 'end': So AD, while B has *կատարեալ* 'perfect'.

2.0.1 *քաղաքական* 'political': This is the reading of AD. B has *ի քաղական*. The word *քաղական* is corrupt.

2.1.1 *է չափաւորելն ըստ* 'is to be moderate according to': The three manuscripts have slightly different texts. A, which we have followed, is structured exactly like the preceding and following phrases in all three manuscripts, except that B omits the *է* 'is' in the third phrase.

տնաւրինականն 'economic': B has the shortened form *տնօրին*: see above, commentary on §1.4.11 for other examples of such shortening.

հոգացողութիւն 'care': D has a corrupt reading *հոգւոց ուղղութիւն* 'uprightness of souls'. This is due to wrong division and subsequent correction.

2.2.3 *կենդանեաց* 'beings': I.e., living beings. This is the reading of AB; *կենդեաց* of C is corrupt.

2.3.1 *նախադրի* 'is prefaced': This is the reading of BC. A has *նախատադրի* which does not occur in *NBH* but may well exist with a meaning similar to *նախադրի*.

բերականութիւն 'grammar': This word is plural in manuscript B for no obvious reason. In the following discussion it is always singular.

տեսակք 'kinds': This is the reading of A and it could also be translated 'species'. Manuscripts BD have lost the pluralizing *ք*: see above comment on §1.0.1 for this variant.

հմտութիւն 1° 'practical (ἐμπειρία)' 1°: The orthographic and graphic variants of B and D are inconsequential. B gives this and the next two nouns in the genitive case. This type of variation is discussed in the commentary to §1.6.11.

հմտութիւն 2° ' practical (ἐμπειρία)' 2°: The reading *հմատութին* in D is a graphic error.

2.3.2 B has numbered the six parts referred to in this section, using Armenian numbers. We have written the numerals out in full in our transcription and they appear thus also in the apparatus.

ներկուն 'expert': For no obvious reason, D places this word after *բառ*.

առոգանութեան 'prosody': D has an alternative orthography.

զրուցատրութիւն 'explanations': This word is genitive in B. See above, commentary on §1.6.11.

ստուգաբանութեան 'etymology': This word is plural in D. The same is true of the following *համեմատութեան*(ն) 'comparison' which is plural in BD.

2.3.3 *առասպելավարձութիւն* 'the composition of stories': This word is genitive-dative in B, see commentary on §1.6.11 above.

ըստ ընտրութեան 'according to the choice': BD omit by homoeoteleuton.

շարադրութեան ըստ 'composition (σύνθεσις), according to': BD transpose these words and B has the genitive plural.

ոտից 'of ... metrical feet': B has *տառից* 'of letters', the genitive plural, presumably by contamination from the start of this section.

վարման 'employment': Manuscript B omits and D has *նման*, a corruption engendered by the graphic similarity of *վ / ն*.

2.3.4 *եւ են մասունք բանի* 'there are ... parts of speech': These words are omitted by B, corruptly, through homoeoteleuton of *բանի* — *բանի* 'speech — speech'.

ընդունելութիւն 'participle': This word is in the genitive in B, cf. §1.6.11 above. The following *նախադրութիւն* 'preposition' is similar.

2.3.5 *որ* 'which'1°: This is the reading of AD; B has *ներ* 'into'.

ընդունելութիւն 'participle': This word is in the genitive in B, cf. §1.6.11 above.

են եւ որ 'are ... and which': This is the reading of A. B reads *եւ են որ* 'and there are those which'; D reads *է եւ են որ* 'is and there are those which'. See §4.2.2.

*ըստ*1° 'according to': Manuscript B adds *ամենայն* 'all', a quite common variant which recurs in B later in this section, preceding the word *անուանն* 'noun'. See also §§1.4.1, 1.5.14, 2.3.7, 4.2.4 (all in B) and *Testament of Reuben* 2:4, 4:5, 4:8, 6:4, *Testament of Simeon* 4:4, 6:6, 7:3 (reflected as additions or omissions). The same variant recurs in B later in this section, preceding the word *բայ*.

նախդիր են 'are prefixes': So Xačʻikyan emends the readings of ABD. The three manuscripts read these two words as a single verb, *նախադրեն* (AD) or *նախդրեն* (B). Xačʻikyan's emendation is persuasive, because it is minimal, being a question of word division and minor orthographic correction. The phrase thus formed fits the structure of the sentence.

*են եւ որ*2° 'and ... there are those which': This is the reading of manuscript A. Manuscripts B and C read *եւ են որ*: see discussion below on §4.2.2.

մակագգ 'related': This is plural in B. However, in similar phrases throughout this section, the singular is found. On the disappearance of the pluralizing *ք* in such phonetic contexts, see comments on §1.0.1. The reading of D arises from graphic confusion of *գ* / *ղ*, see above §1.1.3.

*եւ որ*2° 'and which'2°: B has *են եւ են որ* 'there are, and there are those which'; cf. commentary on §4.2.2.

իրաւք 'things': B has *իրոքն*, with *ո* instead of *o*. D is corrupted to *իւրով*: see *4 Ezra* 3:16, 3:17, *Testament of Levi* 4:1.

աւդոյ 'of atmosphere': This is the reading of BD, while A has *ուզա* which is clearly corrupt for it.

2.3.6 *նախերգութեան* 'proëmium': Xačʻikyan has *նախերդութիւն* by error.

2.3.7 *բաժանին* 'are divided': This is the reading of D. A has the plural active form *բաժանեն*. See §1.5.5 on this reading. This seems to be secondary, for the middle voice is used in the numerous similar cases throughout the book. B has the singular, see §1.1.1 commentary for similar instances.

բաղխողական 'deliberative': B has abbreviated, as it sometimes does, to a single syllable: see §1.4.11. For the spelling of the variant *ղխ/խ* compare *4 Ezra* 6:1E, 6:43, 6:47, 6:53, 7:55, 13:10, cf. *Testament of Levi* 1:1. The form *բաղճասական* of B is clearly a corruption.

պատմութիւն 'narrative': B has this word in the genitive, see above §1.6.11.

տեսարանի 'scene': This is the reading of manuscript A. D has *տեսարանի* which means the same. B has *տեսականի* 'visible thing'. It adds *ամենայն* 'all' preceding this word, see §2.3.5 commentary.

կացրդական2° 'declamatory': B has *կացրուր*, a corruption of the text of the other manuscripts. Its sentence means 'it corroborates'.

պարսաւել 'for blame': B reads *պատուեալ* 'honored', by corruption. B and D stop here and both resume with §4.2.0.

2.4.0-2 These sections exist only in manuscript A.

2.5.0   After the title, B offers a note on the origin of its text *յայլ գրոց* 'from another manuscript' or 'writing'. This section exists only in B and D. Observe that, unlike the preceding, this section is formulated as an address directed to a hearer in the second person singular. We base our edition predominantly on B.

2.5.1   *զբովանդակութիւն* 'content': D does not have the *nota accusativi*.

առեալ 'having received': The verb *առեալ* seems to make better sense here than the reading of B *տուեալ* 'having given'.

2.5.2   *ծանուցիս* 'you are ... informed': This is the reading of D. B's *Vorlage* was difficult for the copyist to read, so after he wrote the first few letters, he left a *vacat*. He then misread the third letter and instead of *ռ* he wrote *ա*, and similarly he wrote *զ* for the following *ց*.

յայտնութիւն 'manifestation': This is the reading of D. B has a genitive, see above, §1.6.11.

կանգնեաց 'established'. This is the reading of B. It is impossible to decide between it and *կարգեաց* 'ranked' (D).

2.5.3   *իցեն* 'there are': D has *ինչ են* 'whatever they are'.

ջուրս 'waters': The locative of B is correct in context. *ջուրցս* of D is corrupt for this.

աւդք 'winds': The plural of B is preferable to the singular of D, since the following verb, *ելանեն* 'go out', is also plural.

գնացք 'paths': The word *նոցա* follows in D. No explanation of the omission in B can be found. A slight indication that *նոցա* is secondary may be found, that it might have been introduced by analogy with the preceding text.

ընդ երկինս 'through the heavens': This or *յերկինս* 'in the heavens' of D is possible. For other cases of variation of *ի* / *ընդ* see *Abel Cain* 43; *Testament of Reuben* 4:2 and commentary.

2.5.4 *անհանգիստ* 'restless': So manuscript D. This reading is also preferred by Xač'ikyan. For examples of the loss of the privative, as in *հանգիստք*, the reading of B, see §1.1.1.

ներքին 'internal': The sea is external to the world, but the heavens are inside it. Manuscript B has *արտաքին* 'outside'.

վնաս եւ շարժմունս 'damage and earthquakes': This reading of B, with the accusative, seems preferable to the nominative of manuscript D. According to D, then, 'damages and movements / earthquakes do also much benefit'. This does not make a great deal of sense; Xač'ikyan, however, prefers the reading of D. For other instances of the omission of *մ* in *շարժմունս*, the reading of B, see §1.5.12.

օգուտ 'help': So manuscript D; B has *անգամ* 'time'.

ջուրց 'waters': This form, as well as the form *ջրոց* found above, are both possible. We have not sought consistency here, but follow the dominant reading of the manuscript tradition in each case. In manuscript B, for example, observe the variation of the spelling within this paragraph.

2.5.5 *բովանդակութիւնք* 'contents': We have accepted the emendation to the plural in light of the preceding plural *այսորիկ*. Manuscripts B and D omit from here to §4.2.0.

3.0.0-3.1.0 Xač'ikyan supplied a general title here *յաղագս բանականին* 'On the Rational'.

3.1.0 From here to §4.1.3 B and D omit and the only witness is A. We note where Xač'ikyan has changed its text. Some of the variants in the apparatus are the result of the normalization of orthography in the text, and are not discussed in this commentary. This is the practice wherever A is the sole witness.

3.1.1 *գոլ եւ* 'to exist and': Xač'ikyan omits *եւ* 'and' for no obvious reason. This is not noted in his apparatus and might be a typographical error.

եւ ... 'and ...': The preceding *երեքին* 'three' requires a third division, but it is lost from the text. The editors have supplied *եւ* ... 'and ... '.

3.1.2   *սահմանականն* 'definitive': Xač'ikyan omits the article, for no obvious reason.

3.1.4   *ի կատարմանէ* 'from its perfection': Xač'ikyan omits *ի* 'from' for no obvious reason.

կամ 'or': The last letter is lost in a lacuna in the manuscript.

3.1.5   *արհեստ* 'craft'; The letters *հե* and most of the *տ* are lost through water damage. This restoration is also made by Xač'ikyan.

3.1.6   *անդունդ* 'the abyss': So manuscript A. Xač'ikyan has *անունդ*.

3.1.12   *յանախտական* 'freedom from sufferings': Xač'ikyan has added the article, presumably because of *պարզն* preceding.

3.1.14   *մակացութեանց* 'eruditions': The abbreviation of *-ւթեան-* has been lost through dampness or some other physical deterioration, which has also affected the word *պատասխանականն* 'the responsive' in §3.2.3.

գործականն 'the practical': Xač'ikyan has emended to the synonymous *գործնականն*. The variation between these two spellings is to be noted:

	գործնական	*գործական*
1.6.9	C D	A B
1.6.9bis	B C D	A
1.6.12	B D	A
2.0.0	A B D	
3.1.14		A
5.4.1		A

գործական is thus to be found in A in all instances except the title in §2.0.0. There is no way of deciding the preferable reading here and so A is maintained.

3.1.15   *իմաստասիրութիւն* 'philosophy': Xač'ikyan has justly emended the text of A *իմաստութիւն* 'wisdom' to *իմաստասիրութիւն* 'philosophy', literally 'loving wisdom'. He bases himself, doubtless, on the continuation of the phrase *սիրել զիմաստութիւն* 'to love wisdom' and the definition of *իմաստասիրութիւն* 'philosophy' offered immediately following. The two words are only found in this context in pseudo-Zeno.

3.2.1   *ենթակայն եւ* 'the subject': The word *եւ* 'and' follows 'subject' but has not been translated. Xač'ikyan omits *եւ* 'and' without noting it. It certainly seems secondary if compared with the other phrases in this section. There is, however, enough fluidity in its use throughout the work to make us hesitant about omitting it. See §3.3.1.

ստորոգեայն 'the predication': Xač'ikyan has emended *-ն* to *-ս* for no apparent reason, and without noting it.

3.2.2 *Հարցական* 'interrogative': Xač'ikyan has added *-ն* for stylistic conformity. However, many such instances of the addition and omission of *-ն* are to be observed.

3.2.3 *ըստ ստորասութեան* 'according to the affirmation': The word *ըստ* 'according to' is added by Xač'ikyan, clearly filling a lack in the text.

3.3.1 *ըստ այլում եւ ժամանակի* 'according to that and tense': Xač'ikyan omits the word *եւ* 'and', thus making the phrase conform with the others in this section and changing its meaning. See comment on §3.2.1, a very similar instance.

3.3.2 *կարգեցան* 'were assigned their place': Here, in view of the clearly plural subject, we follow the emendation of Xač'ikyan. The manuscript has the singular.

4.0.0 A general title has been added by Xač'ikyan, *յաղագս տեսականի* 'On Theory'.

4.1.0 Xač'ikyan has rewritten the title and reads *յաղագս խնդրականի եւ դիտաւորականի* 'On Inquiry and Speculation'. He has also shortened the longer titles found in manuscript A throughout the latter part of the document. We have preserved them all.

4.2.0 Here B and D resume. B breaks off at the end of a page and in the middle of a word in §4.2.8. It has lost a page or pages. D continues to §4.2.15 and then stops again.

ստորոգութեան էակացս 'the category of existing things': So A alone. B has shortened the words to single syllables, as is sometimes its habit, see comment on §1.4.11. D has *ի ստորոգութիւնն* 'for the category' and omits *էակացս* 'of beings'.

4.2.1 *բանզի* 'for': B has *զի* 'for' and D has *եւ* 'and'. These variants are found elsewhere, see *Testament of Reuben* 5:6 for the first and *Good Tidings* 58, *4 Ezra* 7:77, 10:10, 13:58, *Testament of Levi* 6:3 note, *Testament of Simeon* 2:13, 4:3, *Testament of Levi* 1:2 for the second.

ուր — ուր 'where — where': D has lost the intervening words by haplography.

գոյացութիւն2° 'essence': D has *գոյութիւն* 'existence': see §4.2.6 below.

4.2.2   *նախկին* 'precedence': In B, by a corruption, the body of the *խ* with *-կին* taken as an abbreviation was read as **ո(եաս)կ(ա)նի*, which was subsequently corrected to *տեսակն է*.

բարձմանն 'removal': B has *բաժանմանն* 'division'. No obvious explanation is available.

որոշի 'is distinguished': B has the active: compare *ասի* 'is said' further on in this section, which is active *ասէ* 'he / it says' in manuscript B. See §4.2.5 below.

*է որ*1° 'there is that which': This phrase, which is repeated throughout this section and elsewhere in the book as well, shows variation. In the first instance here, for example, the relative *որ* 'that which' is omitted by D; in the third, the following *ոչ* 'not' is omitted by B, while *որ ոչ* is corrupted into *որով* in D ('by which'). For variation in this sort of phrase, see also §§1.4.8, 1.4.9, 1.4.10, 1.6.1, 1.6.6, 1.6.7, 2.3.5tris, 4.2.6, 4.2.11.

*ասի*1° 'is said': B has the active *ասէ* 'he says', cf. *որոշի* above.

4.2.4   *ըստ*1° 'according to'1°: B adds *ամենայն*: see §2.3.5 commentary.

որ ի միոյ 'which ... from one': Corrupted into *յորմէ* 'from which' in B and *որ միոյ* in D.

եւ սեռակնագոյնք 'and most generic': Omitted from D by homoeoteleuton. A has *եռակնագոյնք* which is corrupt.

տեսակ եւ 'species and': The *եւ* 'and' following this is attested only in D. We have followed Xač'ikyan and accepted it into the text. We assume, therefore, that both A and B are corrupt, independently. Otherwise, we might hypothesize that A is corrupt and that B and C each corrected its text.

4.2.5   *եւ*1°: This introductory word is repeated in B by dittography caused by the end and the start of a line.

ի ներքոյ 'under': The form in D seems to be correct. Manuscripts A and B omit *ի* for no obvious reason.

դասի 'is arranged': B has an active verb form, see above §4.2.2.

սահմանաւ ունի 'has ... by definition': The reading *սահմանաւ*, accepted by Xač'ikyan, is found in D. The corruption in B *սահման անուանի* arises from *սահմանաւ(ն) ունի*, perhaps having the article, which is found in A. In D, an *ի* precedes, for no particular reason. In A, a variant case ending *-ու* is found and the preposition *ի* follows.

իբրեւ 'like': A has the similar adverb *իբր*.

սահմանի 'is defined': A has *սահման է* by corruption: compare the variant *սահման* in B earlier in this section.

վերնագոյնսն 'the highest things': Manuscripts B and D are independently corrupt.

4.2.6 *գոյացութիւն* 'being': A has the more or less synonymous *գոյութիւն*: see §4.2.1 above.

եւ է, որ 'and there is that which': See above §4.2.2 for discussion of variants of this and very similar phrases.

հասարակապար ասին 'are commonly said': D has the non-existent *հասարակապարին*, a corruption of these two words.

4.2.7 *դարձեալ է* 'again there is': This is the reading of A; B omits *դարձեալ*, which phenomenon is found elsewhere, e.g., *4 Ezra* 3:24, 6:1I, 9:27. D omits *եւ* 'and'; also a common variant.

ամենին2° 'of all': Manuscripts BD have the more or less synonymous *ամենայնի*; see also §4.2.10 below.

հակադարձին 'mutual': A small lacuna has damaged this word in B, where the corner of the page has been lost. It would suffice only for the loss of the first letter of the word. The preceding phrase is lost in B by haplography of the first and second occurrences of *է որ* 'there is that which'.

4.2.8 *ստորոգութեանցն* 'of the categories': B ends after the first three letters of this word.

սեռս 'genera': D has a singular; the plural found in A is required by context.

4.2.9 *բացասութիւն* 'negation': This is the reading of A. D has *բացութիւն* which means 'opening' and is a rare word.

4.2.10 *երրորդն* 'third': This is corrupted in D by abbreviation into *գ են* = *երեք են* 'there are three'.

տիրագոյն 'most important': D has *տիրակագոյն* which does not exist in the dictionaries.

ամենայն 'all': A has the more on less synonymous *ամեն*: cf. above, §4.2.7.

երկրորդ չորս է 'second is fourfold': D has 'the second ...' (*երկրորդն*). If it did not have the article, we might be led to suppose that *չորս* 'four' was lost by haplography of its abbreviation *դ* with the last letter of *երկրորդ* 'second'. This is not plausible, however, in the present state of the text. Conceivably, the article was added after the loss of *չորս* 'four'.

4.2.11 *տարորոշ* 'discrete': *տարոշ* of D is corrupt through haplography.

մակերեւութիւն1° 'surface': This is the reading of A here and of AD on the second occurrence of the word in this section. D has the synonym *մակերեւոյթ*.

*եւ է որ*2° 'and there is that which3°': For the omission of *է* 'there is' in manuscript A, compare §4.2.6 commentary. Xač'ikyan regards the text from this point until *բան եւ* as secondary and relegates it to the apparatus.

մակարդակ 'plane' seems to be required and not the metathesized form in D, *մակադրակ*, which is not in the dictionaries. Compare the second occurrence of the word in this section.

4.2.12 *առընչին* 'the relative': So Xač'ikyan emends the *առաջին(ն)* '(the) first' of AD.

ունակութիւն 'condition': This is the reading of D. This and the next word are plural in A. The plural ending of the second word is surmounted by erasure dots in A and in fact both were regarded as erroneous and already corrected by the original scribe.

4.2.13 *յարանունաբար ի* 'derivative by': So A, correctly. That text has been corrupted in D to *յարանուն եւ բարի* 'derivative and good'.

գրոցն 'the books': Xač'ikyan has *դրոցն*.

4.2.14 *ամենայնին* 'the all': So manuscript A. *ամենայնումն*, the reading of D, is contaminated from the end of the preceding *միայնում*.

4.3.0 Here D stops and the only witness is A.

զանազանութեան 'distinction': Xač'ikyan emends this to *ընդդիմակայիցն* 'opposites'. He does this because the first paragraph of this section commences with the word *ընդդիմակայքն*, and generally the name of the section echoes the first word of the ensuing text. The reading of the manuscript, however, is clear.

4.3.3 *վերաբերութիւն* 'relationship': This is Xač'ikyan's emendation of the manuscript's *բերաբերութիւն*.

անուան 'of the name': Xač'ikyan emends, surprisingly, to the orthography *անւան* or else that is a typographical error.

4.3.4 *վերաբերութեան* 'relativity': Thus we emend the orthography of the manuscript *վերբերութեան*.

5.1.0 To judge from the customary structure of this section of pseudo-Zeno, at least one initial sentence is lost here.

5.1.2 *զբնականութիւնն* 'the nature': Xač'ikyan has emended *զբնականութիւնն* 'the nature, naturalness' of the manuscript to *բնակութիւն* 'the dwelling'. For similar corruptions, see §1.2.1.

դժուարափոխ 'difficult to change': Xač'ikyan emended the text *դժուարափոխի* of A to *դժուարափոխիփոխ*, presumably positing the loss of a final syllable. However, we have restored *դմուապակիրիս*, assuming a graphic variation of *փ* / *խ*. The reason for this decision is the variant in §1.2.3 in which B reads *փրիփի* where the other manuscripts read *փրիխի*. Here, there is no text in B.

5.1.8 *յատուկ* 'particular': In his text, Xač'ikyan has emended this reading of the manuscript, for no obvious reason, to the non-classical orthography *Հատուկ*.

5.2.3 *ասին եւ* 'are said ... and': So Xač'ikyan convincingly restores the lacuna in A.

5.2.7 *բանգի*: The manuscript has *Գ* = 'three' preceding this linking word. It is probably corrupt, since the third member of the present list already exists in §5.2.6. The same phenomenon recurs also §1.3.1.

նախադասութիւնան 'in (their) precedences': There is physical damage in the manuscript which has carried away a few letters. This is the restoration of Xač'ikyan.

5.3.0 *առանձին* 'a separate section': Or 'on its own'. This word, which is found at the end of most of the section titles in this part of the book, may indicate that they come from another manuscript.

5.3.1 *ոլորումն* 'extension': So emending the unusual orthography of A *ոլրումն*.

5.3.5 *զաւրութիւնք* 'the powers': So Xač'ikyan has very convincingly restored the lacuna.

...մանց: This lacuna in the manuscript cannot be restored.

5.4.0 Xač'ikyan has abbreviated this title.

5.4.1 *ոչ կատարած*1° 'not end': The manuscript does not have *ոչ* 'not'. In it as it stands, then, there is a repetition of the phrase, for it occurred in the preceding line. Xač'ikyan has emended this double reading by introducing *ոչ* 'not' in the second instance, and that seems correct to us.

5.4.4 *երկրորդ* 'second': This emendation of Xač'ikyan is to be accepted, considering the preceding *առաջին* 'first' and the following *երրորդ* 'third'.

5.5.0 Xač'ikyan omits *առանձին* 'a separate section'.

5.5.3 *առաջին* 'first': So the manuscript, which started an enumeration that it did not continue. Xač'ikyan has omitted this word.

5.5.4 *բնութեան* 'of nature': So Xač'ikyan has emended the nominative of the manuscript. Such corruptions, engendered by the abbreviated endings of the abstracts in *-ութիւն* are rather common. See §1.6.11 commentary.

5.5.5   *եւ դարձեալ* 'and again': Xač'ikyan omits *եւ* 'and'.

5.6.1   *երկու են* 'there are two': Xač'ikyan has added the word *են* 'are' which is not in the manuscript. To support this emendation, one can cite similar expressions in §§1.5.1, 1.6.2, 4.1.1, 4.4.12, cf. §§2.3.1. There is no such definitional formula in pseudo-Zeno without the verb *են* 'are'.

5.6.4   *է*3° 'there is2°': Xač'ikyan omits this word for no obvious reason.

5.7.2   *չորք* 'four': This refers apparently either to the preceding or to the following list of four items.

բացկանայ 'occurs': This word is damaged in the manuscript.

5.8.0   *առանձին* 'a separate section': In the manuscript, the letters *անձ* are largely lost. The text of manuscript D resumes here.

5.8.1   *անբաւին* 'the infinite': The privative is lost in A. On this phenomenon, see §1.1.1 above.

5.8.2   *ի յաւիտենականէ* 'and the eternal': D has the abstract noun *յաւիտենականութենէ* 'from eternity'.

անցական 'passing': D has *առանցական* which does not appear in NBH.

անբնական 'unnatural': Manuscript A has the reading *անբնակ* 'uninhabited'. With this, compare the readings assembled in §1.1.1 commentary.

այլ է ոչինչ 'but it is nothing': This is omitted by D through a homoeoteleuton *ինչ* — *ինչ*.

բնդունայն 'idle': This seems to be preferable to *ունայն* 'void' of D, cf. the following *անկայր*.

5.9.1   *անբաւ է* 'the infinite is': This has been corrupted into *անբաւին* in D.

5.9.2   *անեղ* 'ungenerated': D has *աղեղ* 'bow' corruptly. Xač'ikyan emends to *անել* which seems to us unnecessary.

դարձեալ 'again': D has omitted everything from *բառ* to the end of the book.

ունայնագունից 'than the most void': The privative *ան-* is to be found in the only manuscript, A. It is omitted, however, by Xač'ikyan with justification, in view of the structure of the surrounding phrases. On the addition and omission of the privative, see commentary on §1.1.1.

5.9.4   *արարածոյն* 'the creation': Xač'ikyan makes this into a plural.

5.9.7   *որովք* 'of which': Xač'ikyan has emended to the singular, which seems unnecessary.

երեակք 'the triads': Xač'ikyan adds *որով* 'of which', but the text of the manuscript can be translated as it stands.

0.0.0 OF ZENO THE PHILOSOPHER

1.0.0 *On Useful Kinds*

1.0.1 Now, there are six useful kinds (γένη):
positions (θέσεις),
ranks (τάξεις),
orbits (κύκλοι),
measures (μέτρα),
powers (δυνάμεις),
influences (ἐνεργεῖαι).

1.1.0 *On Positions* (θέσεις)

1.1.1 Now, 'positions'[1] is divided into six species.
The first is the non-existence of the void (τὸ κενόν) contained by the unbounded,[2] and within it by means of construction it has the floating sphere,[3] of equal diameter, which has been modified by motion.[4]

1.1.2 The second is the heaven which is constituted of impassible fire and light,[5] enclosed by the void (τῷ κενῷ) and it is both matter and nature of incorporeal living beings.[6]

1.1.3 Third, the firmament of the watery vault[7] contained underneath the highest,[8] in order perpetually to prevent burning and

---

[1] I.e., cosmological positions.

[2] 'contained by the unbounded' seems at first blush to be pleonastic; compare, however, §1.3.1. The void contained by the unbounded is equivalent to 'infinite void'. Note David, *Prol.*, 6.10-17 where God, mover of the heavens, is ἀσώματος, which more or less corresponds to κενός and ἄπειρος.

[3] The sphere is the whole cosmos; the heaven is a layer.

[4] Though half a circle moving creates a sphere, it is better to assume that 'motion' has imparted further structure to the cosmos.

[5] In this section, the non-existent is described as becoming the incorporeal. The 'impassible fire and light' may be an *interpretatio* of the Aristotelian first element, the aether.

[6] These may be angels (cf. §1.2.2) as remote descendants of Platonic ideas, cf. Plato, *Timaeus* 30c-31a, νοητὰ ζῷα, or souls. Moreover, the idea that all the elements (including fire) are inhabited by living beings is found in Plato, *Tim.* 39a; Here the highest element, fire, is inhabited by the star-gods. Also cf. Plotinus, *Enn.* 2.1.6-8.

[7] This is biblical in origin, see Genesis 1:6-7.

[8] I.e., the heaven.

again, enclosing the separating out[9] and the flux of the sensible things.

1.1.4 Fourth, position of the sea which, held firm by the air, stays without overflowing its shores and enclosed underneath the firmament, the constitutor and the habitation of reptiles and of the enormous marine animals.[10] And (it stays) around the earth, to heal infirmities and give health to bodily living beings through the impact of the winds on the various senses.

1.1.5 The fifth[11] is the compound of the earth which has been established firmly on its sides by density, by means of mountains and hills, fields and valleys, by means of thick and dense airs, and enclosed at the edges by the waters of the sea, it stays in a quadrangular form. Within the heart of the earth fire-filled streams of airs and waters are running through all of its veins, whence springs and winds have come up through earthquakes.[12] And similarly (i.e., the same goes for) the beds of seas and rivers. And the begotten things both which are in the waters and which are on the dry land, it[13] is the bringer into being and cause of life of all of them.

1.1.6 The sixth is the interior of the world, which is coagulated from the airs by swelling within a constraint, in the hollow (caused by) the separation of three established things,[14] to constitute junction and binding together of the world, which is the cause of life and is (its) habitation.

1.1.7 And the borders of the constellations (are) within it underneath the firmament,[15] for the stars orbit unerringly, each according to its constellation driven by the airs, in which[16] they have been ordered according to time and according to the boundary of places.

---

[9]   See §1.5.1

[10]   For 'the constitutor... animals' see Genesis 1:21, and cf. note 7.

[11]   See Schmidt, 18, citing Περὶ κόσμου 2.391b, 13f; 3.392b, 14ff.

[12]   Or 'motions'. See Schmidt, 18, citing Seneca, *Nat. quaest.* III.15, Περὶ κόσμου 4.395b, 18ff. The parallels to Περὶ κόσμου and Seneca indicate that here pseudo-Zeno is dependent on a tradition widely used in antiquity. The latter is extensively cited by Stobaeus in his *Anthology*. It is, perhaps, more likely that pseudo-Zeno depends on Plato, *Phaedo* 111c-112a.

[13]   Probably the earth.

[14]   The reference is to the whole cosmos. 'Three established things' translates a word cited by *NBH* only from here. Perhaps these are the three constituent parts of the world from §§1.1.3, 1.1.4 and 1.1.5.

[15]   Cf. §1.1.3.

[16]   I.e., constellations. That stars may be moved by air curents is an Epicurean suggestion, see Epicurus, *Ep. Pythocl.* 93. and especially Lucretius 5.637-49. Note that the planets too are moved in this way, below §1.3.5.

1.2.0 *On Ranks* (τάξεις)

1.2.1 'Ranks' is divided according to three:
according to virtue,
according to law,
according to nature.

1.2.2 For angels[17] and men share the understanding of the arrangement (scil., of things) according to virtue and according to law.[18]

But according to nature, each of those who are customarily in the world are in (their) natural boundaries.

1.2.3 Now those (angels and men)[19] who do not conduct themselves according to virtue and according to law, disorders and catastrophes encounter (them) and dog the life of that selfsame one. And he who moves outside against the natural (παρὰ φύσιν) truly becomes[20] the dissolution and corruption of (his) nature.

1.2.4 But constellations are ranked in the encompassings of airs and in the paths[21] of the aerial motion. They do not proceed around one another and each is not moved from its own position.[22]

1.3.0 *On Orbits* (κύκλοι)

1.3.1 The 'orbits of the sphere' is constituted according to three ways[23] which is (i.e. are):
modelling,
appearance,
eternal existence.

---

[17] Compare David, *Prol.* 24.9-10: both men and angels are rational living beings, and therefore have and know virtue and law. David 38.25, 38.32 and 39.9 talks of ἐπιστημονικαὶ ἀρεταί and *ibid.* 38.32-33 of φυσικαὶ ἀρεταί.

[18] David, *Prol.* 30.23 has the expression κατ' ἀρετὴν ζῶν. The idea of life according to virtue and according to nature is originally Stoic and becomes a commonplace. Here pseudo-Zeno seems to refer to angels. These beings are referred to in §§1.1.2, 1.5.4.

[19] If the bracketed explanation is correct (cf. preceding sentence), and it is the translators', this refers to fallen angels.

[20] I.e., suffers.

[21] Or: orbits. For the 'airs' see §1.1.7.

[22] The fixed stars are meant.

[23] The Armenian *լծումանք* translates Greek τροπαί, i.e. 'turnings'. The Armenian translator mistranslated Greek τροποί 'ways'. We have incorporated this proposal into our translation.

For the world is modelled in the unbounded, and is seen by means of[24] the void in colour and form and in species of kind.

1.3.2 Again, (it is) in that very eternally existent according to (the) model,[25] as a result of which that which appeared is unchanging by nature.

In the same way, again, the sphere has perfection together with diversity.[26]

1.3.3 The orbits of the heavens must be understood to mean the circumferences of the airs, and not the firmament of the watery vault[27]—which is the separating one—and not the third heaven, but the airs which are encircled underneath the firmament. They are ranged according to a sevenfold division underneath one another

1.3.4 in spherical fashion, surrounding the deep,[28] equally, according to the fourfold directions of the world in which the constellations are divided. And in all the places of the airs they are spread out all over in two half-spheres[29] with unceasing revolution in orientation from East to West, which are moving in the same paths.

1.3.5 The planets are seven, divided according to the seven boundaries of the airs, which are these: Saturn, Jupiter, Mars, Sun, Venus, Mercury, the Moon. Because they (are) self-moving, they orbit in orientation from West to East, they orbit and according to each of the constellations they bring the times into being by their orbits.

1.4.0[30] *On Measures* (μέτρα)

1.4.1 'Measures of the world' is divided according to four:
according to place,
and according to colour,
and according to shape,
and according to numbering.

---

[24]　I.e., thanks to the activity of.

[25]　I.e. a sort of transcendental Model (παράδειγμα) as in Plato's *Timaeus*, where the Demiurge looks at the eternal Model. The Creator will not destroy his handiwork, e.g., *Tim.* 41ab.

[26]　Referring to constellations and planets.

[27]　Cf. §1.1.3.

[28]　I.e., interior.

[29]　Viz., of day and night.

[30]　Behind §1.4 is a mathematical sequence in an odd order: geometry – arithmetic –astrology (the latter replacing astronomy).

1.4.2 Place is threefold: upper, lower, middle.[31] And it is differentiated by directions: the upper and so forth.

Colour is said to be fourfold: white, blue, black, clear. And from them are constituted shades, nuances, brilliances, effulgences and various others on a single substrate.[32]

1.4.3[33] Shape (σχῆμα)[34] is said to be three-fold: triangular, quadrangular, and circular. From these, shape is differentiated into various species.

Number (ἀριθμός) is divided three-fold:

for there is that which is called even—it is divided by kinds in an equal way;

and there is that which is odd according to the inequality of the unequal species;[35]

and moreover, that which is constituted from the indivisible.[36]

But those things which are not in accordance with these[37] are called unbounded and indefinite (ἀμέτρως).[38]

1.4.4[39] The borders of the constellations are set by means of the time of the planets (and) by the number of revolutions.[40]

The constellations of the twelve months[41] were discriminated in a threefold way:

according to the four directions of the world,

according to matter,[42]

and according to the phase of the solstices and equinoxes,[43]

according to the parts of the earth,

according to the limbs of the body,

according to the coming into being.

Which they call:

---

[31] Cf. the division of the cosmos, §§1.1.3-1.1.7.

[32] I.e., for each colour.

[33] This section deals with geometry followed by arithmetic.

[34] There is a close parallel in the *Divisiones Aristotelae*, §64 (ed. Mutschmann, p. 63).

[35] That is, e.g., 7 = 3 + 4.

[36] The ἕν is indivisible in arithmetic.

[37] I.e., matter.

[38] The Armenian անչափ means basically 'without measure', perhaps ἀμέτρως. This is indefinite matter, which has neither shape nor number.

[39] The astrological material which follows is discussed at length by Schmidt, pp. 20-24, who is very good on the parallels in Greek astrological literature.

[40] See §1.3.5.

[41] That is, the signs of the zodiac.

[42] I.e., the four elements mentioned in the sequel.

[43] See below: literally 'halves, hemi-'s'.

1.4.5 Ram, Taurus, Gemini to the East, which is air and the vernal equinox;

Cancer, Leo, Virgo to the North, which is fire and the summer solstice;

1.4.6 Libra, Scorpio, Sagittarius to the West, which is earth and the autumnal equinox;

Capricorn, Aquarius, Pisces to the South, which is water and the winter solstice.

1.4.7 But, being sympathetic with the earth and with human limbs:

Ram (is) of the Persians, which is the head,

Taurus (is) of the Babylonians, which is the neck,

Gemini (is) of the Cappadocians, which are the shoulders,

Cancer (is) of the Armenians, which are the lungs,

1.4.8 Leo (is) of the Asians, which is \ BCD the thorax \ A the right arm \ ,

Virgo (is) of the Helladians and Greeks, and they are \ BCD the arms \ A the left arm \ ,

1.4.9 Libra (is) of the \ BCD Arabians \ A Cilicians \ and they are the fists,

Scorpio (is) of the Italians, and they are the legs,

Sagittarius (is) of the Cretans, and they are the groin,

1.4.10 Capricorn (is) of the Syrians,[44] and they are the thighs,

Aquarius (is) of the Egyptians, and they are the knees,

Pisces (is) of the Indians and of the Red Sea, and they are the feet.

1.4.11 But according to coming into being

there are six male ones:

Ram, Gemini, Leo, Libra, Sagittarius, Aquarius;

and six female ones which are:

Taurus, Cancer, Virgo, Scorpio, Capricorn, Pisces.

1.5.0[45] *On Powers* (δυνάμεις)

1.5.1 There are four species (εἴδη) of powers:

there are bringings forth (ἐκφοραί),

---

[44]   Or: Assyrians.

[45]   §§1.5.1-2 are about coming into being, §§1.5.3-4 about what does not come into being, at least not in the way ordinary things do, including souls. §§1.5.5-1.5.13 are (mostly) about the body, its constitution, its diseases (some of which are caused by the *diaita* or way of life) and health (health at 11.5.12), and its dissolution in death in two ways.

there are flowings forth (ἐκχύσεις),
there are separatings forth (ἐκκρίσεις),
and there are givings forth (ἐκδόσεις).

From these the coming into being[46] and the healing (τὸ ἰατρικόν) is constituted.

1.5.2 For the coming into being is divided into three species:
into moist things (τὰ ὑγρά),[47]
into dry things (τὰ ξηρά),[48]
into amphibious things (τὰ ἀμφίβια).

It is brought forth
according to time,
according to matter,
and according to place (χώρα).

1.5.3 But the coming out of the soul is unchanging (ἄτρεπτος) and complete separation, and a creation from outside (θυράθεν). It is generation (γένεσις) according to the mixtures (συμμίξεις?)[49] of matter in a bodiless way (ἀσωμάτως), but the constitution of (its) nature is not according to time nor according to direction, nor according to density of matter from the flux. And it is not made differently (ἑτεροῖος), but that which is differentiated[50] (is so) in accordance with the passibilities (πάθη) or mixtures of (the) body.

1.5.4[51] However, that which is not brought forth in accordance with the production of body, the substance of its nature is not of such a kind, but some other higher growth of nature, and (it is) unchanging, without birth, from impassible (ἀπαθούς) fire and light,[52] incorporeal, immortal in (its) life. At the same time it has received its

---

[46] Observe that Greek γένεσις means 'coming into being' or 'geniture'. In §§1.4.4, 1.4.11, 1.5.2 we also translate 'coming into being'.

[47] In the sea, etc. In §1.1.2 pseudo-Zeno mentions other 'incorporeal living beings', inhabitants of the heaven which is made of fire and light. He thus includes three elements, perhaps inhibited from mentioning the inhabitants of the fourth element, air, by his Christianity.

[48] On land, in the air.

[49] In Plato's *Timaeus* the immortal World Soul as well as the immortal (parts of the) human souls are mixtures created (before time begins) out of the most important kinds, viz. indivisible and divisible Being, Same and Different.

[50] Referring to the human soul only. The lower parts are in relation to the body, which is in the flux.

[51] This section perhaps refers to Platonic Ideas, see §1.1.2 above.

[52] See §1.1.2.

genesis[53] from a single matter, (it is) nonetheless innumerable (ἀναρίθμητος) in multitude.

1.5.5 Medicine (ἡ ἰατρική) is according to membrane and the brain (ὁ ἐγκέφαλος), blood and bile, and from it the nerves and sinews and bones and veins and flesh and skin are constituted. For the joining and the mixture (κρᾶσις) is divided into male and female parts.

1.5.6 The variety of the mixture is divided into three:
according to the body, thin and delicate;
and according to the colour, reddish, brown, blond, bronze;
and according to the hair, frizzy, straight, curly and thin or thick;
and according to flavours and smells, bitter, sweet, sour and sharp.

1.5.7 The bile and the blood are the height of the materials and the foundation of the changes and they are distinguished according to time through modifications (κατὰ τρόπους). From them health and serious illnesses arise. For, according to an equally balanced blending (ἰσόρροπος εὐκρασία *vel sim.*) health comes into being; but according to excess, various illnesses (arise).

1.5.8 For, from (excesses of) the black bile, being moonstruck (somnambulating) (arises); and from imbalance of blood (?),[54] leprosy; and from severity of blood of the womb, sterilities; and from coldness of the shoulders, impotence of the male.

1.5.9 These are constituted according to the excesses.

1.5.10 But the styles of life (ἤθη τοῦ βίου), having been punished (κολαζόμενα) by nature, are necessarily strengthened, so that envy and love of honour and desire (ἐπιθυμία) receive support (= become a σύμμαχος), and from those wars and battles are constituted. And plans (βουλαί) having been accepted for the benefit of one's self, one begets thoughts of the reason and of activity.[55] For in the one case one gains benefit according to the body, in the other case according to the soul.

1.5.11 But death is the dissolution of senses and a destruction and separation of the materials. For there is that (death) which is through accident, according to the mixtures and there is that which is natural according to the passions.[56] The accident happens according to time

---

[53] Cf. § 1.5.1. The single matter is the impassible fire-and-light.
[54] *մխատատարենէն* is an unknown word.
[55] Or: influence.
[56] Or: παθήματα.

in war or from other snares, or from depletion by the sufferings of illness in the middle of life.

1.5.12 But the natural (death)[57] is according to power, until the diminution of the strength of warmth, and it is known from birth according to time through the circling of the planets.[58] But according to the strength of the qualities of matter the cause of the sensible body and the air are different, because according to the good mixture (εὐκρασία) and from the dynamic seed of the earth, by which it is touched and nurtured, good health(s) and growth(s) are constituted.

1.5.13 The opposite of these (is) various pains and the mixture of which is the cause of death,[59] which occurs according to the bitterness of movement of the air, in times of the external things (τὰ ἔξωθεν) according to the qualities of matter, and according to the mixture of the body, to occur, by impressions on the heart, and become a destruction of life (being alive).

1.5.14 Therefore, those coming into beings which are not according to time and power, are miracles of the Uncreated One and not of the nature of material things.

1.6.0 *On Influences* (ἐνεργεῖαι)

1.6.1 'Influence of natures' is divided into three, for
there are those which are nurturers,
and there are those which make wise,
and there are those which make erudite.[60]

1.6.2 Now, there are two species of nurturers—matter and time, for in four ways, according to equality of coincidences, they water the seeds of varieties of seedlings and shoots.

1.6.3 But those (influences) which make wise are divided into two,
      according to appearances,
      and according to sounds.
The appearance is divided into three,
      into colour, into shape and into form.

---

[57] The φυσικὸς ... θανατὸς καθ᾽ ὃν ἅπαντες τελευτῶμεν according to David, *Prol.* 31.16-7.

[58] The reference here is to astrology.

[59] See §1.5.11.

[60] Probably ἐπιστήμονα, cf. §3.1.5.

Colour is divided according to four,

> black, white, blue, and clear.

The mixtures are constituted of these into various appearances of colours.

1.6.4 Similarly the shapes are differentiated into four, according to the impact of the divisible, which is:

> triangle and quadrangle,
>
> length[61] and circle.

But in shape the circle is perfect according to shape and according to the movement of the world, returning again to the same (place).

1.6.5 But the form is in the countenance; and countenance, in the individual; and the individual, in species; while the species (is) in kind. And there is indeed a form upon births and comings forth and creations, which are differentiated after having been brought forth in the indefinite, (into) similar and dissimilar, by means of unpaired time and movement.

1.6.6 But exceptionally, that which does not accept the natural state appears as if above all four *pathos*-receiving elements both the lower and the upper, and above the supernal region for, having been produced, they are differentiated according to the generation of matter. And of them there are those which are voluntary and there are those which are involuntary, and that which is neither voluntary nor involuntary (is) necessity, for it is constrained by no-one.

1.6.7 But sound is elemental, divided into four species,

> non-living,[62]
>
> sensible,[63]
>
> reasonable,[64]
>
> and reasonable in a special sense.[65]

The non-living, by the intermediary of inflations are signals of bodies and knocking of material.

The sensible[66] are symbols to each other for the sake of the species of knowledge.[67]

---

[61] I.e., line.

[62] ἄψυχον, referring to things.

[63] αἰσθητικόν, referring to animals and humans.

[64] λογικόν, referring to humans alone.

[65] Referring to νοῦς or διάνοια 'understanding'. The four terms just listed are taken up in the latter part of this section, where 'non-living', 'sensible', 'reasonable' and 'intelligible' (see note 68) occur.

[66] I.e. sounds made by living beings.

[67] I.e. communication among living beings.

The notations of the reasonable are the symbols of sounds, and the sounds (are the symbols) of the intelligible ones, the comprehension of reality and (of) the reality of the unreal (i.e. the incorporeal).

1.6.8 But the intelligible[68] is constituted of the visible and the sound customary among humans, according to the combination and the recent knowledge.[69]

These do not truly compose those of the divine, but are sometimes used improperly (scil., of the divine).

1.6.9 But erudition (ἐπιστήμη) is art and it is divided into four species,

into the practical and into the reasonable,

into the theoretical and into the comprehensible.[70]

And[71] the practical (πρακτικόν),

into administrative (οἰκονομικόν),

into moral (ἠθικόν),

and into political (πολιτικόν).

And the reasonable (λογικόν),[72]

into the probative (ἀποδεικτικόν),

into the dialectical (διαλεκτικόν),

into the sophistical (σοφιστικόν),[73]

into the divisible (διαιρετικόν),

into the analytical (ἀναλυτικόν),

into the definitional (ὁριστικόν).

1.6.10 And the theoretical, by means of which (is) the searchable,[74]

into the intentional,

into the inseparable definition,

into the categories of beings,

into the opposites,

---

68 I.e., the 'reasonable in a special sense'; see §1.6.7 above.

69 Perhaps this means that concepts ('the intelligible') are constituted according to the visible (more or less equivalent to αἴσθησις or ὄψις) and sound customary among humans (συνήθεια, i.e. ordinary language). So, concepts are formed on the basis of the apprehension of things and of language, which are combined with what we already know.

70 I.e., γνῶσις, the highest discipline of all, which also includes the study of nature (φυσιολογικόν): viz., of time, perfection, beginning, end, nature, being, matter, movement and infinity.

71 See Schmidt, pp. 14-15. He cites Elias, *Prolegomena* (*Comm. in Aristot. Gr.* 18.1) 26-34; David, *Prolegomena* (*Comm. in Aristot. Gr.*) 75.

72 I.e., logic.

73 I.e., the refutation of fallacies.

74 I.e., the solution of problems.

into a cause of ascription, under which, partly (is) reference,
into the quality of the dogmatic.

1.6.11 To the comprehensible (belong):
evil and good, time, perfection, beginning and end, nature,
definitional and efficient, being, matter and movement, void, infinity.
For having been divided also by definition, they are separated.

1.6.12[75] The divisions[76] of the practical are:
will, propensity, selection, anger, desire.
(The divisions) of the reasonable (λογικόν) (are):
noun and verb, word and explicit word,[77] affirmation and negation.

1.6.13 (The divisions) of the theoretical (are):
sensibility, imagination, thought, reasoning, mind.
(The divisions) of the comprehensible (are):
mental distinctions, understandings and thoughts, knowledge
(γνῶσις) and prescience (πρόγνωσις).

1.6.14 The composition of skills is unsearchable nature, indivisible
in assembling, which means man in whom all apparent things are
divided, constituable and unconstituable and mathematical.[78]

1.6.15 The constituable and unconstituable are with one another
in two parts, by class and by subclass. The mathematical are in the
constitutable ones and the unconstituable ones; the diagonals are
constituted.[79] Hence the hexad is perfect.[80] **1.6.16** There are two
constituable with one another and one diagonal.[81]

Again, man is divided according to nature and according to passion:
according to faith,
according to hope,
and according to love.[82]

---

[75] On this and the next section, see Schmidt, pp. 25-26, citing David.

[76] Armenian *սահման* means 'border' and consequently, that contained within a
border. We have chosen to translate it 'division' here, though that English word
usually reflects Armenian *բաժանումն*. It often means 'definition,' but here that
meaning seems difficult.

[77] I.e., name, appellation.

[78] The meaning of this section is quite unclear.

[79] Diagonals are constituted, presumably of $c^2 = a^2 + b^2$ where c is the
hypotenuse.

[80] ἑξὰς τέλειος ἀριθμός David, 22.22ff, 22.32, 53.10ff. Perfect numbers are those
whose parts, when put together (συντιθέμενα) are equal to the whole: e.g., 1 + 2 +
3=6: David 22.34, 53.12. Imperfect numbers (ὑπερτέλειοι, ἐλλιπεῖς or ἀτελεῖς are
those whose parts, when put together, are more or less than the whole: e.g., 12,
whose parts 6 + 4 + 3 + 1 = 16 (more than 12) and 8, whose parts 4 + 2 + 1 = 7 (less
than 8).

[81] A triangle is the image here.

[82] The last three elements are Christian, derived from 1 Corinthians 13:13, 1

1.6.17 Now, we have said this much about the useful kinds, which have been produced above time—positions, ranks, orbits, measures, powers, influences—for the sake of fixing the definitions of the nature of time, the movements of the orbiting planets, which are the bringers into being of time.

1.6.18 But, the fixed stars are symbols of places, of progressions and of distinctions of times, and (if) it happens that the paths of the orbits is[83] slanted, at once it exerts influence upon the philosopher's knowledge. They are the definitions of the first thing/word of the triad, which is divine reason, which they said to be partial.

2.0.0 *On the Practical Realm to which has been added On the Perfection of Speech.*

2.0.1 A thing (πρᾶγμα) is economic, moral, political

2.1.0 *On the Economic*

2.1.1 Now the economic is divided into what is moderate (τὸ σῶφρον), into what is fitting, into domestic.
For the moderate is concerned with restricting in terms of value,
the fitting is the measuring with respect to abundance,
and the domestic is provision with respect to availability.[84]
And the economic means care of ...[85]

2.2.0 *On the Moral*

2.2.1 The moral is to present an example by the disposition towards life of virtue or of evil.

2.2.2 And (the moral) is assigned to reptiles according to their nature, and to the wild animals and domestic animals according to their food, and to the birds and fishes according to habit.

2.2.3 And the term moral is also used for the ethos of thinking[86]

Thessalonians 1:3, 5:8.

[83] Thus the Armenian text.

[84] Or: prosperity.

[85] *կազթեանց*, an unknown word.

[86] The dominant meaning of the Armenian word is 'sensitive, that which senses'. We have chosen a somewhat different meaning within its semantic range and which suits better here.

beings. And that which causes character (ἠθοποιητικόν) is that which is compounded according to time, for, having been added,[87] it is exemplified by seedlings and plants.

2.3.0 *On the Political*[88]

2.3.1 To political matters grammar is prefaced. There are three kinds of grammar: practice (ἐμπειρία), grammar, poetry.
And practical (ἐμπειρία) is said of partial things, **2.3.2** and (its) parts are six:[88a]
expert reading according to prosody,
explanations of stories according to available literary models,
ready explanations of languages and of ancient histories,
the finding of etymology,
information on analogies,
the judgement on literary works (κρίσις ποιημάτων).
2.3.3 Grammar is said of the composition of stories (μῦθοι)
according to the choice of letters,
according to sounds and according to syllables (συλλήψεις),
according to words (λέξεις) and according to composition (σύνθεσις),
according to the employment of simple metrical feet.
2.3.4 Poetry is according to the parts of speech. There are eight parts of speech:[89] noun, verb, participle, article, pronoun, preposition, adverb, conjunction.

And noun and verb are completed by declension and by syntax and according to protasis.[90]
2.3.5 There are those which are participle (μετοχή)
and which are article according to verb,
and there are those which are prefix,
and there are those which are replacement according to the noun,[91]
and there are those which are related (συγγενής),[92]
and there are those which bind.[93]
And speech is guided with things by sound through air.

---

[87] Or: compounded, made.
[88] This section draws on the grammar attributed to Dionysius Thrax, see following notes and also p. 26 above.
[88a] Compare Dionysius Thrax, §1.
[89] Compare Dionysius Thrax, §11.
[90] Or: priority, precedence.
[91] I.e., pronouns.
[92] I.e., to the verb; that is, adverbs.
[93] I.e., conjunctions.

2.3.6 The political is composed according to proëmium, according to structure and according to persuasion.[94] **2.3.7** The headings of its[95] parts are divided into deliberative (συμβουλευτικός), forensic (δικανικός), declamatory (ἐπιδεικτικός or πανηγυρικός).[96]

For the deliberative is narrative according to (future) time,
and the forensic is a sub-part[97] according to (an) event,
and the declamatory is for praise or for blame.

2.4.0 *On Mimetic Representation* (μίμησις)

2.4.1 Mimetic representation is the giving of form, improperly (καταχρηστικῶς) for illusion and it occurs according to these:

from ignorance and weakness thoughts and knowledge of others are measured;[98]

2.4.2 and from agitation and joy the opinions of the others become doubted;
and according to praise and according to facilitation a confusion and circumvention of the wise occurs;
and it is according to political life.

2.5.0 *On Content* [99]

2.5.1 When you hear content, consider it thus; see how heavens and earth are mixed in a family relationship, having received a command from Heaven for air to be mixed with earth.

2.5.2 Now, you are securely informed, that which is between heaven and earth is the force of water and the manifestation of winds; see how it assembled, it coagulated around itself and established its own constraint.

---

[94] Persuasion is part of an old definition of rhetoric, quoted by David, *Prol.* 20.7: πειθοῦς δημιουργός.

[95] I.e., persuasion's.

[96] David, *Prol.* 72.4-5 follows the traditional division of rhetoric: it διαιρεῖται … εἰς δικανικόν which is περὶ τὸν παρεληλυθότα (χρόνον = past), into συμβουλευτικόν which is περὶ τὸν μέλλοντα χρόνον καταγίνεται (future) and into πανηγυρικόν which is περὶ τὸν ἐνεστῶτα (χρόνον = present). With the reversal of the order of the first two elements, this is the same list as in pseudo-Zeno.

[97] Armenian տեղի < τόπος, i.e. 'part' or 'section' of an art or discipline.

[98] քննեալ չափին is a hendiadys and so is translated.

[99] Style and vocabulary both show that this section is most probably from a different source to the rest of the work.

2.5.3 Now, three things one must say water (to be), and what these are we shall say: storage-chambers, strength, flavour.[100] Now, we shall say clearly there is a storage-chamber in waters, from which winds[101] go out, the Haṙasapʻ and the Kʻarsapʻ, the Sarsapʻ and the Nazat.[102] Their exits are from the sea, and their paths through the heavens; having passed by their storage-chambers and their paths, I shall make (them) clear.

2.5.4 Water has a broad seat, enclosed in a storage-chamber; the winds (are) restless, their exit is the outermost parts of the sea, and their path in the outer waters. For sea, which has no hidden (part) is external, but it is internal to the heavens which are above it; and between waters and earth are winds. And frequently they cause damage and earthquakes and much help to wells and (to) veins of waters. Heavens are established above earth.

2.5.5 These are the contents, the contents of all things which I tell you, and the Word of God is Lord.

3.0.0 *On …*

3.1.0 *On Definitions and Divisions which They Added about Nature*

3.1.1 Now, it is necessary first for division to exist and then definition.[103] For division is threefold:
the inferior
and the superior
and …[104]
It is divided into four species:
into special and into partial,[105]

---

[100] Or: odour.

[101] A different Armenian word from that used in §2.5.2. Here and in §2.5.4 the word used also means 'atmospheres'. See next paragraph.

[102] These names are obscure.

[103] David gives the reverse, first definition and then division, like in pseudo-Zeno's section title. A similar reversal of two terms occurs in §4.1.14.

[104] A third division seems required. If we examine David 55.8-16 we find a three-fold division. The first two elements are in reverse order there: ὑποδιαίρεσις as δεύτερα τομή, διαίρεσις as πρώτη τομή, and the third term, corresponding to the missing term in Armenian, was ἐπιδιαίρεσις.

[105] Or: species (viz., of a kind) and parts (viz., of a whole), see διαίρεσις ἀπὸ γένους εἰς εἴδη, e.g. David, *Prol.* 65.16-7.

into similar and into dissimilar;[106]

and again a union of opposites, which is singular.[107]

3.1.2 The 'definitive' is divided into four species by logic, as follows:

what is it? [108]

whence is it?

and of what sort are they?

and why is it?

3.1.3 The sections of an example are divided by the diversity of their parts as follows, according to these (criteria): [109]

The first, what is[110] definition, divided into unmarried out of a kind, and into a constituent out of varieties; by what is the hypothetical differentiated, which is collected[111] from the accidents.[112]

3.1.4 The second. Whence is[113] 'definition' known?—From the agrarian proof.[114]

From which was it taken?—From (its) subject[115] and from (its) goal.[116]

Which is the perfect definition and which imperfect?[117]

---

[106] This might be ἀπὸ ὅλων εἰς μέρη ὁμοιομέρη καὶ εἰς ἀνομοιομέρη.

[107] This is the division of a single genus into opposite species, cf. David, *Prol.* 65.21 ff. ὅταν τὸ ζῷον διέλωμεν εἰς λογικὸν καὶ ἄλογον· τὸ γὰρ ζῷον (one) γένος ἐστι καὶ διαιρεῖται εἰς (opposite) εἴδη.

[108] The first, third and fourth of these traditional (Aristotle, *Posterior Analytics* II.1, where also as first issue we find the εἰ ἐστι) heuristic and problem-defining issues are paralleled by e.g. David, *Prol.* 1.15 (τί ἐστι; ὁποιόν τί ἐστι; διὰ τί ἐστι). Pseudo-Zeno leaves out the equally traditional εἰ ἐστι mentioned by David (as one is allowed to whenever irrelevant, i.e. whenever existence is not in doubt) and replaces it with the issue πόθεν ἐστι (see §3.1.4 for an example of this), which too is already encountered in Aristotle.

[109] I.e., those listed in §3.1.2.

[110] I.e., τί ἐστι;

[111] See note 120 below for another similar phrase.

[112] Compare David, Elias and Ammonius.

[113] I.e., πόθεν ἔστι

[114] Schmidt, p. 28 cites Elias and, even closer to pseudo-Zeno, David, *Prol.* 15.11-12 πόθεν λέγεται ὁρισμός; ἰστεὸν ὅτι ὁρισμὸς λέγεται ἀπὸ μεταφορᾶς τῶν ἐν τοῖς γηδίοις ὁροθεσίων. Has Armenian here mistranslated ὁροθεσίων as "proof"? In the Armenian version of David, the sense of the Greek is preserved.

[115] I.e., field in this analogy.

[116] Literally: completion, execution. Thus, e.g., the subject (ὑποκείμενον) of medicine is human bodies and its aim is health. One may define medicine either by indicating its field or its goal or both. David, *Prol.* 16.14-5 ἰστέον ὅτι οἱ ὁρισμοὶ λαμβάνονται ἢ ἀπὸ τοῦ ὑποκειμένου ἢ ἀπὸ τοῦ τέλους ἢ ἀπὸ τοῦ συναμφοτέρου. See also Schmidt, p. 28.

[117] David, *Prol.* 19.9ff. ποῖος τέλειος ὁρισμὸς καὶ ποῖος ἀτελής;

The perfect is the one which receives the natural, according to the inflections of nouns and verbs,[118] to guide to tranquillity[119] whatever thing exists.

The imperfect is that which is collected[120] from accidents, which is a symbol of the noun or of the verb.

3.1.5 The definitions of philosophy are:[121]

knowledge of the existing (things),

knowledge of the divine

and of the human things,

contemplation of death,

conformity to God,

art of arts and science of sciences.

(So is) philosophy,[122] the love of wisdom. This makes six.

3.1.6 And again, it is divided according to four:

the near subject (is) the depth and the near perfection (is) silence;[123]

the far subject (is) mind and the far perfection (is) truth;

and according to growth—word and life;

and according to veracity—man and collecting,

which the Pythagoreans revere. For that which is, is constituted of four, by four movements.[124]

3.1.7 Why are there six definitions of philosophy?[125]

First, it is because of the existing things,

for there is that which is named and exists not,

and there is that which is not named, but exists.[126]

And second, because of calculation (ἀριθμητική),[127]

---

[118]   Cf. §2.3.4.

[119]   Probably means: you do not have to bother or look further afield because the definition is perfect.

[120]   Literally: 'goes around', cf. §3.1.3.

[121]   Cf. Elias, *Prol.* 7.26-7 and particularly David, *Prol.* 20.25 ff., etc. See Schmidt, p. 30, citing David, *Prol.* 23, 4: γνῶσις τῶν ὄντων ... γνῶσις τῶν θείων τε καὶ ἀνθρωπίνων πραγμάτων ... μελέτη θανάτου ... ὁμοίωσις θεῷ.

[122]   See §3.1.14.

[123]   The terminology seems to reflect that in David 21.25ff. which speaks of προσεχὲς and conversely πόρρω ὑποκείμενον and τέλος. Compare Schmidt, pp. 29 and 30.

[124]   The Pythagoreans are the only Greek philosophers mentioned by pseudo-Zeno. The 'four' is the *tetraktys*, see §3.1.8.

[125]   David, *Prol.* 21.1-2.

[126]   This answers the question 'Why are there six definitions of philosophy?' because the other five follow from the first. See David, *Prol.* 22.2-27 and 23.3ff. With this and the preceding line compare David, *Prol.* 21.4-9.

[127]   David, *Prol.* 21.3.

because six is perfect through its (consisting of) two halves both by threes
and by its being half a dozen.[128]

3.1.8 The tetraktys is even. Its chapters[129] are constituted of the odds and evens,[130] according to this art.[131]

3.1.9 The tens are: 4, 10, 100, 1000, 4, 3, 2, 1: And this is said to be partial in the sight of the intellect.
The triad is odd and it is a symbol of the even-oddness,[132] and in this fashion it is (made) perfect by seeings and by sayings.

3.1.10 And again the number of the triad is defined according to this art:
even is listening to God,[133]
and odd is talking with God,
and the two (of them) is the study of God who is the first one and the last.[134]

3.1.11[135] The first is the knowledge of the things that exist, which are encompassed by the senses, and the knowledge of the divine and the human situations, for not every god is worship and not every human being is a minister.

3.1.12 The second is the tearing of humans away from life's suffering and their being taken into serenity and freedom from sufferings[136] and conformity to God through capability and knowledge and the good. The like(ness) is in accordance with human nature, and is not the true God,[137] **3.1.13** for God's capability and knowing and beneficence are infinite, while the human (are) according to their capacity, for only wishing and longing and choosing are constituted as the likeness of God.[138]

---

[128] This is equivalent to David 22.18ff though his explanation is different.

[129] I.e., 1 + 2 + 3 + 4. Perhaps κεφάλαια.

[130] Odd are 1 and 3; even are 2 and 4.

[131] I.e., arithmetic.

[132] 1 + 2; David 52.6 says: εἰς μονάδα καὶ δυάδα διαιρεῖται.

[133] The even number 2 can be depicted as two points and is receptive because something can be inserted between these points; it is therefore seen as feminine. The impenetrable odd (the 1) is active and masculine. This is a Pythagoran doctrine, a variety of which is already cited Aristotle, *Metaphysics* A ch. 5.

[134] 'who is the first one and the last' is a Christian phrase.

[135] Schmidt, p. 31 deals with §§3.1.11-3.1.14 not completely satisfactorily.

[136] Or: impassibility. Compare David, *Prol.* 22.7 and 25.1-2: νέκρωσιν ... τῶν παθῶν.

[137] See the argument in Elias, *Prol.* 17.22ff.

[138] Compare David, *Prol.* 24.32-33 ὁμοίωσις τῷ θεῷ κατὰ τὸ δυνατόν ἀνθρώπῳ. Also 35.20ff τῷ τε ἀγαθῷ καὶ τῷ γνωστικῷ καὶ τῷ δυνατῷ, where the difference between god and man is stated as well.

3.1.14 The third is the art of arts and the erudition of the eruditions.[139] Now, to the arts belongs the practical,[140] while art is the rational, and to the eruditions belongs the theoretical,[141] while erudition (is) intelligible[142] just like 'king of kings' and 'god of gods'.[143]

3.1.15 Philosophy (is) loving wisdom, in veracity. For all philosophy is divided threefold:

into listening as if to God,

and in talking as if to God,

and in scrutinising as if (scrutinising) God.[144]

3.1.16 The invention of definitions is according to the rational arts and the cause is the ingenious mind of the world, which is God.

3.2.0 *On Proof and Logic*

3.2.1 The probative (ἀποδεικτικός) consists of syllogism, and syllogism (consists) of that which is primary in order and that which is secondary in order.[145]

That which is primary in order and that which is secondary in order (consist of) subjects and predicates.

The subject (consists) of subordinated parts,[146] while the predicate is different (from the subject)[147] which, as mentioned above, becomes (included in the predicate).[148]

---

[139] Alternatively translate 'science of sciences'. David, *Prol.* 39.23ff: τέχνη τεχνῶν, which formula βασιλεῖ παρείκασε τὴν φιλοσοφίαν, and ἐπιστήμη ἐπιστήμων which θεῷ αὐτὴν παρεικάζομεν.

[140] The poetical seems to be omitted.

[141] The arts 'do' something, especially the βαναύσοι τεχναί, but there are also λογικαὶ τεχναί, and these are subordinate to ἐπιστημαὶ and φιλοσοφία. Thus, art is a sub-species of science, in that it is subordinate to it and dependent on it.

[142] I.e., is to be understood as. David, *Prol.* 39.22 has τί βούλεται 'what does it mean?'

[143] See note 139.

[144] Normally, philosophy is divided into three parts: logic, ethics and physics. But here the 'becoming like God' is the main theme.

[145] This means the first and second premises in the syllogism ('major' and 'minor'). Note that pseudo-Zeno fails to mention the conclusion of the syllogism.

[146] The predicate is said of the subject, so the subject is subordinate to (included in) the predicate.

[147] The form of the Armenian word is odd. It is perhaps a 'doubled' form, i.e., and oblique ending -*g* added to the ablative ending -*մէ*. We translate this word as if it had the preposition *յ*- and not *ք*-. See p. 21 above.

[148] Or "(consists) of other (parts included) in the above-metioned syllogism" Both translations are possible. The word *շարասութիւն* is unknown. Made up of *շար*- and *աս*- it presumably reflects something like συν + λεγ-. The word for syllogism,

3.2.2 The dialectical is differentiated into question and answer, in opposition (to one another).

(The) interrogative is diversified by tone and brevity: and it is called investigative, topical, and studious.

3.2.3 The responsive is diversified by introduction and arguments, and is called demonstrative and relevant and plausible, and again, (it is) according to the affirmation and according to the negation and is called a firm assertion in opposition to the things which were asked.[149]

3.3.0 *On Fallacy and Analysis*

3.3.1 Fallacy is according to homonym and synonym,
according to such and such a number,
according to this and according to that both tense and meaning,[150]
according to one variety and another of movement and place.

3.3.2 The analytical is the taking apart and the dissolving of materials and parts and speech.

These are the species of the art of logic, which were assigned their place in nature.

4.0.0 *On ...*

4.1.0 *On Inquiry* (διαζητικόν) *which They Added from Theory*

4.1.1[151] There are four species of inquiry.
For there is that which (is) one sound and the thing is varied;
and there is that which is one thing and its sound;
and, again, that which shares sound and thing;
and there is that which is connected by only a single sound or by a syllable.

---

however, was used at the start of this section. In addition, the preceding verb, *ի վերոյն անցեալ* is obscure. It could reflect Greek ἀναβαίνω which may mean 'return to the beginning of a discourse'. Alternatively it maybe a Hellenizing usage the meaning of which remains unclear. The translation is conjectural.

149 Literally: said, pronounced.
150 *զաւրութիւն* = δύναμις which may be translated 'meaning'.
151 Schmidt, 32.

4.1.2 There is said to be sort and species
Sort is according to subdivision of the variety of the thing and of the
sound;
and species is according to the commonality of the sound and of the
thing;
and number according to the connection of sound or syllable.
4.1.3[152] Speculative is constituted
of thing
and of meaning
and of speech[153]
and of the written.
For the thing is the representation of the non-thing;[154]
and the meaning, of the thing;
while the speech (is the representation) of the meaning;
and the writings are the representations of the speech.
It is called simple and composite:
for there is that which is meaning and speech,
and there is that which is composite speech and meaning.

4.2.0 *On Inseparable Definition and the Category of Existing Things*

4.2.1 There are two species of inseparable definition: (viz. involving) substance and accident;
for where there is substance, (there is) also accident
and where there is accident, (there is) also substance.
4.2.2 Substance is distinguished from accident according to
precedence and removal.[155]
Again, there is that which is differentiated into four:
there is that which is said to be about (a) subject,
and there is that which is said to be in (a) subject,
and there is that which is not in (a) subject,
and there is that which is said to be not about (a) subject, according
to the first substance.[156]

---

[152] Schmidt, 32-33 makes reference to the treatment of the first words of Περὶ
ἑρμενείας in the commentaries on Aristotle.

[153] So we translate Armenian *ձայն* here. Compare also §3.3.2 and here in the
following. The word may also mean 'sound, voice'.

[154] That which is anterior to the thing, such as form.

[155] This means that when you take away the substance you take away the
accident, but not conversely.

[156] See Schmidt, p. 33, going back to Aristotle, *Cat.* 2, 1a20ff. He cites the

4.2.3 The category of the existing things is first of all divided into four:

into sort[157] and into species;

into (specific) difference (διαφορά) and into proper (ἴδιον).

4.2.4 Genus is said to be three-fold:

according to the generation of substance,[158]

and according to the multiplication of lineage, which is shown as growth from one;[159]

and[160] according to itself (viz. in the logical sense) it is divided into five species in three ways, which are called most specific (εἰδικώτατον) and most generic (γενικώτατον), which is substance, (viz. into)[161] body (σῶμα) and bodiless (ἀσώματον),

living (ἔμψυχον) and non-living (ἄψυχον),

perceptive (αἰσθητόν) and non-perceptive (ἀναίσθητον),

possessed of reason (λογικόν) or irrational (ἄλογον),

species (εἶδος) and individual (ἄτομον).

4.2.5 Species is divided four-fold:[162]

there is that which is arranged under genus (τὸ τασσόμενον ὑπὸ τὸ γένος),

and there is that which has genus by definition,[163] and genus is said to be around it like a substrate (ὑποκείμενον).

Again, species and genus are defined in their quiddity and according to the pair of multiplicity;

and there is that which is given species in the highest things and is given genus within.[164]

---

following: τῶν ὄντων (1) τὰ μὲν καθ' ὑποκειμένου λέγεται, ἐν ὑποκειμένῳ δὲ οὐδενί ἐστι ... (2) καθ' δὲ οὐδενὸς (3) τὰ δὲ τε λέγεται καὶ ... (4) τὰ δὲ ἐν ὑποκειμένῳ ἐστὶν οὔτε καθ' ὑποκειμένου τινὸς λέγεται ...

[157] Better: kind. This is the Armenian word used as the translation of γένος. Similarly in the next section.

[158] Cf. 'the origin of each individual', ἡ ἑκάστου τῆς γενέσεως ἀρχή Porphyry, *Isagoge*, 1.

[159] τὸ πλῆθος τῶν ἀπὸ μίας ἀρχῆς, i.e., γένος in the genealogical sense.

[160] See Schmidt, p. 34. The three ways are not evident in the following. Might they be: 1. highest genus, 2. in betweens (generic/species), 3. lowest species (ἄτομον)?

[161] οὐσία qua γένος.

[162] See Porphyry, *Isagoge*, p. 3.14-19.

[163] Porphyry, p. 3.18-18 ἐν τῷ ποῖόν τι ἐστι.

[164] Porphyry, p. 2.10-13; i.e., species in relation to the genus above it and genus in relation to the species below it.

4.2.6 Difference (διαφορά) is divided three-fold:
into substance,[165]
and into accident(s),
separable, and inseparable.[166]
There is that which is incorruptible, and there is that which moves with difficulty, and commonly these are said about opposites.

4.2.7 The proper is spoken of in a fourfold manner: [167]
for there is that which is of alone,
and there is that which is of all,
and, again, there is that which is of alone and of all,
and there is that which is mutual (i.e. forms a combination), according to the perfecting of the particular.

4.2.8[168] Second, 'of the categories' is divided into ten genera, which is substance, quality, quantity, relation, where, when, exist, have, make, bear.

4.2.9 There are partial things (i.e. terms) which are perfected according to combination (in a proposition), for this may be an affirmation or a negation and true or false; and they (the propositions) are named general and particular.[169]

4.2.10 Now, third, (is that which is) principal and most important, prior and perfect in all ways,[170] but the others are all named accidents. It is divided into two:

the first is individual and (is) counted first;

the second (i.e. secondary substance) is fourfold:

species and genus,[171] according to the pair of multiplicity,

---

[165] The *differentia specifica* definies the species.

[166] I.e. (1) ἐν τῷ τῆς οὐσίας λαμβάνοντα λογῷ· (2) ἀχώριστον συμβεβηκός· (3) χώριστον συμβεβηκός· or compare Porphyry, *Isagoge*, p. 9.8-10: τῶν διαφορῶν τὰς μὲν χωριστὰς εἶναι τὰς δὲ ἀχωρίστους. With the next phrase, compare τὸ μὲν γὰρ κινεῖσθαι καὶ τὸ ἠρέμειν καὶ τὸ ὑγαίνειν καὶ τὸ νοσεῖν καὶ ὅσα παραπλήσια (i.e., such opposites) χωριστά ἐστιν.

[167] Compare Porphyry, *Isagoge*, p. Isag. p. 12.13-18, in full: Τὸ δὲ ἴδιον διαιροῦσι τετραχῶς· καὶ γὰρ ὃ μόνῳ τινὶ εἴδει συμβέβηκεν, εἰ καὶ μὴ παντί, ὡς ἀνθρώπῳ τὸ ἰατρεύειν ἢ τὸ γεωμετρεῖν· καὶ ὃ παντὶ συμβέβηκεν τῷ εἴδει, εἰ καὶ μὴ μόνῳ, ὡς τῷ ἀνθρώπῳ τὸ εἶναι δίποδι· καὶ ὃ μόνῳ καὶ παντὶ καὶ ποτέ, ὡς ἀνθρώπῳ παντὶ τὸ ἐν γήρᾳ πολιοῦσθαι. τέταρτον δέ, ἐφ' οὗ συνδεδράμηκεν τὸ μόνῳ καὶ παντὶ καὶ ἀεί, ὡς τῷ ἀνθρώπῳ τὸ γελαστικόν.. For example, man is 'laughing' but does not always laugh: he is a laughing animal.

[168] Schmidt, p. 34 deals with §§4.2.8 and 4.2.9. This statement is dependent on Aristotle's *Cat.* 4, 1b 26.

[169] Terms or propositions.

[170] See next note.

[171] In Aristotle's *Categories* the primary substance (οὐσία), i.e., the independently existing individual entity (e.g., this particular man) is distinguished not only as first

and the partial is (thus) because of its being alone.[172]

4.2.11[173] Quantity is that thing which is discrete;

and there is that which is continuous;

and those others, which have position.

Discrete are word and number;

continuous are line, surface, plane, place and, indeed, time.

and it is (the case) that line, plane, place, surface and time have position.

Word and number have a certain classification and it is particular in all respects.[174]

4.2.12 The relative has four species: condition (ἕξις), sense perception (αἴσθησις), knowledge (ἐπιστήμη), position (θέσις).

4.2.13 Location and inclination and subjacency are said to be derivative by the writings and by the particular, according to opposedness.

4.2.14[175] Quality is said to be fourfold:

according to condition (ἕξις),

and according to logic,

according to strength,

and according to property (πάθος),[176]

according to bitterness and according to sweetness,

according to form and according to shape.

It is particular according to its being alone and according to the all.

4.2.15 The where (ποῦ) and the when (πότε) are said to be according to quantity;

and the being and having, according to the relative;

and the making and bearing, according to quality.[177]

---

category from the nine other categories (the accidents) but also from secondary substance, which is a species (Man) or genus (Living Being). It is not clear why pseudo-Zeno calls species and genus fourfould; perhaps he includes the *differentiae specificae*.

[172] This pertains to §4.2.9.

[173] See Schmidt, 34.

[174] See Schmidt pp. 34-5. He cites Aristotle, *Cat.* 4b22: ἔστι δὲ διωρισμένον μὲν οἷον ἀριθμὸς καὶ λόγος, συνεχὲς δὲ οἷον γραμμή, ἐπιφάνεια, σῶμα, ἔτι δὲ παρὰ ταῦτα χρόνος καὶ τόπος.

[175] See Schmidt, p. 35, citing Aristotle, *Cat.* 8b26ff. He rightly calls attention to the lateness of this list, i.e., quality before quantity, but in pseudo-Zeno's actual treatment quantity comes before quality (§4.2.14).

[176] Better: weakness.

[177] This perhaps shows that the abstract here is made not from Aristotle's *Categories* alone, but from a commentary as well.

4.3.0 *On Distinction*[178]

4.3.1[179] The oppositions are said to be fourfold.
There is that which is relative;
and there is that which is contrary;
and there is that which is innate[180] and lacking;[181]
and there is that which is the affirmative and the negative;[182]
and the one without precedence against another.[183]
The cause of the putting on is classified by proëmium.[184]

4.3.2 For it is according to time (κατὰ χρόνον), that a thing is said
to be more ancient (πρεσβύτερον) or earlier (πρότερον) than something recent;[185]
　　and mind precedes thought;
　　and seeings precede those things seen;
　　and letters[186] precede syllables;
　　and the one precedes the two and is said to be without
　　opposition.[187]

4.3.3 Partial relationship is without opposition and without
declension of tense:
but according to one part of time the things that come into being are
related,
according to the declination of the name of the species of the
derivatives,
according to the mode of doctrine.

4.3.4[188] According to movement (it) is divided into six species,
which are: coming into being, destruction, growth, diminution,
transformation, change according to place.[189] And (it) is said to be

---

[178]　Here we have the beginning of the so-called postpredicamenta. See
Aristotle, *Cat.*, chaps. 10 ff. The word translated 'distinction' here is the same word
translated 'variety' in §§1.5.6 and 4.1.2.

[179]　Schmidt, p. 35

[180]　Or: having; cf. Aristotle, *Cat.*, *ibid.* ἕξις.

[181]　Innate (i.e., present *ab initio*) as well as lacking is στέρησις.

[182]　Cf. Aristotle, *Cat.*, 10, 11b17; Schmidt, p. 35.

[183]　What is meant is that a is opposite to b = b is opposite to a: see Aristotle, *Cat.*,
12b3-5, 12-13.

[184]　This sentence is obscure. Perhaps it means: the God mentioned in Chapter
1 determines what happens. "putting on" might be also "ascription".

[185]　Schmidt, p. 35, citing Aristotle, *Cat.*, chap. 12.

[186]　Here we emend *ւнաщ* 'song' to *ւншн* 'letter', following Aristotle. *Cat.* 14b.1.2
τὰ στοιχεῖα πρότερα τῶν συλλαβῶν.

[187]　Cf. Aristotle, *Cat.*, 12b1-2, 14a29 ff.

[188]　Aristotle, *Cat.*, chap. 14; Schmidt, p. 35.

[189]　The sentence is cited from Aristotle. *Cat.* 14, 15a13-14.

according to opposition[190] and according to putting on,[191] and according to partial relationship.

4.3.5 Now, these are the diversifying (subjects) of the first and the second (parts) of the *Categories*, those of genus and of species, of difference and particularity, of essence and of quantity, of relativity and quality.

These are the species of the theoretical which are arranged in the existent. The second part is completed by this art, which is called speaking with God.

5.0.0 *On …*

5.1.0 *On …*

5.1.1 …[192] and again, it is differentiated by grade: at the beginning, good and at the conclusion, evil. But that which is in the middle is distinguished by the constituents[193] according to four species:

according to introductions

and according to words

and according to activities, which means sin or righteousness.

5.1.2 The fourth, because there is that which by nature is good and evil,[194] and there is that which is improper.

By nature there is that the dwelling (of) which is incorruptible and difficult to change, for although it receives change, it is established again in the same (condition) in its natural border.[195]

5.1.3 The improper is that which does not constitute the naturalness of a boundary and, moreover, it is easily moved in encounters with the subject.

5.1.4 Now, the good is characterised by nature, while the evil is without nature and boundary. For the good, if it is changed into evil,

---

[190] I.e., growth is opposed to diminution.

[191] Putting on: i.e., being given form.

[192] From 'fourth' in §5.1.2 and 'fifth' in §5.1.5 it may be inferred that a section has been lost containing at least the first, the second and part of the third members of this list. Xǎik'yan introduces the titles 'On the Intellect' for this part of the book and 'On Good and Evil' for §5.1.1. See Schmidt, p. 36.

[193] The Armenian word *բաղկանաց* is not in *NBH*. It must mean something like 'constituents'; see §5.2.5 where the same word occurs.

[194] From §§5.1.2-5.1.4 it is evident the sense is 'and there is evil'. Three things are listed.

[195] Or: definition.

it does not remain only evil, but is changed by nature again into the same (i.e., the good). But the evil receiving the change to good, at the same time is constituted by nature.

5.1.5 Fifth, that according to the species of division, the good is specified by substance[196] and the evil by accident. Again it is divided equally into four:

for there is that which (is) good,

and there is that which (is) evil,

and there is that which (is) evil and good,

and there is that which (is) neither evil nor good.[197]

5.1.6 Now, there are those of them which are passible internally and act externally. For it is to be understood that good and evil receive their constitution from movement and from matter.

Movement, having been defined, is differentiated from matter by priority, which is the creator of good,

but matter, subsequent to movement, is the constitutor of the evil.

5.1.7 But substance[198] is according to four mixtures:

of command

and of duration

and of shadow

and of appearance.

These are delimited by double definition:

command is the cause of duration, from which good is said (to be),

but shadow is the cause of appearance, from which evil is said (to be).

5.1.8 And again, the particular and unmixed command is in their midst, remaining without border, but duration takes its place from the shadow, and appearance takes definition from the shadow.

5.1.9 In the same borders the existent received its constitution, through kinds and through species and through effects and through births and through forms and through colours.

5.1.10 Now the evil is made known, disruptor and definer of the good, while the good (is) wholly incorruptible and accepting change of the evil.

---

[196]   Or: essence.

[197]   Aristotle, *Cat.*, 12a24., Plato *Euth.* 281e4, *Gorg.* 467e3, *Lysis* 217b3, 219a2, and Stoic ἀδιαφορά.

[198]   Or: essence.

5.2.0 *On Knowledge of Perfect Expression*[199]

5.2.1 Perfect expression is of parts and of individuals and of species and of sorts and of numbers. For each one of them receives its perfection, but together they are said to be most perfect. Those which are constituted of each other are imperfect and not a perfect expression.

5.2.2 First, according to other problems, the borders each receive perfection in time according to the parts of revolution, 1, 2, 3, 5, 3, 12, 24, 5, 7, 11, 91, 365, 52, 12, 3, 15, 19, 28, 10.

5.2.3 But together they, in the higher section, are said to be most perfect, and receive the reordering, which (are) 532, 3 ..., which come into being from one another, according to the declension of the expressions and the parts of the name,[200] are categorised as imperfect.

5.2.4 Second, the perfect expression is differentiated according to beginning and ending. Because all the things that will come into being and have come into being are said to be perfect according to their completion. And perfection is not according to declensions, but in each of the boundaries, whatever thing was going to come into being was completed and whatever thing had to come into being receives perfection.

5.2.5 But there is also in between a tense in the (expression) according to the present. Now, according to careful reflection they constitute the most perfect expression in two ways. At the beginning it is not perfect, for those things which introduce, or say, or act (are) in the middle of the compositions;[201] alternatively, it is indeed not contested.[202]

5.2.6 Third, now, according to the indicative nature[203] by subject and by perfection,[204] according to the proximate and according to the diversity of the fourfold, by each of them they are called perfect ones, but general sections being very perfect of the nine-fold borders.

5.2.7 Accordingly the creative is he who alone establishes the species which are imperfect and not a perfect expression. According

---

[199] *բան* is taken to reflect Greek λεκτόν here and is so translated. See Schmidt, p. 36.
[200] Or: noun.
[201] This is a rare Armenian word, see n. 193 above.
[202] The sense of this and the following section remains unclear.
[203] Perhaps this means 'mood'.
[204] Perhaps this indicates the aspect of the action.

to the One Who Is is the division of the existent things in (their) precedences in categori(es). In each of them (is that which is) perfect and that (which is) most perfect of all.

5.2.8 Fourth, according to the division of the accidents concerning the real accident and existing in the subject, being incomplete and not perfect.

5.2.9 Fifth, according to the supreme and according to art is the tetraktys, from which all things, having received their composition, are bounded. In their individuality[205] they are said to be perfect.

5.2.10 According to the infinite: unmixedness is said to be sublime. And again, from the three, indeed, are those which, going towards dissolution and decay, are always an imperfect and not perfect expression.

5.2.11 Now, the perfection of an expression was seen to be threefold by vision, according to parts, which are bordered each for itself. But the whole ones are most perfect; and those existences which learn from each other are an imperfect and not a perfect expression.

5.2.12 Because the sublime thing is constituted in perfection and not from the imperfect, for the imperfect things are parts of the perfect which are composed.

Up to here is the knowledge of the perfect expression.

5.3.0 *On Time: a separate section*[206]

5.3.1 Time is extension according to all (its) parts in a threefold way and counter-procession by disposition. (These are) measures of the movements[207] of each and corresponding to the revolutions of the orbits, in which the numbers are constituted and ended, which are 5, 8, 12, 24, 5, 7, 12, 91, 354, 11, 12, 3, 5, 8, 15, 19, 28, 10, 190, 456, 532, 13, 704.

5.3.2 Such are the numbers of the orbits, that have been shown in order: parts,[208] hours, days, weeks, months, seasons, years, cycles, eras, completions of times. According to these, too, the numbers are fitted in, because there are those which are constituted of each other; and there are those which start, and others receive the completion.

---

[205] Or: eachness.
[206] Schmidt, p. 36.
[207] Cf. Greek ἀγωγή.
[208] I.e., minutes.

5.3.3 Again, those which are completed are constituted in the others, or the revolutions.[209] And the number 19 by means of 28 completely perfect species, which are circles. 13 and 84 are the intercalation years, which is not set in order in the sense-perceptible living conduct of the world.

5.3.4 According to the perfection of the 13 the fullness and dissolution of flowing and the variety of species of the whole universe is constituted. And, of necessity, becoming does not take place into non-flowing and non-diverse species, namely that which is timeless.

5.3.5 First. According to others, time is divided in five species, that is:

the beginning of the universe,
and the completion of natures,
and the powers of the revolutions,
and the measures of the mean,
and the sections of ...[210]

Now, those which follow this are called timeless.

5.3.6 Second. In nature according to the Creator there is a differentiation into four kinds, which are additions to the substrates of each, which are said to be universal. Time is not constituted of anything which is prior or posterior, but borders of each are made clear to the senses by time according to the powers of mixtures or affections. Because resolution of the senses is constituted by both these. Because, moreover, that which does not occur according to these is called timeless.

5.3.7 Third. According to the essence it exists[211] in the divisions of accidents, according to a continual sequence of positions and ordering (διάταξις). Because it is continuous with itself, beyond the accidents and beings. Things higher than those are called timeless.

5.3.8 Fourth. The constitution of time is according to the four: from matter and movement to be present at borders of the void through structure, by a command of the uncreated nature.

5.3.9 Time has appeared threefold by theory according to all, for it is that which according to lengthening has been taken, because of births of multitudes of individuals and (because of the) differentiation of the duration of the accidents. But (things which are) before

---

[209] Nominative plural.
[210] Something is missing from the text.
[211] *բնաւորեցաւ գոլ* is taken here as equivalent of πέφυκεν.

the universe and after are called timeless, and they are not constituted.

5.4.0 *On Theology of Beginning and of End: a separate section*

5.4.1 Beginning and ending (are) material, theoretical, fundamental, practical, and they are divided according to creation and time.
For beginning is according to the creation
and end is according to time.
For there is beginning which is end,
and there is end which (is) beginning,
and there is beginning which is not end,
and there is that which (is) neither end nor beginning.
5.4.2 And it is according to other questions (ζητήματα). For[212] in nature there is distinction according to the number 4:[213]
for there is that which is a near beginning and a near end,
and that which is a far beginning and a far end.[214]
Beginning is distinguished according to superfluity,
and end according to precision.
5.4.3 First: in the case of existence, beginning is distinguished according to being and end according to accident.
5.4.4 Second: again (it is distinguished as) being general and partial:
for there is that which is a beginning,
and there is that which (is) an end in substrate,
and there is that which (is) a beginning and at the same time an end,
and there is that which (is) neither a beginning nor an end.
5.4.5 Third: it is differentiated both according to movement and according to matter:
for beginning according to movement is prior,[215]
and end according to matter is posterior.

---

[212] Perhaps here reflecting the word ὅτι, so that what follows is the citation from the ζητήματα

[213] See §§3.1.4 and 3.1.6. Schmidt on p. 38 talks of tetra-lemmata, but the justification of pseudo-Zeno is the Pythagorean tetraktys.

[214] Cf. §3.1.6

[215] Armenian *նախ էին զոլով* is clear in the manuscript. It should probably be emended to *նախկին զոլով* 'is prior'.

5.4.6 For all this exists according to the number 4 in a double division:

from matter

and from movement

and from void, which is beginning and end and the mean,

(and from) change (τροπή) according to movement and according to matter.

And tense/time by the theory of the number three:

  imperfect (παρατατικός),

  pluperfect,

  aorist;

which is according to the measures of the cycle[216] of the void.

5.4.7 And according to the infinite (there is) being (which is) without beginning, without end, unchanging, timeless, not present, not past, not future. Again, he is Creator of the compositions of beginning and end and what is contained in between.

5.4.8 Now, beginning and end were revealed through the understanding of the number three; because there is that which is without beginning and there is that which (is) without end. But beginning and end are constituted in the middle by numerous divisions.[217]

5.5.0 *On Nature* (περὶ φύσεως): *a separate section*

5.5.1 Nature is determined (ὡρισμένον) and *qualitative* (ποιόν).[218]

The determined is natural and fixed,

  while the *qualitative* is unnatural and unfixed.

For the natural consists of kinds and of the constituent differentiations,

  and the unnatural is the movement of the species,

  and the transformation of the like and the unlike.

And the numbers are equally constituted of simple individuals.[219]

---

[216] Perhaps 'circumference'; alternatively 'declension'.

[217] 'Numerous divisions' are found all over the treatise. The cycle of the void contains the cosmos in the 'middle'.

[218] Throughout this section and in §5.5.3 the Armenian text reads արարչական 'creative' where we would expect 'qualitative'. This is probably due to a confusion of the Greek words ποιόν and ποιητικόν. We have so translated and italicized these instances.

[219] I.e. numbers consist of units or 'ones'.

5.5.2 Again, it is the natural which is determined by the genus and the constituent differentiations; [220]

and there is that which is determined by name,

and there is that which becomes more according to the diminishing of terms, and grows less according to multiplicity.[221]

5.5.3 First. According to the existence: the definitions differ according to essence and the *qualitative* according to accidents. And again,

there is that which is definitive,

and there is that which is *qualitative*, which is in the substrate,[222]

and there is that which is definitive and at the same time *qualitative*,

and again there is that which is neither definitive nor *qualitative*.

5.5.4 And the constitution of nature is according to a fourfold division.

For the infinite is simple and uncompoundable,

and matter

and movement are mixed and numerous in their compounding,

and the void is the ground for distinction in the middle.

5.5.5 Now, nature is threefold in division:

for there is that which is simple according to the definitive,

and there is that which is composite according to the *qualitative*,

and again, there is that which, in the middle, (is) sharing.

5.6.0 *About Essential: a separate section*

5.6.1 There are two species of essentials: the sensible-perceptible and the intelligible. For from the sense-perceptible the imperceptible (issues), and from the intelligible, the unintelligible.

For essence is said (to derive) from the imperceptible, and accident from the unintelligible. And essence (is) general and accident (is) partial. Again, accident (is) the general, but substance (is) partial.

5.6.2 First. It is differentiated in a fourfold manner:

for the infinite is called general according to essence,

and the void, partial according to accident,

and matter, partial according to essence,

and movement, general according to accident.

---

[220] I.e., definition per genus et differentiam.

[221] Name determines just as definition does; it is more general in incomplete definition and less general in complete definition (David).

[222] Or: subject

5.6.3 Second. The essence of the essential is divided in a fourfold manner:

for the infinite is called He Who Is,[223] without beginning and interruption;

and movement and matter, existence by force of beginning and ending;

and the void is called that which is not and non-existence, but is declined of the necessary by means of noun and verb.

5.6.4 Existence has shown itself in a threefold manner:

for there is that which is perceptive according to the sense-perceptible and the unintelligible,

and there is that which, again, (consists) of the two,

according to essence,

and according to accident.

5.7.0 *On The Creating and Eternally Forth-Flowing Tetrad, which is of Theological Movement and Matter: a separate section*

5.7.1 All is movement, in motions matter (exists), and again, all (is) matter and in material things movements (are found). Such are things and intelligibles, those which are reasoned, and those which are carried out. For (that) which (is) movement (is) also matter, and (that) which is matter (is) also movement, **5.7.2** since they are creators in respect of each other.

For the heating of matter and its cooling and (its) getting moist and (its) drying out occurs[224] through movement, i.e. four, but the coming into existence of movement and (its) destruction, the growing and diminishing, its qualitative change and changing occurs[225] through matter.

5.7.3 First. It is differentiated for movement, in the existence according to rarefaction in the void. But (there is difference) in the existence of matter, according to the thickness of movement, and the receiving of the appearance from[226] the void.

5.7.4 Second. According to the infinite it is unmoving and immaterial, for it is called unmixed. Since movement and matter are constituted from the unmoving and the immaterial, but cessation is

---

[223] Or: that which is.
[224] Or: is constituted.
[225] Or: is constituted.
[226] Or: out of.

derived from both movement and matter, which is a simile so to speak.

5.8.0 *On the Void: a separate section*

5.8.1 The unintelligible non-thing is called 'void'; irrational and non-active, and is a separation from partial and universal mind.[227] For it is (found) in mixtures with matter and with movement. Externally it is called infinite by its capacity to be the universe,[228] and having become capable according to the infinite, it is called so in a threefold way.

5.8.2 The composition of the void is according to these, for out of existence and the thing, non-existence and the non-thing is said (to occur); and out of unchanging being and the eternal, the passing and the unnatural. But not as some have considered that it is something, but it is nothing, since even to have an opinion on it is called idle and barren.

5.9.0 *On the Infinite.*

5.9.1 The infinite is that which in all respects is infinite, which is called totality,[229] indivisible and without species. And there are thoughts and designs, conceptions and sciences and theories, universal and without measure. But according to others it is according to the hexad and according to the tetrad. For the infinite is neither good nor bad, neither beginning nor end, and neither movement nor matter.

5.9.2 In accordance with these it is said (to be) ungenerated, for it does not receive its existence from something else, nor from itself. And again, the infinite exists according to the second one: more superior things than the most superior, more atemporal than the most atemporal things, more natural than the most natural, more essential than the most essential things, more void than the most void, more infinite than the most infinite things.

5.9.3 In accordance with these (properties) it is called the most incomprehensible of the things that exist, for the limit of (its) being researched is located in the endless beyond. For according to these

---

[227] Or: thoughts.
[228] Or: all things.
[229] Or: universe.

(properties) there does not exist comprehension of the nature of the secondary infinite.[230]

5.9.4 According to the tetrad, only the knowledge of the Creator of the creation (flows forth) out of the reason of God towards the races of the angels and men, and out of God's speaking to the angels and to men. Theologising (is about) three Gods each with its own separate nature, for there is (one) which is called the parent, there is one which is the offspring and there is the one which goes forth.

5.9.5 But this (theology) appears in accordance with the nature of man, on account of the compassion of the Father and the love of humanity[231] of the Son and the mercifulness of the Spirit. For they are three, they are one in nature, will and creatorship.

5.9.6 Likewise, also in accordance with (the nature of) the angels, the three persons are glorified: the creator and the establisher and the constructor, to whom they say, 'Holy, Holy, Holy, all together is the Lord of hosts. Glory and honour and praise to the ungenerated One and the incomprehensible One and the eternal One, now and in all eternity.'

5.9.7 The hexads, which are defined by each other, are finished; and the tetrads (are finished too) of which the accounts (logoi) are the summaries,[232] and the triads of the accounts (logoi) are called partial, and the twelve was completed in its parts, and was found to be transcended by the monads, according to each of the parts of the species and sorts.

5.9.8 For this is the understanding of every triad[233] and is the knowledge of the universal art of philosophy and the definitions[234] of the objects of study; so we leave the art of the invincible philosophers[235] to those who are going to be penalised in this world.

6.1.1 God, God, God, glory to you now and in eternity.

---

[230] See §5.9.2.

[231] φιλανθρωπία.

[232] So accepting Xačik'yan's emendation. Without it, read, 'the triads, by which they are called partial ones of the accounts (λόγοι)'.

[233] Or: admonition, counsel. Alternatively, 'for every triad has its meaning and (is) ...'.

[234] Or: rules.

[235] This proves that the treatise belongs with the school of David the Invincible, and so explains why, as we have seen, David is a major source.

LIST OF WORDS IN THE TRANSLATION

This concordance contains most words in the translation excluding words which are very common or of no particular importance for the specific content of the work. The words are in strict alphabetical order.

abundance	2.1.1	aorist	5.4.6
accident	1.5.11 1.5.11 4.2.1	apparent	1.6.14
	4.2.1 4.2.1 4.2.2	appearance	1.3.1 1.6.3 5.1.7
	4.2.6 5.1.5 5.2.8		5.1.7 5.1.8 5.7.3
	5.4.3 5.6.1 5.6.1	appearances	1.6.3 1.6.3
	5.6.1 5.6.2 5.6.2	appeared	1.3.2 5.3.9
	5.6.4	appears	1.6.6 5.9.5
accidents	3.1.3 3.1.4 4.2.10	Aquarius	1.4.6 1.4.10 1.4.11
	5.2.8 5.3.7 5.3.7	Arabians	1.4.9
	5.3.9 5.5.3	arguments	3.2.3
act	5.1.6 5.2.5	arm	1.4.8 1.4.8
active	5.8.1	Armenians	1.4.7
activities	5.1.1	arms	1.4.8
activity	1.5.10	arrangement	1.2.2
added	2.0.0 2.2.3 3.1.0	art	1.6.9 3.1.5 3.1.8
	4.1.0		3.1.10 3.1.14 3.1.14
additions	5.3.6		3.3.2 4.3.5 5.2.9
administrative	1.6.9		5.9.8 5.9.8
adverb	2.3.4	article	2.3.4 2.3.5
aerial	1.2.4	arts	3.1.5 3.1.14 3.1.14
affections	5.3.6		3.1.16
affirmation	1.6.12 3.2.3 4.2.9	ascription	1.6.10
affirmative	4.3.1	Asians	1.4.8
agitation	2.4.2	assertion	3.2.3
agrarian	3.1.4	atemporal	5.9.2 5.9.2
air	1.1.4 1.4.5 1.5.12	autumnal	1.4.6
	1.5.13 2.3.5 2.5.1		
airs	1.1.5 1.1.5 1.1.6	Babylonians	1.4.7
	1.1.7 1.2.4 1.3.3	bad	5.9.1
	1.3.3 1.3.4 1.3.5	balanced	1.5.7
alive	1.5.13	barren	5.8.2
amphibious	1.5.2	battles	1.5.10
analogies	2.3.2	bear	4.2.8
analysis	3.3.0	bearing	4.2.15
analytical	1.6.9 3.3.2	beds	1.1.5
ancient	2.3.2 4.3.2	before	5.3.9
angels	1.2.2 1.2.3 5.9.4	begets	1.5.10
	5.9.4 5.9.6	begotten	1.1.5
anger	1.6.12	beings	1.1.2 1.1.4 1.6.10
animals	1.1.4 2.2.2 2.2.2		2.2.3 5.3.7
answer	3.2.2	beneficence	3.1.13

compounded	2.2.3	creative	5.2.7
compounding	5.5.4	creator	5.1.6 5.3.6 5.4.7
comprehensible	1.6.9 1.6.11 1.6.13		5.9.4 5.9.6
comprehension	1.6.7 5.9.3	creators	5.7.2
conceptions	5.9.1	creatorship	5.9.5
conclusion	5.1.1	Cretans	1.4.9
condition	4.2.12 4.2.14 5.1.2	criteria	3.1.3
conduct	1.2.3 5.3.3	curly	1.5.6
conformity	3.1.5 3.1.12	customary	1.6.8
confusion	2.4.2	cycle	5.4.6
conjunction	2.3.4	cycles	5.3.2
connected	4.1.1		
connection	4.1.2	damage	2.5.4
consist	3.2.1	days	5.3.2
consisting	3.1.7	death	1.5.11 1.5.11 1.5.12
consists	3.2.1 3.2.1 3.2.1		1.5.13 3.1.5
	5.5.1 5.6.4	decay	5.2.10
constellation	1.1.7	declamatory	2.3.7 2.3.7
constellations	1.1.7 1.2.4 1.3.4	declension	2.3.4 4.3.3 5.2.3
	1.3.5 1.4.4 1.4.4	declensions	5.2.4
constituable	1.6.14 1.6.15 1.6.16	declination	4.3.3
constituent	3.1.3 5.5.1 5.5.2	declined	5.6.3
constituents	5.1.1	deep	1.3.4
constitutable	1.6.15	defined	3.1.10 4.2.5 5.1.6
constitute	1.1.6 5.1.3 5.2.5		5.9.7
constituted	1.1.2 1.3.1 1.4.2	definer	5.1.10
	1.4.3 1.5.1 1.5.5	definition	1.6.10 1.6.11 3.1.1
	1.5.9 1.5.10 1.5.12		3.1.3 3.1.4 3.1.4
	6.8 1.6.15 3.1.6		4.2.0 4.2.1 4.2.5
	3.1.8 3.1.13 4.1.3		5.1.7 5.1.8
	5.1.4 5.2.1 5.2.12	definitional	1.6.9 1.6.11
	5.3.1 5.3.2 5.3.3	definitions	1.6.17 1.6.18 3.1.0
	5.3.4 5.3.6 5.3.6		3.1.5 3.1.7 3.1.16
	5.3.9 5.4.8 5.5.1		5.5.3 5.9.8
	5.7.4	definitive	3.1.2 5.5.3 5.5.3
constitution	1.5.3 5.1.6 5.1.9		5.5.3 5.5.5
	5.3.8 5.5.4	deliberative	2.3.7 2.3.7
constitutor	1.1.4 5.1.6	delicate	1.5.6
constrained	1.6.6	delimited	5.1.7
constraint	1.1.6 2.5.2	demonstrating	1.6.9
construction	1.1.1	demonstrative	3.2.3
constructor	5.9.6	dense	1.1.5
contemplation	3.1.5	density	1.1.5 1.5.3
content	2.5.0 2.5.1	depletion	1.5.11
contents	2.5.5 2.5.5	depth	3.1.6
contested	5.2.5	derivative	4.2.13
cooling	5.7.2	derivatives	4.3.3
corruption	1.2.3	derive	5.6.1
counted	4.2.10	derived	5.7.4
countenance	1.6.5 1.6.5	designs	5.9.1
counter	5.3.1	desire	1.5.10 1.6.12
creating	5.7.0	destruction	1.5.11 1.5.13 4.3.4
creation	1.5.3 5.4.1 5.4.1		5.7.2
	5.9.4	determined	5.5.1 5.5.1 5.5.2
creations	1.6.5		5.5.2

envy	1.5.10	exit	2.5.4
equal	1.1.1 1.4.3	exits	2.5.3
equality	1.6.2	expert	2.3.2
equally	1.3.4 1.5.7 5.1.5 5.5.1	explanations	2.3.2 2.3.2
		explicit	1.6.12
equinox	1.4.5 1.4.6	expression	5.2.0 5.2.1 5.2.1 5.2.4 5.2.5 5.2.5 5.2.7 5.2.10 5.2.11 5.2.11 5.2.12
equinoxes	1.4.4		
eras	5.3.2		
erudite	1.6.1		
erudition	1.6.9 3.1.14 3.1.14	expressions	5.2.3
eruditions	3.1.14 3.1.14	extension	5.3.1
essence	4.3.5 5.3.7 5.5.3 5.6.1 5.6.1 5.6.2 5.6.2 5.6.3 5.6.4	external	1.5.13 2.5.4
		externally	5.1.6 5.8.1
essential	5.6.0 5.6.3 5.9.2 5.9.2	facilitation	2.4.2
		faith	1.6.16
essentials	5.6.1	fallacy	3.3.0 3.3.1
established	1.1.5 1.1.6 2.5.2 2.5.4 5.1.2	false	4.2.9
		family	2.5.1
establisher	5.9.6	father	5.9.5
establishes	5.2.7	feet	1.4.10 2.3.3
eternal	1.3.1 5.8.2 5.9.6	female	1.4.11 1.5.5
eternally	1.3.2 5.7.0	fields	1.1.5
eternity	5.9.6 6.1.1	fifth	1.1.5 5.1.5 5.2.9
ethos	2.2.3	filled	1.1.5
etymology	2.3.2	finding	2.3.2
even	1.4.3 3.1.8 3.1.9 3.1.10 5.8.2	finished	5.9.7 5.9.7
		fire	1.1.2 1.1.5 1.4.5 1.5.4
evens	3.1.8		
event	2.3.7	firmament	1.1.3 1.1.4 1.1.7 1.3.3 1.3.3
evil	1.6.11 2.2.1 5.1.1 5.1.2 5.1.4 5.1.4 5.1.4 5.1.4 5.1.5 5.1.5 5.1.5 5.1.5 5.1.6 5.1.6 5.1.7 5.1.10 5.1.10		
		first	1.1.1 1.6.18 3.1.1 3.1.3 3.1.7 3.1.10 3.1.11 4.2.2 4.2.3 4.2.10 4.2.10 4.3.5 5.2.2 5.3.5 5.4.3 5.5.3 5.6.2 5.7.3
excess	1.5.7		
excesses	1.5.8 1.5.9	fishes	2.2.2
exemplified	2.2.3	fists	1.4.9
exerts	1.6.18	fitted	5.3.2
exist	3.1.1 3.1.11 4.2.8 5.9.3 5.9.3	fitting	2.1.1 2.1.1
		five	4.2.4 5.3.5
existence	1.1.1 1.3.1 5.4.3 5.5.3 5.6.3 5.6.3 5.6.4 5.7.2 5.7.3 5.7.3 5.8.2 5.8.2 5.9.2	fixed	1.6.18 5.5.1
		fixing	1.6.17
		flavour	2.5.3
		flavours	1.5.6
		flesh	1.5.5
existences	5.2.11	floating	1.1.1
existent	1.3.2 4.3.5 5.1.9 5.2.7	flowing	5.3.4 5.3.4 5.7.0
		flowings	1.5.1
existing	3.1.5 3.1.7 4.2.0 4.2.3 5.2.8	flows	5.9.4
		flux	1.1.3 1.5.3
exists	3.1.4 3.1.7 3.1.7 5.3.7 5.4.6 5.7.1 5.9.2	fold	1.4.3 1.4.3 4.2.4 4.2.5 4.2.6 5.2.6
		follow	5.3.5

planets	1.3.5 1.4.4 1.5.12 1.6.17	property	4.2.14
plans	1.5.10	proposition	4.2.9
plants	2.2.3	propositions	4.2.9
plausible	3.2.3	prosody	2.3.2
pluperfect	5.4.6	protasis	2.3.4
poetry	2.3.1 2.3.4	provision	2.1.1
political	1.6.9 2.0.1 2.3.0 2.3.1 2.3.6 2.4.2	proximate	5.2.6
		punished	1.5.10
position	1.1.4 1.2.4 4.2.11 4.2.12	putting	4.3.1 4.3.4
		Pythagoreans	3.1.6
positions	1.0.1 1.1.0 1.1.1 1.6.17 5.3.7	quadrangle	1.6.4
		quadrangular	1.1.5 1.4.3
possessed	4.2.4	qualitative	5.5.1 5.5.1 5.5.3 5.5.3 5.5.3 5.5.3 5.5.5 5.7.2
posterior	5.3.6 5.4.5		
power	1.5.12 1.5.14		
powers	1.0.1 1.5.0 1.5.1 1.6.17 5.3.5 5.3.6	qualities	1.5.12 1.5.13
		quality	1.6.10 4.2.8 4.2.14 4.2.15 4.3.5
practical	1.6.9 1.6.9 1.6.12 2.0.0 2.3.1 3.1.14 5.4.1	quantity	4.2.8 4.2.11 4.2.15 4.3.5
practice	2.3.1	question	3.2.2
praise	2.3.7 2.4.2 5.9.6	questions	5.4.2
precede	4.3.2 4.3.2	quiddity	4.2.5
precedence	4.2.2 4.3.1		
precedences	5.2.7	races	5.9.4
precedes	4.3.2 4.3.2	Ram	1.4.5 1.4.7 1.4.11
precision	5.4.2	ranged	1.3.3
predicate	3.2.1	ranked	1.2.4
predicated	3.2.1	ranks	1.0.1 1.2.0 1.2.1 1.6.17
predicates	3.2.1		
prefaced	2.3.1	rarefaction	5.7.3
prefix	2.3.5	rational	3.1.14 3.1.16
preposition	2.3.4	reading	2.3.2
prescience	1.6.13	ready	2.3.2
present	2.2.1 5.2.5 5.3.8 5.4.7	real	5.2.8
		reality	1.6.7 1.6.7
prevent	1.1.3	realm	2.0.0
primary	3.2.1 3.2.1	reason	1.5.10 1.6.18 4.2.4 5.9.4
principal	4.2.10		
prior	4.2.10 5.3.6 5.4.5	reasonable	1.6.7 1.6.7 1.6.7 1.6.9 1.6.9 1.6.12
priority	5.1.6		
probative	3.2.1	reasoned	5.7.1
problems	5.2.2	reasoning	1.6.13
proceed	1.2.4	receive	1.5.10 5.1.6 5.2.2 5.2.3 5.3.2 5.9.2
procession	5.3.1		
produced	1.6.6 1.6.17	received	1.5.4 2.5.1 5.1.9 5.2.9
production	1.5.4		
progressions	1.6.18	receives	3.1.4 5.1.2 5.2.1 5.2.4
proëmium	2.3.6 4.3.1		
pronoun	2.3.4	receiving	1.6.6 5.1.4 5.7.3
proof	3.1.4 3.2.0	recent	1.6.8 4.3.2
propensity	1.6.12	red	1.4.10
proper	4.2.3 4.2.7	reddish	1.5.6
properties	5.9.3 5.9.3	reference	1.6.10

summaries	5.9.7		4.1.3 4.1.3 4.3.2
summer	1.4.5		5.2.4 5.2.4 5.2.12
sun	1.3.5		5.8.1 5.8.2
superfluity	5.4.2		5.8.2
superior	3.1.1 5.9.2 5.9.2	things	(41) 1.1.3 1.1.5
supernal	1.6.6		1.1.6 1.2.2 1.4.3
support	1.5.10		1.5.2 1.5.2 1.5.2
supreme	5.2.9		1.5.13 1.5.14 1.6.14
surface	4.2.11 4.2.11		2.3.1 2.3.5 2.5.3
surrounding	1.3.4		2.5.5 3.1.5 3.1.5
sweet	1.5.6		3.1.7 3.1.11 3.2.3
sweetness	4.2.14		4.2.0 4.2.3 4.2.5
swelling	1.1.6		4.2.9 4.2.11 4.3.2
syllable	4.1.1 4.1.2		4.3.3 5.2.4 5.2.5
syllables	2.3.3 4.3.2		5.2.7 5.2.9 5.2.12
syllogism	3.2.1 3.2.1		5.3.7 5.3.9 5.7.1
symbol	3.1.4 3.1.9		5.7.1 5.9.2 5.9.2
symbols	1.6.7 1.6.7 1.6.7		5.9.2 5.9.2 5.9.3
	1.6.18	thing / word	1.6.18
sympathetic	1.4.7	thinking	2.2.3
synonym	3.3.1	third	1.1.3 1.3.3 3.1.14
syntax	2.3.4		4.2.10 5.2.6 5.3.7
Syrians	1.4.10		5.4.5
		thorax	1.4.8
take	5.3.4	thought	1.6.13 4.3.2
taken	3.1.4 3.1.12 5.3.9	thoughts	1.5.10 1.6.13 2.4.1
takes	5.1.8 5.1.8		5.9.1
taking	3.3.2	three	1.1.6 1.2.1 1.3.1
talking	3.1.10 3.1.15		1.4.3 1.4.3 1.5.2
Taurus	1.4.5 1.4.7 1.4.11		1.5.6 1.6.1 1.6.3
tearing	3.1.12		2.3.1 2.5.3 4.2.4
tell	2.5.5		4.2.4 4.2.6 5.2.10
ten	4.2.8		5.4.6 5.4.8 5.9.4
tens	3.1.9		5.9.5 5.9.6
tense	3.3.1 4.3.3 5.2.5	threefold	1.4.2 1.4.4 3.1.1
tense / time	5.4.6		3.1.15 5.2.11 5.3.1
term	2.2.3		5.3.9 5.5.5 5.6.4
terms	2.1.1 4.2.9 5.5.2		5.8.1
tetrad	5.7.0 5.9.1 5.9.4	threes	3.1.7
tetrads	5.9.7	time	1.1.7 1.4.4 1.5.2
tetraktys	3.1.8 5.2.9		1.5.3 1.5.4 1.5.7
theological	5.7.0		1.5.11 1.5.12 1.5.14
theologising	5.9.4		1.6.2 1.6.5 1.6.11
theology	5.4.0 5.9.5		1.6.17 1.6.17 1.6.17
theoretical	1.6.9 1.6.10 1.6.13		2.2.3 2.3.7 4.2.11
	3.1.14 4.3.5 5.4.1		4.2.11 4.3.2 4.3.3
theories	5.9.1		5.1.4 5.2.2 5.3.0
theory	4.1.0 5.3.9 5.4.6		5.3.1 5.3.5 5.3.6
thick	1.1.5 1.5.6		5.3.6 5.3.8 5.3.9
thickness	5.7.3		5.4.1 5.4.1 5.4.4
thighs	1.4.10		5.5.3
thin	1.5.6 1.5.6	timeless	5.3.4 5.3.5 5.3.6
thing	2.0.1 3.1.4 4.1.1		5.3.7 5.3.9 5.4.7
	4.1.1 4.1.1 4.1.2	times	1.3.5 1.5.13 1.6.18
	4.1.2 4.1.3 4.1.3		5.3.2

together	1.1.6 1.3.2 5.2.1	unpaired	1.6.5
	5.2.3 5.9.6	unreal	1.6.7
tone	3.2.2	unsearchable	1.6.14
topical	3.2.2	untitled	6.1.1
totality	5.9.1	upper	1.4.2 1.4.2 1.6.6
touched	1.5.12	useful	1.0.0 1.0.1 1.6.17
tranquillity	3.1.4		
transcended	5.9.7	valleys	1.1.5
transformation	4.3.4 5.5.1	value	2.1.1
translation	6.1.1	varied	4.1.1
treatise	6.1.1	varieties	1.6.2 3.1.3
triad	1.6.18 3.1.9 3.1.10	variety	1.5.6 3.3.1 4.1.2
	5.9.8		5.3.4
triads	5.9.7	various	1.1.4 1.4.2 1.4.3
triangle	1.6.4		1.5.7 1.5.13 1.6.3
triangular	1.4.3	vault	1.1.3 1.3.3
true	3.1.12 4.2.9	veins	1.1.5 1.5.5 2.5.4
truly	1.2.3 1.6.8	venus	1.3.5
truth	3.1.6	veracity	3.1.6 3.1.15
twelve	1.4.4 5.9.7	verb	1.6.12 2.3.4 2.3.4
two	1.3.4 1.6.2 1.6.3		2.3.5 3.1.4 5.6.3
	1.6.15 1.6.16 3.1.7	verbs	3.1.4
	3.1.10 4.2.1 4.2.10	vernal	1.4.5
	4.3.2 5.2.5 5.6.1	Virgo	1.4.5 1.4.8 1.4.11
	5.6.4	virtue	1.2.1 1.2.2 1.2.3
			2.2.1
unbounded	1.1.1 1.3.1 1.4.3	visible	1.6.8
unceasing	1.3.4	vision	5.2.11
unchanging	1.3.2 1.5.3 1.5.4	void	1.1.1 1.1.2 1.3.1
	5.4.7 5.8.2		1.6.11 5.3.8 5.4.6
uncompoundable	5.5.4		5.4.6 5.5.4 5.6.2
unconstituable	1.6.14 1.6.15 1.6.15		5.6.3 5.7.3 5.7.3
uncreated	1.5.14 5.3.8		5.8.0 5.8.1 5.8.2
underneath	1.1.3 1.1.4 1.1.7		5.9.2 5.9.2
	1.3.3 1.3.3	voluntary	1.6.6 1.6.6
understanding	1.2.2 5.4.8 5.9.8		
understandings	1.6.13	war	1.5.11
understood	1.3.3 5.1.6	warmth	1.5.12
unequal	1.4.3	wars	1.5.10
unerringly	1.1.7	water	1.4.6 1.6.2 2.5.2
unfixed	5.5.1		2.5.3 2.5.4
ungenerated	5.9.2 5.9.6	waters	1.1.5 1.1.5 1.1.5
unintelligible	5.6.1 5.6.1 5.6.4		2.5.3 2.5.4 2.5.4
	5.8.1		2.5.4
union	3.1.1	watery	1.1.3 1.3.3
universal	5.3.6 5.8.1 5.9.1	way	1.3.2 1.4.3 1.4.4
	5.9.8		1.5.3 5.3.1 5.8.1
universe	5.3.4 5.3.5 5.3.9	ways	1.3.1 1.6.2 4.2.4
	5.8.1		4.2.10 5.2.5
unlike	5.5.1	weakness	2.4.1
unmarried	3.1.3	weeks	5.3.2
unmixed	5.1.8 5.7.4	wells	2.5.4
unmixedness	5.2.10	west	1.3.4 1.3.5 1.4.6
unmoving	5.7.4 5.7.4	white	1.4.2 1.6.3
unnatural	5.5.1 5.5.1 5.8.2	wild	2.2.2

INDEX OF ANCIENT SOURCES CITED IN
THE NOTES TO THE TRANSLATION

The note numbers given in the index below refer to the notes on the translation.

PART FOUR

INDEXES AND TOOLS

CONCORDANCE OF THE ARMENIAN TEXT OF PSEUDO-ZENO

ագարակային adjective [1]
       ագարակայնոց 3.1.4
ազգ noun [2]
       ազգս 5.9.4
       ազգի 4.2.4
ազդումն noun [6]
       ազդումն 1.6.1 1.6.18
       ազդմունք 1.0.1 1.6.17
       ազդմանց 1.6.0
       ազդմամբք 1.5.13
ախտ noun [4]
       ախտի 1.6.16 3.1.12 4.2.14
       ախտից 1.5.11
ախտաժետութիւն noun [1]
       ախտաժետութեանց 1.1.4
ախտաստացական adjective [1]
       ախտաստացականից 1.6.6
աձանց adjective [1]
       աձանցից 4.3.3
աձանցական adjective [1]
       աձանցականք 5.3.6
ակամայ adjective [2]
       ակամայ 1.6.6(2x)
աղբիւր noun [2]
       աղբերք 1.1.5
       աղբերս 2.5.4
աղեղնատր adjective [3]
       աղեղնատր 1.4.6 1.4.9 1.4.11
աճելութիւն noun [1]
       աճելութիւն 4.3.4
աճեմ verb [1]
       աճել 5.7.2
աճումն noun [3]
       աճումն 1.5.4 4.2.4
       աճմունք 1.5.12
ամ noun [2]
       ամք 5.3.2 5.3.3
ամանակ noun [3]
       ամանակ 5.2.5 5.4.6
       ամանակի 1.6.17
ամառնային adjective [1]
       ամառնային 1.4.5
ամենայն adjective [19]
       ամենայն 1.1.5 1.2.2 1.3.4 3.1.11(2x) 3.1.15 4.2.10 5.2.4
       5.3.1 5.7.1(2x) 5.9.8
       ամենայնի 4.2.10 4.2.11 4.2.14
       ամենայնէ 5.2.7
       ամենայնիւ 5.9.1
       ամենայնք 1.6.14 5.2.9

ամենեքեան noun		[2]
	ամենեցուն 1.1.5 2.5.5	
ամէն adjective		[2]
	ամենի 4.2.7(2x)	
ամիս noun		[2]
	ամիսք 5.3.2	
	ամսոց 1.4.4	
ամլութիւն noun		[1]
	ամլութիւնք 1.5.8	
ամոք adjective		[1]
	ամոքաց 1.5.6	
այժմ adverb		[2]
	այժմ 5.9.6 6.1.1	
այլ adjective		[21]
	այլ 1.4.2(2x) 1.4.3 1.5.4 1.5.11 1.5.12 3.3.1(2x)	
	այլում 3.3.1(2x)	
	այլմէ 5.9.2	
	այլք 2.3.5 4.2.10 5.3.2	
	այլոց 2.4.1 2.4.2 5.2.2 5.3.3 5.3.5 5.4.2 5.9.1	
այլ conjunction		[16]
	այլ 1.3.3 1.5.3(2x) 1.5.4 1.6.8 4.2.2 4.3.3 5.1.4 5.2.4 5.2.	
	5 5.3.4 5.3.6 5.6.3 5.8.2(2x) 5.9.5	
այլայլակ adjective		[1]
	այլայլակ 1.5.3	
այլայլեմ verb		[1]
	այլայլել 5.7.2	
այլայլութիւն noun		[1]
	այլայլութիւն 4.3.4	
այլապէս adverb		[2]
	այլապէս 3.3.1(2x)	
այլմէ noun		[1]
	այլմէց 3.2.1	
այծեղջիւր noun		[3]
	այծեղջիւր 1.4.6 1.4.10 1.4.11	
այն demonstrative pronoun		[1]
	այնք 4.2.11	
այս demonstrative pronoun		[19]
	այս 5.9.5	
	այսմ 5.3.5	
	այսք 1.5.9 1.6.8 1.6.18 3.3.2 4.3.5 5.3.9	
	այսորիկ 1.3.5 2.5.5 5.1.7 5.7.1	
	այսորիկ 1.4.3 2.4.1 5.3.6 5.8.2 5.9.2 5.9.3(2x)	
այսչափ adjective		[1]
	այսչափ 5.3.2	
այսպէս adverb		[6]
	այսպէս 1.1.5 1.5.4 3.1.2 3.1.3 3.1.14 5.8.1	
այսքան adjective		[2]
	այսքան 1.6.17 5.2.12	
անախտական adjective		[1]
	անախտական 3.1.12	
անամանակ adjective		[1]
	անամանակ 5.4.7	
անանջատական adjective		[1]
	անանջատական 4.2.6	

աննանցեալ adjective   [1]
  աննանցեալ 5.4.7
աննապական adjective   [1]
  աննապական 5.1.10
աննապատնի adjective   [1]
  աննապատնի 5.4.7
աննասուն noun   [1]
  աննասնոց 2.2.2
աննարութիւն noun   [1]
  աննարութինք 1.5.8
անբաղկացելի adjective   [3]
  անբաղկացելիս 1.6.15
  անբաղկացելիք 1.6.14 1.6.15
անբան adjective   [2]
  անբան 4.2.4 5.8.1
անբաւ adjective   [19]
  անբաւ 1.6.11 5.5.4 5.6.2 5.6.3 5.8.1 5.9.1(3x) 5.9.2
  անբաւս 3.1.13
  անբաւի 1.3.1 5.2.10 5.4.7 5.7.4 5.8.1 5.9.0 5.9.3
  անբաւէ 1.1.1
  անբաւք 1.4.3
անբաւագոյն adjective   [2]
  անբաւագոյն 5.9.2
  անբաւագունից 5.9.2
անբնական adjective   [3]
  անբնական 5.5.1(2x) 5.8.2
անգամ noun   [1]
  անգամ 2.5.4
անգոյ adjective   [1]
  անգոյ 5.8.2
անգոյութին noun   [1]
  անգոյութին 1.1.1
անդադար adjective   [1]
  անդադար 1.3.4
անդամ noun   [1]
  անդամոց 1.4.4
անդէմ adjective   [1]
  անդէմ 1.6.10
անդունդ noun   [2]
  անդունդ 3.1.6
  անդնդովք 1.3.4
անդրէն adverb   [4]
  անդրէն 1.3.2 1.6.4 5.1.2 5.2.3
անեղ adjective   [4]
  անեղ 5.9.2
  անեղի 1.5.14 5.3.8 5.9.6
անեղծանելի adjective   [2]
  անեղծանելի 4.2.6 5.1.2
անզանազան adjective   [1]
  անզանազան 5.3.4
անզգալի adjective   [2]
  անզգալի 5.6.1
  անզգայոյ 5.6.1
անզգայուն adjective   [1]
  անզգայուն 4.2.4

անդոյզ adjective [1]
　　անդոյզ 1.6.5
անդուգութիւն noun [1]
　　անդուգութեան 1.4.3
անթուելի adjective [1]
　　անթուելի 1.5.4
անժամանակ adjective [5]
　　անժամանակ 5.3.4 5.3.5 5.3.6 5.3.7
　　անժամանակք 5.3.9
անժամանակացոյն adjective [2]
　　անժամանակացոյն 5.9.2
　　անժամանակացունից 5.9.2
անիմանալի adjective [3]
　　անիմանալի 5.6.1
　　անիմանալոյ 5.6.1 5.6.4
անիմացուած noun [1]
　　անիմացուած 5.8.1
անիր adjective [4]
　　անիր 5.8.1 5.8.2
　　անիրի 1.6.7 4.1.3
անխառն adjective [2]
　　անխառն 5.1.8 5.7.4
անխառնութիւն noun [1]
　　անխառնութիւն 5.2.10
անխնդրելի adjective [1]
　　անխնդրելի 1.6.14
անկատար adjective [10]
　　անկատար 3.1.4(2x) 5.2.7 5.2.8 5.2.10 5.2.11
　　անկատարէ 5.2.12
　　անկատարք 5.2.1 5.2.3 5.2.12
անկատարած adjective [2]
　　անկատարած 5.4.7 5.4.8
անկարգութիւն noun [1]
　　անկարգութիւնք 1.2.3
անկենդանական adjective [2]
　　անկենդանական 1.6.7(2x)
անկենդանի adjective [1]
　　անկենդանի 4.2.4
անկրական adjective [2]
　　անկրական 1.1.2 1.5.4
անհանգիստ adjective [1]
　　անհանգիստ 2.5.4
անհաս adjective [1]
　　անհասի 5.9.6
անհասացոյն adjective [1]
　　անհասացոյն 5.9.3
անհաստատ adjective [1]
　　անհաստատ 5.5.1
անհատ adjective [10]
　　անհատ 1.6.5 1.6.14 4.2.4 4.2.10
　　անհատս 5.5.1
　　անհատի 1.6.5
　　անհատից 1.4.3 5.2.1 5.3.9 5.9.7
անհարթ adjective [1]
　　անհարթ 1.4.3

անհասանութ adjective [1]
    անհասանութ 5.3.4
անհուն adjective [2]
    անհունս 1.6.5 5.9.3
անձն noun [2]
    անձին 1.5.10
    անձինս 5.9.6
անմահ adjective [1]
    անմահ 1.5.4
անմման adjective [1]
    անմման 5.9.1
անմարմին adjective [3]
    անմարմին 1.1.2 1.5.4 4.2.4
անմարմնաբար adverb [1]
    անմարմնաբար 1.5.3
անմեկնելի adjective [3]
    անմեկնելի 1.6.10 4.2.0 4.2.1
անմոլար adjective [1]
    անմոլարք 1.6.18
անյաղթ adjective [1]
    անյաղթ 5.9.8
անյեղլի adjective [3]
    անյեղլի 1.5.3 1.5.4 5.4.7
աններգործեալ adjective [1]
    աններգործեալ 5.8.1
աններկայ adjective [1]
    աններկայ 5.4.7
աննիւթ adjective [2]
    աննիւթ 5.7.4
    աննիւթէ 5.7.4
աննման adjective [3]
    աննման 3.1.1
    աննմանք 1.6.5
    աննմանից 5.5.1
անշարադրելի adjective [1]
    անշարադրելի 5.5.4
անշարժ adjective [2]
    անշարժ 5.7.4
    անշարժէ 5.7.4
անշարժելի adjective [1]
    անշարժելի 1.3.2
անորիշ adjective [1]
    անորիշ 5.4.6
անուանադրեմ verb [1]
    անուանադրեն 1.4.4
անուն noun [10]
    անուն 1.6.12 2.3.4(2x)
    անուան 2.3.5 3.1.4 4.3.3 5.2.3
    անուանց 3.1.4
    անուամբ 5.5.2 5.6.3
անչափ adjective [2]
    անչափ 5.9.1
    անչափք 1.4.3
անպակասաբար adverb [1]
    անպակասաբար 1.5.3

անշատական adjective [1]
    անշատական 4.2.6

անսահման adjective [1]
    անսահման 5.1.8

անխառ adjective [1]
    անխառ 1.1.7

անակիցն adjective [2]
    անակիցն 5.4.7 5.4.8

անվայր adjective [1]
    անվայր 5.8.2

անտեսակ adjective [1]
    անտեսակ 5.9.1

անցական adjective [1]
    անցական 5.8.2

անցանեմ verb [2]
    անցեալ 2.5.3 3.2.1

աշխարհ noun [11]
    աշխարհ 1.3.1
    աշխարհի 1.1.6(2x) 1.2.2 1.3.4 1.4.1 1.4.4 1.6.4 3.1.16
    5.3.3 5.9.8

աշխանային adjective [1]
    աշխանային 1.4.6

ապա adverb [1]
    ապա 3.1.1

ապականեմ verb [1]
    ապականել 5.7.2

ապականութիւն noun [1]
    ապականութիւն 4.3.4

ապացոյց noun [1]
    ապացուցի 3.2.0

ապացուցական adjective [2]
    ապացուցական 1.6.9 3.2.1

աշ noun [1]
    աշ 1.4.8

առ preposition [2]
    առ 1.6.7 5.9.4

առ ի preposition [5]
    առ ի 1.6.18 2.2.1 2.4.1 3.1.4 3.1.13

առադրեմ verb [5]
    առադրի 2.2.2
    առադրեցին 2.0.0 3.1.0 4.1.0
    առադրեալ 2.2.3

առակաբար adverb [1]
    առակաբար 5.7.4

առանձին adjective [6]
    առանձին 5.3.0 5.4.0 5.5.0 5.6.0 5.7.0 5.8.0

առանձնական adjective [1]
    առանձնական 3.1.1

առանձնանամ verb [1]
    առանձնանան 1.6.11

առանձնաւորութիւն noun [1]
    առանձնաւորութեամբ 5.9.4

առանց preposition [8]
    առանց 1.1.4 1.5.4 4.3.1 4.3.2 4.3.3(2x) 5.1.4 5.6.3

առաջին adjective [17]

    առաջին 1.1.1 3.1.3 3.1.7 3.1.10 3.1.11 4.2.2 4.2.3 4.2.10(2x) 4.3.5 5.2.2 5.3.5 5.4.3 5.5.3 5.6.2 5.7.3

    առաջնոյ 1.6.18

առասպելաւարձութիւն noun [1]

    առասպելաւարձութիւն 2.3.3

առաւելութիւն noun [4]

    առաւելութեան 1.5.7 3.1.6 5.4.2

    առաւելութեանց 1.5.9

առաւելում verb [1]

    առաւելու 5.5.2

առաքինութիւն noun [4]

    առաքինութեան 1.2.1 1.2.2 1.2.3 2.2.1

առընդդեմ adjective [1]

    առընդդեմ 5.3.1

առժամայն adverb [1]

    առժամայն 1.6.8

առինչ noun [2]

    առինչ 4.2.8

    առնչի 4.2.12

առինչունակ adjective [2]

    առինչունակի 4.2.15 4.3.5

առինչունակապէս adverb [1]

    առինչունակապէս 4.3.1

առիծ noun [3]

    առիծ 1.4.5 1.4.8 1.4.11

առկայ adjective [1]

    առկայ 5.3.7

առձեռն adjective [1]

    առձեռն 2.3.2

առնեմ verb [5]

    առնեն 2.5.4

    առնի 1.5.3

    արարից 2.5.3

    առնել 4.2.8 4.2.15

առնում verb [20]

    առնու 1.3.2 3.1.4 5.1.2 5.2.4 5.5.5

    առնուն 5.2.1 5.2.2 5.2.3 5.3.2

    էառ 5.9.7

    առչիր 2.5.1

    առեալ 1.5.4 2.5.1 5.2.9 5.3.9

    առնուլ 5.1.4 5.1.6 5.1.8 5.7.3

    առնլով 5.1.9

առոգանութիւն noun [1]

    առոգանութեան 2.3.2

առողջութիւն noun [4]

    առողջութիւն 1.1.4 1.5.7

    առողջութիւնք 1.5.7 1.5.12

առոյգ adjective [1]

    առոյգ 1.5.12

ասացութիւն noun [1]

    ասացութեամբ 5.7.4

ասեմ verb [73]

    ասեմ 2.5.5

    ասեն 5.2.5 5.9.6

        ասի 1.4.2 1.4.3(2x) 1.6.14 2.1.1 2.2.3 2.3.1 2.3.3 3.1.7(2x)
3.1.9 3.2.2 3.2.3(2x) 4.1.2 4.1.3 4.2.2(2x) 4.2.4 4.2.5 4.2.7
4.2.14 4.3.2(2x) 4.3.4 4.3.5 5.1.1 5.1.7(2x) 5.2.10 5.3.5 5.3.6
5.6.1 5.6.2(2x) 5.6.3(2x) 5.7.4 5.8.1(3x) 5.8.2(2x) 5.9.1 5.9.2
5.9.3 5.9.4
        ասին 1.4.3 4.2.4 4.2.6 4.2.9 4.2.10 4.2.13 4.2.15 4.3.1 5.2.1
5.2.3 5.2.4 5.2.6 5.2.9 5.3.6 5.3.7 5.3.9 5.9.7
        ասացին 1.6.18
        ասացուք 2.5.3(2x)
        ասացեալ 1.6.17
        ասել 1.3.3 2.5.3

ասիացի noun   [1]
        ասիացիք 1.4.8

ասրի noun   [1]
        ասրոց 1.4.10

աստեղատուն noun   [5]
        աստեղատունք 1.2.4 1.3.4 1.4.4
        աստեղատանց 1.1.7 1.4.4

աստղ noun   [1]
        աստեղք 1.1.7

աստուած noun   [23]
        աստուած 3.1.10 3.1.11 3.1.12 3.1.14 3.1.15 3.1.16 6.1.1(3x)
        աստուածս 5.9.4
        աստուծոյ 1.6.18 2.5.5 3.1.5 3.1.10(2x) 3.1.12 3.1.13(2x)
3.1.15(2x) 5.9.4(2x)
        աստուծոց 3.1.14

աստուածաբանական adjective   [1]
        աստուածաբանական 5.7.0

աստուածաբանեմ verb   [1]
        աստուածաբանել 5.9.4

աստուածային adjective   [3]
        աստուածայնոց 1.6.8 3.1.5 3.1.11

աստուածխաւսութիւն noun   [2]
        աստուածխաւսութիւն 4.3.5
        աստուածխաւսութեան 5.4.0

ատենական adjective   [2]
        ատենական 2.3.7(2x)

արաբացի noun   [1]
        արաբացոց 1.4.9

արական adjective   [2]
        արական 1.5.5
        արականք 1.4.11

արարած adjective   [1]
        արարածոյ 5.9.4

արարիչ noun   [3]
        արարիչ 5.9.4 5.9.6
        արարչի 5.3.6

արարչական adjective   [9]
        արարչական 1.6.11 5.5.1(2x) 5.5.3(4x)
        արարչականի 5.2.7 5.5.5

արարչութիւն noun   [3]
        արարչութեան 5.4.1(2x)
        արարչութեամբ 5.9.5

արգանդ noun   [1]
        արգանդի 1.5.8

արգել noun [1]
    արգել 2.5.2
արգելում verb [1]
    արգելուլ 2.1.1
արգելումն noun [2]
    արգելման 1.1.3 1.1.6
արդ adverb [26]
    արդ 1.0.1 1.1.1 1.2.3 1.5.14 1.6.2 1.6.17 2.1.1 2.5.2 2.5.3(2x)
    3.1.1 3.1.14 4.2.10 4.3.5 5.1.4 5.1.6 5.1.10 5.2.5 5.2.6 5.2.11
    5.3.5 5.3.9 5.4.8 5.5.5 5.6.4 5.7.1
արդար adjective [1]
    արդար 4.2.9
արդարութիւն noun [1]
    արդարութիւն 5.1.1
արեգակն noun [1]
    արեգակն 1.3.5
արեւելք noun [3]
    արեւելս 1.3.5
    արեւելից 1.3.4 1.4.5
արեւմուտք noun [3]
    արեւմուտս 1.3.4
    արեւմտից 1.3.5 1.4.6
արիւն noun [3]
    արիւն 1.5.7
    արեան 1.5.5 1.5.8
արհեստ noun [17]
    արհեստ 1.6.9 3.1.5 3.1.14(2x) 5.9.8(2x)
    արհեստի 3.1.8 3.1.9 3.1.10 3.3.2 4.3.5
    արհեստիւ 4.3.5
    արհեստից 1.6.14 3.1.5 3.1.14(2x) 3.1.16
արու adjective [1]
    արուի 1.5.8
արտաբերեմ verb [4]
    արտաբերի 1.5.2 1.5.4
    արտաբերեալ 1.6.5 1.6.6
արտաբերութիւն noun [1]
    արտաբերութիւնք 1.5.1
արտադատութիւն noun [2]
    արտադատութեան 1.1.3
    արտադատութիւնք 1.5.1
արտադրեմ verb [1]
    արտադրեցան 1.6.17
արտադրութիւն noun [1]
    արտադրութիւնք 1.5.1
արտահոսութիւն noun [1]
    արտահոսութիւնք 1.5.1
արտաքին adjective [3]
    արտաքին 2.5.4(3x)
արտաքոյ adverb [2]
    արտաքոյ 1.5.3 5.8.1
արտաքուստ adverb [1]
    արտաքուստ 5.1.6
արտաքս adverb [1]
    արտաքս 1.2.3

ազդուտ noun   [1]
    ազդուտ 2.5.4
ազդիմ verb   [1]
    ազդի 1.5.10
աղ noun   [19]
    աղ 1.1.6 1.4.5 1.5.12
    աղոյ 1.5.13 2.3.5
    աղբ 1.3.3 2.5.3 2.5.4(2x)
    աղս 2.5.1
    աղոց 1.1.4 1.1.5(2x) 1.1.6 1.1.7 1.2.4 1.3.3 1.3.4 1.3.5
ազդավարութիւն noun   [1]
    ազդավարութեան 1.2.4
այր noun   [1]
    աւուրբ 5.3.2
այրէն noun   [3]
    այրինի 1.2.1 1.2.2 1.2.3
այրինակ noun   [2]
    այրինակի 2.2.3 3.1.3
այրինակեմ verb   [1]
    այրինակեալ 2.2.1
բաբելացի noun   [1]
    բաբելացող 1.4.7
բազմութիւն noun   [2]
    բազմութեանց 5.3.9
    բազմութեամբ 1.5.4
բազում adjective   [2]
    բազում 2.5.4(2x)
բաժանական adjective   [2]
    բաժանական 1.6.9
    բաժանականին 1.6.4
բաժանեմ verb   [36]
    բաժանի 1.1.1 1.2.1 1.4.1 1.4.3 1.5.2 1.5.5 1.6.1 1.6.3(2x)
    1.6.9 1.6.16 .1.1 3.1.1 3.1.2 3.1.3 3.1.6 3.1.15 4.2.3 4.2.4
    4.2.5 4.2.6 4.2.8 4.2.10 4.3.4 5.3.5 5.4.1 5.4.2 5.6.3
    բաժանին 1.6.3 1.6.14 2.3.7
    բաժանեալ 1.3.4 1.3.5 1.6.7 1.6.11 3.1.3
բաժանումն noun   [10]
    բաժանումն 3.1.1 5.2.7
    բաժանման 1.3.3 3.1.1 5.1.5 5.2.8
    բաժանմամբ 5.4.6 5.5.5
    բաժանմունս 5.3.7
    բաժանմանց 3.1.0
բախումն noun   [1]
    բախման 1.6.7
բաղխունչական adjective   [2]
    բաղխունչական 2.3.7(2x)
բաղկանամ verb   [36]
    բաղկանայ 1.3.1 1.4.3 1.5.1 1.6.8 3.1.6 3.2.1 4.1.3 5.1.3
    5.2.12 5.3.4 5.3.6(2x) 5.5.1 5.5.5 5.7.2(2x) 5.7.4
    բաղկանան 1.4.2 1.5.5 1.5.9 1.5.10 1.5.12 1.6.3 1.6.15
    3.1.8 5.2.1 5.3.2 5.3.3 5.3.9
    բաղկացաւ 5.1.4
    բաղկացան 5.4.8
    բաղկացեալ 1.1.2 1.6.8 5.3.1
    բաղկանալ 1.1.6 3.1.13

բաղկանք noun [2]
    բաղկանաց 5.1.1 5.2.5
բաղկացելի adjective [4]
    բաղկացելիս 1.6.15
    բաղկացելիք 1.6.14 1.6.15 1.6.16
բաղկացութիւն noun [7]
    բաղկացութիւն 5.1.6 5.1.9 5.2.9 5.3.8 5.5.4 5.8.2
    բաղկացութիւնք 5.4.7
բաղկացումն noun [1]
    բաղկացումն 1.5.3
բաղկացուցանեմ verb [1]
    բաղկացուցանեն 5.2.5
բաղկացուցիչ noun [5]
    բաղկացուցիչ 1.1.4 3.1.3 5.1.6 5.5.1 5.5.2
բայ noun [7]
    բայ 1.6.12 2.3.4(2x)
    բայի 2.3.5 3.1.4
    բայիւ 5.6.3
    բայից 3.1.4
բայց conjunction [1]
    բայց 1.6.8
բան noun [23]
    բան 1.6.12(2x) 2.3.5 2.5.5 3.1.6 4.2.11(2x) 5.2.1(2x) 5.2.4 5.2.5 5.2.7 5.2.10 5.2.11 5.2.12
    բանի 1.5.10 1.6.18 2.0.0 2.3.4(2x) 5.2.0 5.2.11
    բանից 5.2.3
բանական adjective [11]
    բանական 1.6.7(2x) 1.6.9(2x) 3.1.14 3.1.16 3.3.2 4.2.4
    բանականի 1.6.7 1.6.12 3.0.0
բանաւորութիւն noun [2]
    բանաւորութիւն 1.6.18
    բանաւորութենէ 5.9.4
բառ noun [2]
    բառից 2.3.3 5.5.2
բառնամ verb [1]
    բարձեալ 1.1.1
բարառնական adjective [1]
    բարառնական 2.2.3
բարեխառնութիւն noun [2]
    բարեխառնութեան 1.5.7 1.5.12
բարերարեմ verb [1]
    բարերարել 3.1.13
բարի adjective [17]
    բարի 1.6.11 5.1.1 5.1.2 5.1.4(3x) 5.1.5(4x) 5.1.7 5.1.10 5.9.1
    բարւոյ 5.1.6(2x) 5.1.10
    բարեաւ 3.1.12
բարկութիւն noun [1]
    բարկութիւն 1.6.12
բարձ noun [1]
    բարձք 1.4.10
բարձումն noun [2]
    բարձումն 1.5.13
    բարձման 4.2.2
բարձրութիւն noun [1]
    բարձրութիւն 1.5.7

բարոյական adjective [5]
    բարոյական 1.6.9 2.0.1 2.2.1 2.2.3
    բարոյականի 2.2.0
բարք noun [1]
    բարուց 2.2.3
բացասութիւն noun [4]
    բացասութեան 3.2.3
    բացասութիւն 1.6.12 4.2.9
    բացասութեամբ 4.3.1
բացատրութիւն noun [1]
    բացատրութիւն 2.3.2
բացերեւական adjective [1]
    բացերեւական 1.6.12
բացերեւիմ verb [2]
    բացերեւեցաւ 1.3.2
    բացերեւեալ 1.3.1
բացերեւութիւն noun [1]
    բացերեւութիւն 1.3.1
բաւական adjective [2]
    բաւականէ 5.8.1
    բաւականաւ 3.1.13
բաւականիմ verb [1]
    բաւականեալ 5.8.1
բերումն noun [2]
    բերման 1.1.4
    բերմանց 5.3.1
բժշկական adjective [1]
    բժշկական 1.5.1
բժշկականութիւն noun [1]
    բժշկականութիւն 1.5.5
բլուր noun [1]
    բլրաւք 1.1.5
բնական adjective [9]
    բնական 1.2.2 1.2.3 1.5.11 1.5.12 3.1.4 5.1.2 5.5.1(2x) 5.5.2
բնականազոյն adjective [2]
    բնականազոյն 5.9.2
    բնականազունից 5.9.2
բնականութիւն noun [5]
    բնականութիւն 1.6.6 5.1.2 5.1.3
    բնականութեան 1.2.1 1.2.2
բնակարան noun [1]
    բնակարան 1.1.4
բնակութիւն noun [1]
    բնակութիւն 1.1.6
բնատրեմ verb [4]
    բնատրեցաւ 5.1.4 5.3.7
    բնատրեցան 1.2.2
    բնատրեալ 1.6.8
բնութիւն noun [35]
    բնութիւն 1.1.2 1.6.11 1.6.14 5.5.1 5.5.5
    բնութեան 1.2.3 1.5.3 1.5.4(2x) 1.5.14 1.6.16 1.6.17 2.2.2
    3.1.0 3.1.12 3.3.2 5.1.4 5.2.6 5.3.6 5.3.8 5.4.2 5.5.0 5.5.4
    5.9.3 5.9.5
    բնութենէ 1.5.10

բնութեամբ 1.3.2 5.1.2(2x) 5.1.4(3x) 5.9.5
բնութեանց 1.6.1 5.3.5

բոլոր adjective [10]
բոլոր 1.1.1 1.3.2 5.3.9 5.4.6 5.9.1
բոլորի 1.3.1 5.3.4 5.3.5 5.3.9 5.8.1

բոլորակ noun [3]
բոլորակ 1.4.3 1.6.4(2x)

բոլորութիւն noun [1]
բոլորութեամբ 1.3.4

բոյս noun [2]
բուսոց 1.6.2 2.2.3

բովանդակութիւն noun [4]
բովանդակութիւն 2.5.1 2.5.5
բովանդակութեան 2.5.0
բովանդակութիւնք 2.5.5

բուրումն noun [1]
բուրումն 2.5.3

բռնադատեմ verb [1]
բռնադատեալ 1.1.6

բռնադատութիւն noun [1]
բռնադատութիւն 1.6.6

գ...ակ noun [1]
գ...ակ 5.2.3

գազան noun [1]
գազանաց 2.2.2

գամիրք name [1]
գամրաց 1.4.7

գանգուր adjective [1]
գանգուր 1.5.6

գարնանային adjective [1]
գարնանային 1.4.5

գետ noun [2]
գետք 1.1.5
գետոց 1.1.5

գերագոյն adjective [1]
գերագունի 1.6.6

գերազանցագոյն adjective [2]
գերազանցագոյն 5.9.2
գերազանցագունից 5.9.2

գերազանցեալ adjective [3]
գերազանցեալ 5.2.10 5.2.12 5.9.7

գերակատար adjective [2]
գերակատար 5.2.6 5.4.6

գթութիւն noun [1]
գթութեան 5.9.5

գիծ noun [2]
գիծ 4.2.11(2x)

գիտելի adjective [1]
գիտելի 1.5.12

գիտեմ verb [1]
գիտել 3.1.13

գիտնական adjective [1]
գիտնականաւ 3.1.12

գիտութիւն noun [10]
գիտութիւն 1.6.13 3.1.5(2x) 3.1.11(2x)

գիտութեան 1.6.18 5.2.0 5.2.12
գիտութիւնք 2.4.1 5.9.1

գիր noun [1]
գրոց 4.2.13

գիտ noun [2]
գիտ 2.3.2 3.1.16

գլխատրեմ verb [1]
գլխատրին 5.9.7

գլուխ noun [3]
գլուխ 1.4.7
գլուխք 2.3.7 3.1.8

գծած noun [1]
գծածք 1.6.7

գնաց noun [3]
գնաց 2.5.4
գնացք 2.5.3
գնացս 2.5.3

գոհութիւն noun [1]
գոհութիւն 5.9.6

գողտր adjective [1]
գողտր 1.5.6

գոմ verb [19]
գոյ 5.9.3
գոն 5.2.1
գոլ 1.1.5 1.2.2 1.6.18 3.1.1 3.1.4 3.1.9 3.1.12 5.2.8 5.2.11
5.3.7 5.4.5 5.6.1
գոլով 1.3.4 5.2.7 5.4.4 5.4.5 5.5.4

գոյ noun [1]
գոյէ 5.8.2

գոյանամ verb [2]
գոյանայ 5.4.6
գոյանան 5.2.3

գոյացութիւն noun [23]
գոյացութիւն 4.2.1(3x) 4.2.2 4.2.4 4.2.6 4.2.8 5.1.7
5.6.1(3x) 5.6.3
գոյացութեան 4.2.2 4.2.4 4.3.5 5.4.3 5.5.3 5.6.2(2x) 5.6.4
գոյացութենէ 5.1.5
գոյացութիւնք 5.2.11
գոյացութեանց 5.3.7

գոյացումն noun [1]
գոյացումն 1.5.4

գոյացուցանեմ verb [2]
գոյացուցանէ 5.2.7
գոյացուցանեն 1.3.5

գոյացուցիչ noun [6]
գոյացուցիչ 1.1.5 5.1.6 5.4.7 5.7.0
գոյացուցիչք 1.6.17 5.7.2

գոյն noun [8]
գոյն 1.3.1 1.4.2 1.6.3(2x)
գունոյ 1.4.1 1.5.6
գունոց 1.6.3
գունովք 5.1.9

գոյութիւն noun [1]
գոյութիւնս 5.9.2

գովեմ verb [2]
  գովի 2.4.2
  գովել 2.3.7
գործական adjective [2]
  գործական 3.1.14 5.4.1
գործնական adjective [4]
  գործնական 1.6.9(2x)
  գործնականի 1.6.12 2.0.0
գռուզ adjective [1]
  գռուզ 1.5.6
գտանեմ verb [2]
  գտանի 5.9.3
  գտաւ 5.9.7
գրեմ verb [2]
  գրեցելոյ 4.1.3
  գրեցեալք 4.1.3
դադարումն noun [2]
  դադարումն 5.7.4
  դադարման 5.6.3
դաշտ noun [1]
  դաշտաւք 1.1.5
դառն adjective [1]
  դառն 1.5.6
դառնամ verb [29]
  դարձեալ 1.1.3 1.3.2 1.4.3 1.6.16 3.1.6 3.1.10 3.2.3 4.1.1
  4.2.2 4.2.5 4.2.7 5.1.1 5.1.3 5.1.4 5.1.5 5.1.8 5.2.10 5.3.3
  5.4.4 5.4.7 5.5.2 5.5.3(2x) 5.5.5 5.6.1 5.6.4 5.7.1 5.9.2
  դառնալ 1.6.4
դառնութիւն noun [2]
  դառնութեան 1.5.13 4.2.14
դաս noun [2]
  դաս 4.2.11
  դասիւ 1.6.15
դասատրութիւն noun [1]
  դասատրութեան 5.3.7
դասեմ verb [3]
  դասի 4.2.5 4.3.1 5.3.3
դատութիւն noun [1]
  դատութիւն 5.2.3
դատումն noun [1]
  դատումն 2.3.2
դար noun [4]
  դար 1.4.3 3.1.8 3.1.10
  դարք 5.3.2
դարկոծատ adjective [1]
  դարկոծատաց 3.1.9
դերանուն noun [1]
  դերանուն 2.3.4
դեմ noun [5]
  դեմս 1.6.5
  դեմք 1.6.5
  դիմաց 3.2.1
  դիմաւք 1.3.4 1.3.5
դժուարաշարժելի adjective [1]
  դժուարաշարժելի 4.2.6

դժուարափոխ adjective   [1]
        դժուարափոխ 5.1.2
դժուարին adjective   [1]
        դժուարինք 1.5.7
դիմադրական adjective   [1]
        դիմադրական 3.1.1
դիմակայութիւն noun   [1]
        դիմակայութեան 4.3.4
դիմեմ verb   [1]
        դիմեալ 5.2.10
դիտատրական adjective   [2]
        դիտատրական 1.6.10 4.1.3
դիր noun   [8]
        դիր 4.2.11(2x)
        դիրք 1.0.1 1.1.1 1.1.4 1.6.17
        դրից 1.1.0 5.3.7
դիւրաշարժ adjective   [1]
        դիւրաշարժ 5.1.3
դիւրացուցանեմ verb   [1]
        դիւրացուցանելոյ 2.4.2
դու   personal pronoun   [2]
        քեզ 2.5.5 6.1.1
դուռն noun   [1]
        դուրս 2.5.3
դրութիւն noun   [2]
        դրութիւն 4.2.12
        դրութեանց 3.1.11
եզիպտացի noun   [1]
        եզիպտացւոց 1.4.10
եզր noun   [1]
        եզերից 1.1.4
ելանեմ verb   [3]
        ելանեն 1.2.4 2.5.3
        ելեալ 1.2.3
ելլադացի noun   [1]
        ելլադացւոց 1.4.8
ելող adjective   [1]
        ելող 5.9.4
ելումն noun   [2]
        ելմանց 1.6.5
        ելումն 1.5.3
ելք noun   [3]
        ելք 2.5.3 2.5.4
        ելիք 5.1.9
եկամուտ adjective   [2]
        եկամուտ 5.3.3
        եկամտաց 1.5.13
եկատրի noun   [3]
        եկատրի 1.4.5 1.4.7 1.4.11
եղանակ noun   [8]
        եղանակ 1.4.5 1.4.6 1.6.10 4.3.3
        եղանակս 2.3.2
        եղանակք 5.3.2
        եղանակաց 1.5.7 1.5.12

եղանիմ verb [2]
        եղաւ 5.1.4
        եղելոց 5.2.4
եղծանելի adjective [1]
        եղծանելի 5.1.10
եղծումն noun [2]
        եղծումն 1.2.3 5.2.10
եղումն noun [9]
        եղումն 5.4.6 5.5.1
        եղման 1.4.4 5.1.10 5.3.1
        եղմանց 1.3.1 1.5.7 1.5.13 5.3.5
եմ verb [322]
        է 1.1.1 1.1.2 1.1.5 1.1.6(3x) 1.3.1 1.3.3(2x) 1.4.2 1.4.3(2x)
        1.4.5(2x) 1.4.6(2x) 1.4.7(3x) 1.4.8 1.5.5 1.5.10(2x) 1.5.11(3x)
        1.5.12(3x) 1.6.4(2x) 1.6.5(2x) 1.6.7 1.6.9 1.6.14 1.6.18
        2.0.1 2.1.1(3x) 2.2.1 2.2.3 2.3.1 2.3.4 2.3.7(3x) 2.4.1 2.4.2
        2.5.2 2.5.3(2x) 2.5.4(5x) 2.5.5
        3.1.1(3x) 3.1.2(3x) 3.1.3 3.1.4(5x) 3.1.7(6x) 3.1.8 3.1.9(2x)
        3.1.10(4x) 3.1.11 3.1.12(2x) 3.1.13(2x) 3.1.14(3x) 3.1.16(3x)
        3.2.1 3.3.1 3.3.2
        4.1.1(4x) 4.1.2(2x) 4.1.3(3x) 4.2.2(6x) 4.2.4 4.2.5(3x) 4.2.6(2x)
        4.2.7(4x) 4.2.8 4.2.10(3x) 4.2.11(7x) 4.2.14 4.3.1(4x) 4.3.2 4.3.4
        5.1.2(4x) 5.1.3 5.1.5(4x) 5.1.6(3x) 5.1.7(2x) 5.2.1 5.2.5(3x)
        5.2.7(2x) 5.2.9 5.2.12 5.3.1(2x) 5.3.4 5.3.5 5.3.6 5.3.7 5.3.8
        5.3.9 5.4.1(7x) 5.4.2(3x) 5.4.4(5x) 5.4.6(2x) 5.4.7 5.4.8(3x)
        5.5.1(4x) 5.5.2(3x) 5.5.3(5x) 5.5.4(2x) 5.5.5(5x) 5.6.1(2x)
        5.6.3(2x) 5.6.4(3x) 5.7.0 5.7.1(3x) 5.7.4(2x) 5.8.1(2x) 5.8.2(2x)
        5.9.1(5x) 5.9.2 5.9.4(3x) 5.9.8
        են 1.0.1 1.1.5 1.1.7 1.2.2 1.2.4 1.3.3 1.3.5(2x) 1.4.3 1.4.7 1.4.8
        1.4.9(3x) 1.4.10(3x) 1.4.11 1.5.1 1.5.7 1.5.14(2x) 1.6.1(4x)
        1.6.2 1.6.6(2x) 1.6.7(3x) 1.6.12 1.6.16 1.6.17 1.6.18 2.3.2
        2.3.4(2x) 2.3.5(9x) 2.5.1 2.5.3 2.5.4(2x) 3.1.2 3.1.5(2x) 3.1.9
        3.1.11 3.3.2 4.1.1 4.1.3 4.2.1 4.2.9 4.2.12 4.3.5(2x) 5.1.6 5.2.12
        5.3.2(3x) 5.3.3 5.3.6 5.4.7 5.6.1 5.7.2 5.9.5(2x) 5.9.8
        իցէ 5.8.2
        իցեն 2.5.3
        էր 5.2.4
        ելով 1.6.8 5.2.6 5.2.8
ենթակայ noun [17]
        ենթակայ 3.1.6(2x) 3.2.1
        ենթակայի 5.1.3
        ենթակայում 1.4.2 4.2.2(2x) 5.2.8 5.4.4 5.5.3
        ենթակայէ 3.1.4 3.2.1 4.2.2(2x) 4.2.5 5.2.6
        ենթակայից 5.3.6
ենթականամ verb [2]
        ենթականալ 5.7.3(2x)
ենթիւ adjective [1]
        ենթիւ 4.1.2
երակ noun [1]
        երակ 3.1.9
երակաբար adverb [5]
        երակաբար 1.4.2 1.4.3 4.2.4 5.6.4 5.8.1
երակի adverb [16]
        երակի 1.4.3 1.4.4 1.6.1 1.6.3 3.1.1 3.1.10 3.1.15 4.2.4 4.2.6
        5.2.11 5.3.1 5.3.9 5.4.6 5.4.8 5.5.5 5.9.8

եռանկիւնի noun   [2]
    եռանկիւնի 1.4.3 1.6.4
երակ noun   [3]
    երակս 1.1.5 2.5.4
    երակք 1.5.5
երան noun   [1]
    երանք 1.4.9
երանգ noun   [1]
    երանգք 1.4.2
երբ adverb   [2]
    երբ 4.2.8 4.2.15
երբեմն adverb   [1]
    երբեմն 1.6.8
երեակ adjective   [1]
    երեակք 5.9.7
երեակ noun   [1]
    երեակ 1.3.5
երեակայութիւն noun   [1]
    երեակայութիւն 1.6.13
երեւիմ verb   [7]
    երեւի 1.6.6 5.9.5
    երեւեցաւ 5.2.11 5.3.9 5.4.8 5.6.4
    երեւեալք 1.6.14
երեւումն noun   [5]
    երեւումն 5.5.5 5.7.3
    երեւման 5.1.7 5.1.8
    երեւմանէ 5.1.7
երեք number   [11]
    երեք 2.3.1 2.5.3 5.9.5
    երիս 1.5.2 1.5.6 5.9.4 5.9.6
    երից 1.1.6 1.2.1 1.3.1 5.2.10
երեքտասան number   [1]
    երեքտասանից 5.3.4
երկակենցաղ adjective   [1]
    երկակենցաղս 1.5.2
երկակի adverb   [3]
    երկակի 1.6.3 5.1.7 5.2.5
երկար adjective   [1]
    երկար 1.6.4
երկարումն noun   [1]
    յերկարման 5.3.9
երկբայանամ verb   [1]
    երկբայացեալ 2.4.2
երկդիմի adjective   [1]
    երկդիմի 5.4.6
երկին noun   [9]
    երկին 1.1.2 1.3.3
    երկինս 2.5.3
    երկնի 2.5.2
    երկինք 2.5.1 2.5.4(2x)
    երկնից 1.3.3 2.5.1
երկիր noun   [10]
    երկիր 2.5.1
    երկրի 1.1.5(2x) 1.4.4 1.4.7 1.5.12 2.5.2 2.5.4(2x)
    երկրաւ 1.1.4

երկմեան adjective   [1]
> *երկմեամբ* 3.1.7

երկմանաբար adverb   [1]
> *երկմանաբար* 1.6.15

երկոտասան number   [1]
> *երկոտասան* 1.4.4

երկոտասանեակ noun   [2]
> *երկոտասանեակ* 5.9.7
> *երկոտասանեկին* 3.1.7

երկու number   [7]
> *երկու* 1.6.2 1.6.16 4.2.1 5.6.1
> *երկուս* 1.3.4 4.2.10 4.3.2

երկոքեան noun   [2]
> *երկոցունց* 3.1.10 5.6.4

երկոքին noun   [1]
> *երկուսին* 5.3.6

երկրորդ   numeral ordinal   [15]
> *երկրորդ* 1.1.2 3.1.4 3.1.7 3.1.12 4.2.8 4.2.10 4.3.5(2x)
> 5.2.4 5.3.6 5.4.4 5.6.3 5.7.4 5.9.3
> *երկրորդի* 5.9.2

երրեակ adjective   [2]
> *երրեկի* 1.6.18
> *երրեկով* 3.1.7

երրորդ   numeral ordinal   [8]
> *երրորդ* 1.1.3 1.3.3 3.1.14 4.2.10 5.2.6 5.2.7 5.3.7 5.4.5

երփն noun   [1]
> *երփունք* 1.4.2

եւ conjunction   [683]
> *եւ* 1.1.1(2x) 1.1.2(3x) 1.1.3(2x) 1.1.4(5x) 1.1.5(12x)
> 1.1.6(2x) 1.1.7(2x) 1.2.1 1.2.2(2x) 1.2.3(5x) 1.2.4(2x)
> 1.3.1(3x) 1.3.2 1.3.3(2x) 1.3.4 1.3.5 1.4.1(2x) 1.4.2(4x)
> 1.4.3(5x) 1.4.4(3x) 1.4.5(2x) 1.4.6(2x) 1.4.7 1.4.8(2x)
> 1.4.9(3x) 1.4.10(3x) 1.5.1 1.5.2 1.5.3(3x) 1.5.4(4x) 1.5.5(10x)
> 1.5.6(7x) 1.5.7(6x) 1.5.8(3x) 1.5.10(5x) 1.5.11(2x) 1.5.11(2x)
> 1.5.12(5x) 1.5.13(2x) 1.5.14(2x) 1.6.1(2x) 1.6.2(2x) 1.6.3(4x)
> 1.6.4(4x) 1.6.5(7x) 1.6.6(7x) 1.6.7(5x) 1.6.8(2x) 1.6.9(6x)
> 1.6.10 1.6.11(5x) 1.6.12(4x) 1.6.13(3x) 1.6.14(2x) 1.6.15(4x)
> 1.6.16(5x) 1.6.18(3x)
> 2.1.1 2.2.2(5x) 2.2.3 2.3.1(2x) 2.3.2(2x) 2.3.3(3x) 2.3.4(5x)
> 2.3.5(6x) 2.3.6 2.3.7(2x) 2.4.1(3x) 2.4.2(6x) 2.5.1 2.5.2(3x)
> 2.5.3(6x) 2.5.4(8x) 2.5.5
> 3.1.0 3.1.1(6x) 3.1.2(3x) 3.1.3 3.1.4(4x) 3.1.5(2x) 3.1.6(7x)
> 3.1.7(6x) 3.1.8 3.1.9(5x) 3.1.10(3x) 3.1.11(3x) 3.1.12(6x)
> 3.1.13(4x) 3.1.14(4x) 3.1.15(3x) 3.1.16 3.2.0 3.2.1(5x)
> 3.2.2(4x) 3.2.3(7x) 3.3.0 3.3.1(7x) 3.3.2(3x)
> 4.1.1(6x) 4.1.2(5x) 4.1.3(10x) 4.2.0 4.2.1(4x) 4.2.2(5x)
> 4.2.3(2x) 4.2.4(9x) 4.2.5(8x) 4.2.6(4x) 4.2.7(4x) 4.2.9(4x)
> 4.2.10(7x) 4.2.11(9x) 4.2.12 4.2.13(3x) 4.2.14(7x) 4.2.15(4x)
> 4.3.1(6x) 4.3.2(6x) 4.3.3 4.3.4(3x) 4.3.5(5x)
> 5.1.1(4x) 5.1.2(3x) 5.1.3 5.1.4 5.1.5(7x) 5.1.6(4x) 5.1.7(3x)
> 5.1.8(4x) 5.1.9(5x) 5.1.10(2x) 5.2.1(5x) 5.2.3(2x) 5.2.4(5x)
> 5.2.5(2x) 5.2.6(2x) 5.2.7(3x) 5.2.8(2x) 5.2.9 5.2.10(3x)
> 5.2.11(2x) 5.2.12 5.3.1(2x) 5.3.2(3x) 5.3.3(2x) 5.3.4(4x)
> 5.3.5(4x) 5.3.6(2x) 5.3.7(2x) 5.3.8 5.3.9(3x) 5.4.0 5.4.1(8x)
> 5.4.2(5x) 5.4.3 5.4.4(7x) 5.4.5(2x) 5.4.6(6x) 5.4.7(3x) 5.4.8(3x)

5.5.1(8x) 5.5.2(4x) 5.5.3(7x) 5.5.4(4x) 5.5.5(2x) 5.6.1(5x)
5.6.2(3x) 5.6.3(5x) 5.6.4(3x) 5.7.0(2x) 5.7.1(7x) 5.7.2(6x)
5.7.3(2x) 5.7.4(5x) 5.8.1(4x) 5.8.2(7x) 5.9.1(10x) 5.9.2(2x)
5.9.4(6x) 5.9.5(3x) 5.9.6(8x) 5.9.7(5x) 5.9.8(3x)
6.1.1

եւթն number [3]
> *եւթն* 1.3.3 1.3.5(2x)

եւս adverb [2]
> *եւս* 1.4.2 5.2.10

զ nota accusativi [57]
> *զ* 1.1.1 1.3.2 1.3.3(3x) 1.3.5 1.5.10 1.6.2 1.6.6 1.6.17(2x)
> 1.6.18(2x) 2.0.0 2.5.1(2x) 2.5.3 2.5.5 3.1.0 3.1.4 3.1.6
> 3.1.10 3.1.12 3.1.15(2x) 4.1.0 4.2.5 4.3.2(5x) 5.1.2(2x)
> 5.1.4 5.1.6(2x) 5.1.8 5.1.9 5.2.1 5.2.2 5.2.3 5.2.4 5.2.5 5.2.7
> 5.2.9 5.3.2 5.3.7 5.3.9 5.5.5 5.7.3 5.9.2 5.9.4 5.9.6(3x) 5.9.7

զ preposition [12]
> *զ* 1.1.4 1.2.4 1.3.4 1.5.4 2.5.2 3.1.10 3.1.15 3.2.1 4.2.2(2x)
> 4.2.5(2x)

զանազան adjective [2]
> *զանազան* 1.6.3 5.3.4

զանազանեմ verb [24]
> *զանազանի* 1.4.2 1.4.3 1.5.3 1.5.6 1.6.4 3.1.3 3.2.2 3.2.3 4.2.2
> 5.1.1 5.1.6 5.2.4 5.3.6 5.4.2 5.4.3 5.4.5 5.5.3 5.6.2 5.7.3
> *զանազանին* 1.5.7 1.6.5 1.6.6
> *զանազանեալ* 4.1.1
> *զանազանեալք* 1.4.2

զանազանիչ noun [1]
> *զանազանիչք* 4.3.5

զանազանութիւն noun [10]
> *զանազանութիւն* 1.5.6
> *զանազանութեան* 4.1.2 4.3.0 5.2.6
> *զանազանութեամբ* 1.3.2 3.1.3
> *զանազանութեանց* 1.6.2 3.1.3 5.5.1 5.5.2

զանցանեմ verb [1]
> *զանցեալ* 5.9.3

զատութիւն noun [1]
> *զատութեանց* 5.3.9

զաւրաւիգն adjective [1]
> *զաւրաւիգն* 1.5.10

զաւրութիւն noun [16]
> *զաւրութիւն* 1.1.4 2.5.2 2.5.3
> *զաւրութեան* 1.5.12(2x) 1.5.14 3.3.1 4.2.14
> *զաւրութեամբ* 2.5.2
> *զաւրութիւնք* 1.0.1 1.6.17 5.3.5
> *զաւրութեանց* 1.5.0 1.5.1 5.3.6 5.9.6

զգալի adjective [5]
> *զգալի* 5.6.1
> *զգալիս* 5.3.3
> *զգալոյ* 5.6.1 5.6.4
> *զգալեացս* 1.1.3

զգայական adjective [3]
> *զգայական* 1.5.12 1.6.7(2x)

զգայութիւն noun [7]
> *զգայութիւն* 1.6.13 4.2.12
> *զգայութիւնս* 1.1.4

   զզայութեանց 1.5.11 5.3.6(2x)
   զզայութեամբք 3.1.11
զզայուն adjective [2]
   զզայուն 2.2.3 4.2.4
գենոն name [1]
   գենոնի 0.0.0
գերուն noun [1]
   գերնոց 1.1.4
զի conjunction [59]
   զի 1.1.7 1.2.2 1.3.1 1.4.3 1.5.2 1.5.5 1.5.7 1.5.10 1.5.11
   1.5.12 1.6.1 1.6.2 1.6.6(2x) 1.6.7 1.6.11 2.1.1 2.2.3 2.3.7
   3.1.1 3.1.13 4.1.1 4.1.2 4.1.3 4.2.2 4.2.5 4.2.7 4.2.9 4.3.1
   4.3.2 5.1.2 5.1.4 5.1.5(2x) 5.1.6 5.2.5 5.2.12 5.3.6(2x)
   5.3.7 5.3.9 5.4.1 5.4.2(2x) 5.4.4 5.4.8 5.5.5(2x) 5.6.1
   5.6.4 5.7.1 5.7.2 5.7.4 5.8.1 5.8.2 5.9.2 5.9.3(2x) 5.9.4
զի interrogative pronoun [3]
   է՞ր 3.1.2 3.1.7
   ի՞ւ 3.1.3
զիարդ adverb [2]
   զիարդ 2.5.1 2.5.2
զի՞նչ interrogative pronoun [2]
   զի՞նչ 3.1.2
   զի՞նչ 3.1.3
զինչէ noun [1]
   զինչէում 4.2.5
զկնի preposition [1]
   զկնի 5.3.9
գոյզ adjective [3]
   գոյզ 1.5.7 4.2.5 4.2.10
գուարթութիւն noun [1]
   գուարթութենէ 2.4.2
գուգակցութիւն noun [1]
   գուգակցութեամբ 2.5.1
գուգեմ verb [1]
   գուգեալք 1.2.2
գրուցատրութիւն noun [1]
   գրուցատրութիւն 2.3.2
է noun [1]
   էին 5.4.5
էագոյն adjective [2]
   էագոյն 5.9.2
   էագունից 5.9.2
էակ noun [14]
   էակ 3.1.6 5.4.7 5.6.3(2x)
   էակի 5.1.9 5.2.7 5.5.3
   էակաց 1.6.10 3.1.5 3.1.7 3.1.11 4.2.0 4.2.3 5.9.3
էական adjective [2]
   էականի 5.3.7
   էականաց 5.2.7
էականութիւն noun [7]
   էականութիւն 1.6.11 5.6.4
   էականութեան 4.3.5 5.4.3 5.6.0 5.6.1 5.6.3
լմրունեմ verb [1]
   լմրունիլ 3.1.12

ընդ preposition [27]
    ընդ 1.1.3 1.1.4 1.1.5(2x) 1.1.7 1.3.3(2x) 1.3.4 1.6.10 1.6.15
    1.6.16 1.6.18 2.5.1 2.5.3 2.5.4 3.1.10 3.1.13 3.1.15 5.1.1 5.2.5
    5.4.6 5.4.7 5.4.8 5.5.4 5.5.5 5.8.1(2x)
ընդդէմ preposition [1]
    ընդդէմ 4.3.1
ընդդիմակայ adjective [1]
    ընդդիմակայք 4.3.1
ընդդիմակաց adjective [1]
    ընդդիմակաց 4.2.6
ընդկայութիւն noun [1]
    ընդկայութիւն 4.2.13
ընդկողմանումն noun [1]
    ընդկողմանումն 4.2.13
ընդհանուր adjective [8]
    ընդհանուր 5.9.1
    ընթանուր 5.2.6 5.4.4 5.6.1(2x) 5.6.2(2x) 5.9.8
ընդունակ adjective [2]
    ընդունակ 5.1.10
    ընդունակք 1.1.5
ընդունայն adjective [1]
    ընդունայն 5.8.2
ընդունելութիւն noun [2]
    ընդունելութիւն 2.3.4 2.3.5
ընդունիմ verb [3]
    ընդունի 1.6.6 3.1.4
    ընկալեալ 1.5.10
ընթացք noun [1]
    ընթացից 1.6.18
ընտրեմ verb [2]
    ընտրեցան 1.4.4
    ընտրել 3.1.13
ընտրողական adjective [1]
    ընտրողական 1.3.3
ընտրողութիւն noun [1]
    ընտրողութիւն 1.6.12
ընտրութիւն noun [1]
    ընտրութեան 2.3.3
ըստ preposition [274]
    ըստ 1.1.7(3x) 1.2.1(4x) 1.2.2(3x) 1.2.3(3x) 1.3.1 1.3.2 1.3.3
    1.3.4 1.3.5(2x) 1.4.1(5x) 1.4.2 1.4.3(4x) 1.4.4(6x) 1.4.5(2x)
    1.4.6(2x) 1.4.7(2x) 1.4.11 1.5.2(3x) 1.5.3(5x) 1.5.4 1.5.5(4x)
    1.5.6(4x) 1.5.7(4x) 1.5.9 1.5.10(2x) 1.5.11(3x) 1.5.12(4x)
    1.5.13(3x) 1.5.14(2x) 1.6.2 1.6.3(3x) 1.6.4(3x) 1.6.6 1.6.8
    1.6.16(5x)
    2.1.1(3x) 2.2.2(3x) 2.2.3 2.3.2(2x) 2.3.3(6x) 2.3.4(2x) 2.3.5(2x)
    2.3.6(3x) 2.3.7(2x) 2.4.1 2.4.2(3x)
    3.1.3 3.1.4 3.1.6(3x) 3.1.8 3.1.9 3.1.10 3.1.12 3.1.16 3.2.3(2x)
    3.3.1(8x)
    4.1.2(3x) 4.2.2(4x) 4.2.4(3x) 4.2.5 4.2.7 4.2.9 4.2.10(3x)
    4.2.11 4.2.13 4.2.14(10x) 4.2.15(3x) 4.3.2 4.3.3(3x) 4.3.4(5x)
    5.1.1(6x) 5.1.5 5.1.7 5.2.2(2x) 5.2.3 5.2.4(3x) 5.2.5(3x)
    5.2.6(3x) 5.2.7(2x) 5.2.8 5.2.9(2x) 5.2.10 5.2.11 5.3.1(2x)
    5.3.2 5.3.4 5.3.5 5.3.6(3x) 5.3.7(3x) 5.3.8 5.3.9(2x) 5.4.1(3x)
    5.4.2(4x) 5.4.3(2x) 5.4.5(4x) 5.4.6(4x) 5.4.7 5.5.2(2x)

5.5.3(3x) 5.5.4 5.5.5(2x) 5.6.2(5x) 5.6.3(2x) 5.6.4(3x)
5.7.3(2x) 5.7.4 5.8.1 5.8.2 5.9.1(3x) 5.9.2(2x) 5.9.3(2x)
5.9.4 5.9.5 5.9.6 5.9.7 5.9.8

թագաւոր noun [2]
  թագաւոր 3.1.14
  թագաւորաց 3.1.14
թաթ noun [1]
  թաթք 1.4.10
թանձրութիւն noun [3]
  թանձրութեան 1.5.3 5.7.3
  թանձրութեամբ 1.1.5
թէ conjunction [4]
  թէ 1.5.4 3.1.2 5.1.4 5.8.2
թէեւ conjunction [1]
  թէեւ 5.1.2
թէկն noun [1]
  թիկանց 1.5.8
թթու adjective [1]
  թթու 1.5.6
թիւ noun [12]
  թիւ 1.4.3 3.1.10 4.1.2 4.2.11(2x)
  թուոյ 3.3.1
  թուով 1.4.4
  թիւք 5.3.1 5.3.2(2x) 5.5.1
  թուոց 5.2.1
թողում verb [1]
  թողլով 5.9.8
թուականութիւն noun [2]
  թուականութեան 1.4.1 3.1.7
թուեմ verb [1]
  թուեալ 4.2.10
թուխ adjective [1]
  թուխ 1.5.6
թոչուն noun [1]
  թոչնոց 2.2.2
ժամ noun [2]
  ժամք 5.3.2
  ժամուց 1.6.18
ժամանակ noun [34]
  ժամանակ 1.6.2 1.6.11 4.2.11(2x) 5.3.1 5.3.5 5.3.6 5.3.9
  ժամանակս 1.3.5 1.5.13
  ժամանակի 1.1.7 1.4.4 1.5.2 1.5.3 1.5.7 1.5.11 1.5.12 1.5.14
  1.6.5 1.6.17(2x) 2.2.3 2.3.7 3.3.1 4.3.2 4.3.3(2x) 5.2.2 5.3.0
  5.3.8 5.4.1(2x)
  ժամանակաւ 5.3.6
  ժամանակաց 5.3.2
ժողովեմ verb [1]
  ժողովեաց 2.5.2
ժողովումն noun [2]
  ժողովումն 3.1.6
  ժողովման 1.6.14
ի preposition [321]
  ի 1.1.1(3x) 1.1.4 1.1.5(5x) 1.1.6 1.1.7(2x) 1.2.2 1.2.4(2x)
  1.3.1(3x) 1.3.2(2x) 1.3.5 1.4.2(2x) 1.4.3(2x) 1.5.2(3x) 1.5.3
  1.5.4 1.5.7 1.5.8(4x) 1.5.10(2x) 1.5.11(2x) 1.5.12(3x)

1.5.13(2x) 1.6.3(5x) 1.6.4(2x) 1.6.5(3x) 1.6.6 1.6.7 1.6.8(3x)
1.6.9(11x) 1.6.10(3x) 1.6.14 1.6.15 1.6.18
2.1.1(3x) 2.2.3(2x) 2.3.7(3x) 2.4.1(2x) 2.4.2(2x) 2.5.3(3x)
3.1.1(2x) 3.1.2 3.1.3(3x) 3.1.4(2x) 3.1.6 3.1.9(3x) 3.1.12
3.1.15 3.2.1(5x) 3.3.2
4.1.0 4.1.1 4.1.3(2x) 4.2.2 4.2.3(5x) 4.2.4(2x) 4.2.5(3x)
4.2.6(2x) 4.2.8(2x) 4.2.13(2x) 4.3.4
5.1.1 5.1.2(2x) 5.1.3 5.1.4(2x) 5.1.5(3x) 5.1.6(4x) 5.1.7(3x)
5.1.8(3x) 5.1.9 5.2.1(5x) 5.2.2 5.2.3(2x) 5.2.5 5.2.6 5.2.7(2x)
5.2.10 5.2.11 5.2.12 5.3.2 5.3.3 5.3.5 5.3.6 5.3.7 5.3.8(2x) 5.4.2
5.4.4 5.4.6(2x) 5.5.1(3x) 5.5.2(2x) 5.5.3 5.5.5(2x) 5.6.1
5.7.1(2x) 5.7.2(2x) 5.7.3 5.7.4(2x) 5.8.1(2x) 5.8.2(3x)
5.9.4(2x) 5.9.7
յ 1.1.1 1.1.2(2x) 1.1.5 1.1.7 1.2.2(2x) 1.2.4 1.3.1(2x) 1.3.4(5x)
1.3.5(2x) 1.4.3 1.4.4 1.4.5 1.4.6 1.5.2 1.5.4 1.5.5(3x) 1.5.6
1.5.7(2x) 1.5.10 1.5.11(2x) 1.5.12(3x) 1.5.13 1.6.5(2x) 1.6.6
1.6.9(3x) 1.6.10(3x) 1.6.14 1.6.15
2.3.2 2.3.7 2.5.1 2.5.3 2.5.4(2x)
3.1.1 3.1.4(3x) 3.1.8 3.1.10 3.1.12 3.1.13 3.2.1
4.1.3(2x) 4.2.2(2x) 4.2.10 4.3.3 4.3.5
5.1.4 5.1.7(3x) 5.1.8 5.1.10 5.2.1 5.2.4 5.2.6 5.2.7(3x) 5.2.8
5.2.9(2x) 5.2.10(2x) 5.2.11 5.2.12 5.3.1(2x) 5.3.2 5.3.4(2x)
5.3.5 5.3.6(2x) 5.4.3 5.4.4 5.4.6(2x) 5.5.1 5.5.3 5.6.1(3x)
5.6.4 5.7.3(4x) 5.7.4(2x) 5.8.2 5.9.2(2x) 5.9.3(2x) 5.9.7

ի ձեռն preposition [8]
    ի ձեռն 1.1.4 1.3.1 1.4.4 1.6.5 1.6.10 2.3.5 4.1.0 5.6.3

ի մէջ preposition [1]
    ի մէջ 2.5.2

ի ներքոյ preposition [1]
    ի ներքոյ 4.2.5

ի ներքուստ adverb [1]
    ի ներքուստ 5.1.6

ի ներքս adverb [1]
    ի ներքս 1.1.6

ի վերայ preposition [10]
    ի վերա 3.1.0
    ի վերայ 1.6.5 1.6.6(2x) 1.6.17 2.0.0 2.3.5 2.5.4 5.3.7
    յ ... վերայ 2.5.4

ի վերոյ adverb [1]
    ի վերոյ 3.2.1

իբր conjunction [1]
    իբր 3.1.15

իբրեւ conjunction [3]
    իբրեւ 3.1.15(2x) 4.2.5

իբրու adverb [1]
    իբրու 3.1.14

իզական adjective [2]
    իզական 1.5.5
    իզականք 1.4.11

իմանալի adjective [4]
    իմանալի 1.3.3 5.1.6 5.6.1
    իմանալոյ 5.6.1

իմանամ verb [1]
    իմացեալք 5.7.1

իմանիմ verb [1]
  իմանին 5.2.11
իմաստ noun [3]
  իմաստք 1.6.13 5.9.1
  իմաստից 2.4.2
իմաստական adjective [1]
  իմաստական 1.6.9
իմաստակութիւն noun [2]
  իմաստակութիւն 3.3.1
  իմաստակութեան 3.3.0
իմաստասէր adjective [2]
  իմաստասիրի 0.0.0 1.6.18
իմաստասիրութիւն noun [5]
  իմաստասիրութիւն 3.1.5 3.1.15(2x)
  իմաստասիրութեան 3.1.5 3.1.7
իմաստնացուցիչ noun [2]
  իմաստնացուցիչք 1.6.1 1.6.3
իմաստութիւն noun [2]
  իմաստութիւն 3.1.15
  իմաստութեան 3.1.5
իմաց noun [1]
  իմացս 1.2.2
իմացական adjective [5]
  իմացական 1.6.9 3.1.14
  իմացականի 1.6.11 1.6.13 3.1.9
իմացուած noun [8]
  իմացուած 1.6.7 1.6.8 4.1.3(3x)
  իմացուածս 1.5.10
  իմացուածի 4.1.3
  իմացուածէ 4.1.3
իմացութիւն noun [1]
  իմացութեամբ 5.4.8
իմացումն noun [4]
  իմացմունք 5.9.8
  իմացմունս 4.3.2
  իմացմանց 1.6.7 1.6.8
իմն indefinite pronoun [3]
  իմն 1.5.4 5.1.1 5.1.7
իննակի adverb [1]
  իննակի 5.2.6
իննետասաներեակ noun [1]
  իննետասաներեակ 5.3.3
ինչ noun [1]
  ինչս 2.5.3
ինչ indefinite pronoun [8]
  ինչ 3.1.4 4.2.11 5.2.4(2x) 5.3.6 5.7.1(2x) 5.8.2
ինքն pronoun [3]
  ինքեան 4.2.4 5.3.7
  ինքենէ 5.9.2
ինքնաշարժ adjective [1]
  ինքնաշարժ 1.3.5
իսկ conjunction [129]
  իսկ 1.4.3 1.4.11 1.5.7 1.5.12 1.6.3 1.6.5 1.6.7 2.1.1 2.3.7 2.5.4
  3.1.10 3.1.13 3.1.14(2x) 3.2.1(3x) 4.1.2 4.1.3 4.2.10 4.2.11
  4.2.15 5.1.4 5.1.6 5.1.7 5.1.8 5.1.10 5.2.1 5.2.2 5.2.5 5.2.6

        5.2.7 5.2.8 5.2.9 5.2.11 5.3.5 5.3.6 5.3.7 5.3.8 5.4.3 5.4.5 5.5.1
        5.5.3 5.5.4 5.5.5 5.6.1(2x) 5.6.2 5.6.3 5.7.2 5.7.4(2x) 5.8.1
        5.8.2

իսկագոյն adjective   [1]
        իսկագոյն 4.2.10

իսկապէս adverb   [3]
        իսկապէս 1.2.3 1.6.5 1.6.8

իտալացի noun   [1]
        իտալացւոց 1.4.9

իր noun   [16]
        իր 1.6.7 2.0.1 4.1.1(3x) 4.1.3
        իրի 1.6.7 4.1.2(2x) 4.1.3
        իրէ 4.1.3 5.8.2
        իրք 5.7.1
        իրաց 2.3.1 3.1.4
        իրաւք 2.3.5

իւր personal pronoun   [4]
        իւր 1.1.1 1.1.7 2.5.2
        իւրում 1.5.10

իւր reflexive pronoun   [1]
        իւրեանց 1.3.5

իւրաքանչիւր indefinite pronoun   [17]
        իւրաքանչիւր 1.1.4 1.1.7 1.2.2 1.3.5 5.2.1 5.2.2 5.2.4 5.3.6
        5.9.4 5.9.7
        իւրաքանչիւրս 5.2.7 5.2.9 5.2.11
        իւրաքանչիւրոց 1.2.4 5.3.1 5.3.6
        իւրաքանչիւրովք 5.2.6

իւրովին adverb   [1]
        իւրովին 2.5.2

լայնանիստ adjective   [1]
        լայնանիստ 2.5.4

լանջք noun   [1]
        լանջք 1.4.7

լեառն noun   [1]
        լերամբք 1.1.5

լեզու noun   [1]
        լեզուաց 2.3.2

լինելոց verb   [1]
        լինելոցք 5.2.4

լինելութիւն noun   [5]
        լինելութիւն 1.5.3 1.5.4 4.3.4
        լինելութեան 1.6.6
        լինելութիւնք 4.3.3

լինիմ verb   [21]
        լինի 1.2.3 1.5.7 1.5.11 1.6.15 2.4.1 2.4.2 3.2.1 4.2.9 5.1.5
        լինին 1.1.5 1.5.7 2.4.2 5.3.2
        եղեալք 5.2.4
        լինել 1.4.7 1.5.10 1.5.13(2x) 5.2.4 5.3.4 5.7.2

լոյս noun   [2]
        լուսոյ 1.1.2 1.5.4

լուծումն noun   [2]
        լուծումն 1.5.11 5.3.6

լուդակ noun   [1]
        լուդակաց 2.2.2

լուապեր adjective [1]
    լուապեր 1.3.5

լուին noun [1]
    լուին 1.3.5

լուանթագ noun [1]
    լուանթագ 1.3.5

լուանուտ adjective [1]
    լուանուտք 1.5.8

լռութին noun [2]
    լռութին 3.1.4 3.1.6

լսեմ verb [3]
    լսիցես 2.5.1
    լսել 3.1.10 3.1.15

լրումն noun [2]
    լրումն 5.3.4 5.9.7

խապէութին noun [1]
    խապէութին 2.4.1

խախտումն noun [1]
    խախտումն 2.4.2

խադամ verb [1]
    խադացեալ 1.1.5

խադացումն noun [1]
    խադացումն 5.3.1

խամութին noun [1]
    խամութենէ 2.4.1

խատն adjective [7]
    խատն 1.5.13 5.5.4
    խատնս 5.8.1
    խատնից 1.5.3 1.5.11 5.1.7 5.3.6

խատնակցութին noun [1]
    խատնակցութեանց 1.5.3

խատնեմ verb [2]
    խատնեալ 2.5.1(2x)

խատնուած noun [4]
    խատնուած 1.5.5
    խատնուածոյ 1.5.6 1.5.13
    խատնուածք 1.6.3

խարտեաշ adjective [1]
    խարտեաշ 1.5.6

խասիմ verb [3]
    խասել 3.1.10 3.1.15
    խասելոյ 5.9.4

խասք noun [1]
    խասք 2.2.3

խեգզետի noun [2]
    խեգզետի 1.4.5 1.4.11
    խեգզետին 1.4.7

խզումն noun [1]
    խզումն 3.1.12

խիտ adjective [1]
    խիտ 1.1.5

խնդիր noun [2]
    խնդրոց 5.2.2 5.4.2

խնդրական adjective   [3]
    խնդրական 1.6.10
    խնդրականի 4.1.0 4.1.1
խոկումն noun   [1]
    խոկումն 3.1.5
խոյ noun   [3]
    խոյ 1.4.5 1.4.7 1.4.11
խոնաային adjective   [1]
    խոնաայինս 1.5.2
խոնաումն noun   [1]
    խոնաումն 5.7.2
խորհուրդ noun   [4]
    խորհուրդ 5.9.8
    խորհուրդք 1.5.10 1.6.13 5.9.1
խուն noun   [1]
    խուն 5.5.4
խորվութին noun   [1]
    խորվութենէ 2.4.2
խստութին noun   [1]
    խստութենէ 1.5.8
ծախեմ verb   [1]
    ծախիլ 1.5.11
ծածուկ adjective   [1]
    ծածուկ 2.5.4
ծանաւթութին noun   [2]
    ծանաւթութին 5.9.4
    ծանաւթութեան 1.6.7
ծնանիմ verb   [1]
    ծնանի 1.5.10
ծնելութին noun   [1]
    ծնելութենէ 1.5.12
ծննդաբաշխական adjective   [1]
    ծննդաբաշխական 1.5.1
ծննդաբաշխութին noun   [2]
    ծննդաբաշխութին 1.5.2
    ծննդաբաշխութեան 1.4.11
ծննդական adjective   [1]
    ծննդականք 1.1.5
ծննդականութին noun   [1]
    ծննդականութեան 1.4.4
ծնող adjective   [1]
    ծնող 5.9.4
ծնունդ noun   [5]
    ծնունդ 5.9.4
    ծննդեան 1.5.4
    ծննդեանց 1.6.5
    ծննդից 5.3.9
    ծննդիւք 5.1.9
ծով noun   [7]
    ծով 2.5.4
    ծովու 1.1.4 1.1.5 1.4.10
    ծովէ 2.5.3 2.5.4
    ծովուց 1.1.5
ծորումն noun   [1]
    ծորման 1.1.4

ծունր noun [1]
    ծունկք 1.4.10
կազթեանք name [1]
    կազթեանց 2.1.1
կազմիչ noun [1]
    կազմիչ 5.9.6
կազմութիւն noun [1]
    կազմութեան 2.3.6
կալումն noun [1]
    կալմունք 1.6.14
կամ conjunction [23]
    կամ 1.5.3(4x) 1.5.4 1.5.6 1.5.11(2x) 2.2.1 2.2.3 2.3.7 3.1.4
    4.1.1 4.1.2 4.2.9(2x) 5.1.1 5.2.5(3x) 5.3.3 5.3.6(2x)
կամ noun [4]
    կամաւ 1.6.6(2x)
    կամք 1.6.12
    կամաւք 5.9.5
կամ verb [5]
    կայ 1.1.4 1.1.5 5.1.4
    կայ 4.2.8 4.2.15
կամիմ verb [1]
    կամել 3.1.13
կանգնեմ verb [1]
    կանգնեաց 2.5.2
կապ noun [1]
    կապ 2.3.5
կապոյտ adjective [2]
    կապոյտ 1.4.2 1.6.3
կապուած noun [1]
    կապուած 1.1.6
կառուցումն noun [2]
    կառուցմամբ 1.1.1 5.3.8
կատարած noun [24]
    կատարած 1.6.11 5.3.5 5.4.1(6x) 5.4.2(2x) 5.4.3 5.4.4(3x)
    5.4.5 5.4.6 5.4.8(2x) 5.9.1
    կատարածի 5.1.1 5.2.4(2x) 5.4.0 5.4.7
կատարելագոյն adjective [5]
    կատարելագոյն 5.2.1 5.2.5 5.2.7
    կատարելագոյնք 5.2.3 5.2.11
կատարելական adjective [2]
    կատարելական 5.2.4
    կատարելականի 5.2.12
կատարելութիւն noun [5]
    կատարելութիւն 1.6.11 5.2.1 5.2.11
    կատարելութեան 2.0.0 4.2.7
կատարեմ verb [27]
    կատարին 4.2.9 5.3.3
    կատարեցաւ 4.3.5 5.2.4
    կատարեցան 5.9.7
    կատարեալ 1.6.4 1.6.15 3.1.4(2x) 3.1.7 3.1.9 4.2.10 5.2.0
    5.2.1(2x) 5.2.5 5.2.7(2x) 5.2.8 5.2.10 5.2.11 5.2.12 5.3.3
    կատարեալք 2.3.4 5.2.4 5.2.6 5.2.9
կատարիլ noun [1]
    կատարիլք 5.2.4

կատարումն noun [13]
    կատարումն 1.3.2 3.1.6(2x) 5.2.2 5.2.4 5.3.2 5.4.2
    կատարման 5.2.12 5.3.4 5.6.3
    կատարմանէ 3.1.4 5.2.6
    կատարմունք 5.3.2

կար noun [1]
    կարիւ 3.1.12

կարգ noun [5]
    կարգք 1.0.1 1.2.1 1.6.17
    կարգաց 1.2.0
    կարգաւք 5.3.2

կարգեմ verb [5]
    կարգեցաւ 4.3.5
    կարգեցան 3.3.2
    կարգեալ 1.1.7 1.2.4 1.3.3

կարեմ verb [1]
    կարել 3.1.13

կարիճ noun [3]
    կարիճ 1.4.6 1.4.9 1.4.11

կարծեմ verb [2]
    կարծեցին 5.8.2
    կարծել 5.8.2

կարծիք noun [2]
    կարծիք 1.6.13 2.4.2

կարճապատութիւն noun [1]
    կարճապատութեամբ 3.2.2

կարմիր adjective [1]
    կարմիր 1.4.10

կացադրութիւն noun [1]
    կացադրութիւնս 1.6.10

կացրդական adjective [2]
    կացրդական 2.3.7(2x)

կեանք noun [6]
    կեանք 3.1.6
    կենաց 1.1.5 1.2.3 1.5.10 1.5.11 3.1.12

կենդանի adjective [4]
    կենդանի 4.2.4
    կենդանեաց 1.1.2 1.1.4 2.2.3

կենդանութիւն noun [3]
    կենդանութեան 1.1.6 1.5.13
    կենդանութեամբ 1.5.4

կենցաղական adjective [1]
    կենցաղական 5.3.3

կերակրեմ verb [1]
    կերակրի 1.5.12

կերպ noun [1]
    կերպի 4.2.14

կերպարան noun [3]
    կերպարան 1.6.3 1.6.5(2x)

կերպարանումն noun [1]
    կերպարանումն 2.4.1

կէս adjective [1]
    կիսով 3.1.7

կէտ noun [1]
    կիտից 1.1.4

կիզողութիւն noun [1]
    կիզողութեան 1.1.3
կիզումն noun [1]
    կիզումն 5.7.2
կիսագունդ noun [1]
    կիսագունդս 1.3.4
կիր noun [3]
    կրից 1.5.3 1.5.11 5.3.6
կիլիկացի noun [1]
    կիլիկացիք 1.4.9
կծու adjective [1]
    կծու 1.5.6
կշեռ noun [4]
    կշեռ 1.4.6 1.4.11 1.5.7
    կշեռն 1.4.9
կող noun [1]
    կողք 1.4.8
կողմն noun [2]
    կողման 1.5.2 1.5.3
    կողմանց 1.1.5 1.3.4 1.4.2 1.4.4
կոճատ noun [3]
    կոճատ 1.4.3 3.1.9 3.1.10
կոճատադար adjective [1]
    կոճատադարուց 3.1.8
կոյս noun [3]
    կոյս 1.4.5 1.4.8 1.4.11
կործանումն noun [1]
    կործանմունք 1.2.3
կոթունք noun [1]
    կոթունք 1.4.9
կրեմ verb [4]
    կրի 1.6.4
    կրին 5.1.6
    կրել 4.2.8 4.2.15
կրետացի noun [1]
    կրետացինց 1.4.9
կրկին adjective [1]
    կրկին 3.1.1
կցորդեմ verb [1]
    կցորդին 5.5.5
հակադարձ adjective [2]
    հակադարձի 4.2.7 4.2.13
հակադարձաբար adverb [1]
    հակադարձաբար 3.2.2
հակադրութիւն noun [3]
    հակադրութեան 4.3.2 4.3.3
    հակադրութեամբ 3.2.3
հակառակ adjective [1]
    հակառակ 1.5.13
համայն adjective [1]
    համայն 5.1.10
համանգամայն adjective [7]
    համանգամայն 1.3.2 1.5.4 5.2.1 5.2.3 5.3.3
    համանգամայնք 5.2.11 5.3.6

Համար noun [1]
  Համար 2.5.1
Համեմատութիւն noun [1]
  Համեմատութեան 2.3.2
Համեստական adjective [2]
  Համեստական 2.1.1 (2x)
Հայ noun [1]
  Հայոց 1.4.7
Հայր noun [1]
  Հաւր 5.9.5
Հանգէտ adjective [1]
  Հանգէտ 5.5.1
Հանգիտութիւն noun [2]
  Հանգիտութեան 1.4.3 1.6.2
Հանդերձ preposition [1]
  Հանդերձ 2.3.5
Հանդիպիմ verb [1]
  Հանդիպին 1.2.3
Հանդիպումն noun [1]
  Հանդիպմանց 1.6.2
Հանրական adjective [1]
  Հանրական 5.8.1
Հասարակ adjective [3]
  Հասարակ 4.1.1 4.1.2
  Հասարակաց 1.4.4
Հասարակաբար adverb [2]
  Հասարակաբար 4.2.6 4.2.9
Հասարակածիր adjective [2]
  Հասարակածիր 1.4.5 1.4.6
Հասողական adjective [1]
  Հասողական 5.6.4
Հասումն noun [1]
  Հասումն 5.9.3
Հաստադիմակայ adjective [1]
  Հաստադիմակայից 1.1.6
Հաստատեմ verb [3]
  Հաստատի 5.1.2
  Հաստատեալ 1.1.4 1.1.5
Հաստատութիւն noun [3]
  Հաստատութիւն 1.1.3 1.3.3 1.5.7
Հաստատուն adjective [5]
  Հաստատուն 1.6.17 5.5.1
  Հաստատնով 1.1.4 1.1.7 1.3.3
Հաստատրանական adjective [1]
  Հաստատրանական 3.2.3
Հաստեմ verb [1]
  Հաստեալ 2.5.4
Հաստիչ noun [1]
  Հաստիչ 5.9.6
Հատ noun [1]
  Հատից 5.2.3
Հատած noun [5]
  Հատած 1.4.3 5.2.3
  Հատածք 3.1.3 5.2.6 5.3.5

Հատուած noun [1]
  Հատուածիւք 5.4.8
Հատումն noun [1]
  Հատումն 1.5.3
Հատուցական adjective [1]
  Հատուցական 3.2.3
Հարաւ noun [1]
  Հարաւոյ 1.4.6
Հարթ adjective [1]
  Հարթ 1.3.4
Հարկաբար adverb [1]
  Հարկաբար 1.5.10
Հարկեմ verb [3]
  Հարկի 1.6.6 5.2.4 5.3.4
Հարցական adjective [1]
  Հարցական 3.2.2
Հարցումն noun [1]
  Հարցմամբ 3.2.2
Հաւանական adjective [1]
  Հաւանական 3.2.3
Հաւատ noun [1]
  Հաւատոյ 1.6.16
Հեռի adjective [4]
  Հեռի 3.1.6(2x) 5.4.2(2x)
Հետեւեմ verb [2]
  Հետեւին 1.2.3 5.3.5
Հիմնական adjective [1]
  Հիմնական 5.4.1
Հինգ number [2]
  Հինգ 4.2.4 5.3.5
Հինգերորդ numeral ordinal [3]
  Հինգերորդ 1.1.5 5.1.5 5.2.9
Հիւանդութիւն noun [3]
  Հիւանդութենէ 1.5.11
  Հիւանդութիւնք 1.5.7(2x)
Հիւթ noun [1]
  Հիւթից 3.3.2
Հիախ adjective [1]
  Հիախոյ 1.4.5
Հմտանամ verb [1]
  Հմտացիս 2.5.2
Հմտութիւն noun [2]
  Հմտութիւն 2.3.1(2x)
Հնագէտ adjective [1]
  Հնագէտ 2.3.2
Հնագոյն adjective [1]
  Հնագոյն 4.3.2
Հնարական adjective [1]
  Հնարական 3.1.16
Հնդիկ noun [1]
  Հնդկաց 1.4.10
Հոգացողութիւն noun [1]
  Հոգացողութիւն 2.1.1
Հոգի noun [3]
  Հոգւոյ 1.5.3 1.5.10 5.9.5

Յոլովեմ verb   [1]
          Յոլովի 5.6.3
Յոլովումն noun   [7]
          Յոլովման 4.3.3(2x) 5.2.3 5.4.6
          Յոլովմամբ 2.3.4
          Յոլովմանց 3.1.4 5.2.4
Յոծ adjective   [1]
          Յոծ 1.1.5
Յող noun   [2]
          Յող 1.4.6 2.5.1
Յողմ noun   [3]
          Յողմք 1.1.5
          Յողմոց 1.1.4 2.5.2
Յոմանուն adjective   [1]
          Յոմանուն 3.3.1
Յոսանուտ adjective   [1]
          Յոսանուտ 5.3.4
Յոռումն noun   [2]
          Յոռման 1.1.3
          Յոռմանէ 1.5.3
Յոռ noun   [1]
          Յոռող 1.5.6
Յուպ adjective   [5]
          Յուպ 3.1.6(2x) 5.2.6 5.4.2(2x)
Յուր noun   [3]
          Յուր 1.4.5
          Յրոյ 1.1.2 1.5.4
Յոստատի noun   [1]
          Յոստատի 2.5.3
Յրայից adjective   [1]
          Յրայիցք 1.1.5
Յրամ ան noun   [5]
          Յրաման 2.5.1 5.1.7 5.1.8
          Յրամանէ 5.1.7 5.3.8
Յրատ noun   [1]
          Յրատ 1.3.5
Յրեշտակ noun   [4]
          Յրեշտակք 1.2.2
          Յրեշտակաց 5.9.4(2x) 5.9.6
Ճախ adjective   [1]
          Ճախ 1.4.8
Ճարդ noun   [1]
          Ճարդ 1.5.6
Ճայն noun   [19]
          Ճայն 1.6.7 4.1.1(3x) 4.1.3(3x)
          Ճայնի 2.3.5 4.1.2(2x)
          Ճայնէ 1.6.8 4.1.3
          Ճայնիւ 3.2.2
          Ճայնք 1.6.7
          Ճայնից 1.6.3 1.6.7 3.3.2 4.1.3 5.1.1
Ճերն noun   [3]
          Ճերն 1.4.8(2x)
          Ճերք 1.4.8
Ճեւ noun   [11]
          Ճեւ 1.3.1 1.4.3(2x) 1.6.3

    ձեւի 1.6.4
    ձեւոյ 1.4.1 1.6.4 4.2.14
    ձեւով 1.1.5
    ձեւք 1.6.4
    ձեւաւք 5.1.9

ձմեռնային adjective [1]
    ձմեռնային 1.4.6

ձոր noun [1]
    ձորովք 1.1.5

ձուկն noun [3]
    ձուկն 1.4.6 1.4.10 1.4.11

ճառ noun [2]
    ճառք 5.9.7
    ճառից 5.9.7

ճառեմ verb [2]
    ճառելոց 3.1.9
    ճառեցելովք 3.2.3

ճշմարիտ adjective [1]
    ճշմարիտ 3.1.12

ճշմարտութիւն noun [1]
    ճշմարտութիւն 3.1.6

ճոխութիւն noun [1]
    ճոխութեան 2.1.1

մագ noun [1]
    մագոյ 1.5.6

մածուցանեմ verb [1]
    մածոյց 2.5.2

մակագրութիւն noun [1]
    մակագրութեան 1.6.10

մակադրութիւն noun [2]
    մակադրութեան 4.3.1 4.3.4

մակագգ noun [1]
    մակագգ 2.3.5

մակարդակ noun [2]
    մակարդակ 4.2.11(2x)

մակացելի adjective [4]
    մակացելի 1.6.9
    մակացելիք 1.6.1 1.6.14 1.6.15

մակացութիւն noun [7]
    մակացութիւն 3.1.5 3.1.14(2x) 4.2.12
    մակացութեանց 3.1.5 3.1.14(2x)

մակբայ noun [1]
    մակբայ 2.3.4

մակերեւութիւն noun [2]
    մակերեւութիւն 4.2.11(2x)

մահ noun [3]
    մահ 1.5.11
    մահուան 1.5.13
    մահու 3.1.5

մաղձ noun [2]
    մաղձ 1.5.7
    մաղձոյ 1.5.5

մասն noun [20]
    մասն 4.3.5
    մասին 4.3.3

	մասունս 1.5.5	
	մասամբ 1.6.10	
	մասունք 2.3.2 2.3.4 5.2.12 5.3.2	
	մասանց 1.4.4 1.4.7 2.3.4 2.3.7 3.1.3 3.3.2 5.2.1 5.2.2 5.2.11 5.3.1 5.9.7	
	մասամբք 5.9.7	
մասնական adjective		[14]
	մասնական 1.6.18 2.3.1 3.1.1 3.1.9 4.3.3 4.3.4 5.4.4 5.6.1(2x) 5.6.2(2x) 5.8.1	
	մասնականք 4.2.9 5.9.7	
մարդ noun		[7]
	մարդ 1.6.14 1.6.16 3.1.6 3.1.11	
	մարդս 1.6.8	
	մարդոյ 1.4.4 1.4.7	
մարդասիրութիւն noun		[1]
	մարդասիրութեան 5.9.5	
մարդիկ noun		[4]
	մարդիկ 1.2.2	
	մարդկան 3.1.12 5.9.4(2x)	
մարդկային adjective		[5]
	մարդկային 3.1.12 5.9.5	
	մարդկայինս 3.1.13	
	մարդկայնոց 3.1.5 3.1.11	
մարմին noun		[8]
	մարմին 4.2.4	
	մարմնոյ 1.5.3 1.5.4 1.5.6 1.5.10 1.5.12 1.5.13	
	մարմնոց 1.6.7	
մարմնական adjective		[1]
	մարմնական 1.1.4	
մարտ noun		[1]
	մարտից 1.5.10	
մարտուցանեմ verb		[1]
	մարտուցեալ 5.2.5	
մեծամեծ adjective		[1]
	մեծամեծաց 1.1.4	
մեկնութիւն noun		[1]
	մեկնութեան 1.1.6	
մեղ noun		[1]
	մեղք 5.1.1	
մէզ noun		[1]
	մզան 1.5.5	
մէջ adjective		[14]
	մէջ 2.5.4 5.1.1 5.2.5 5.3.3 5.4.7	
	մէջս 1.1.1 1.1.7 1.5.11 5.2.5 5.4.6 5.4.8 5.5.4 5.5.5	
	միջի 5.1.8	
մի number		[12]
	մի 1.6.16 4.1.1(4x) 4.3.1 4.3.2 5.9.5	
	միոյ 4.2.4	
	միում 1.4.2 4.3.3	
	միոջէ 1.5.4	
միայն adjective		[6]
	միայն 3.1.13 5.1.4 5.2.7 5.9.4	
	միայնում 4.2.7(2x)	
միայնումն noun		[2]
	միայնումն 4.2.10 4.2.14	

միանգամայն adverb   [2]
    միանգամայն 5.1.4 5.9.6
միատրութիւն noun   [1]
    միատրութիւն 3.1.1
միմեանս reciprocal pronoun   [12]
    միմեանս 1.6.7
    միմեանց 4.3.1 5.2.1 5.2.3 5.2.11 5.3.2 5.7.2 5.9.7
    միմեամբք 1.2.4 1.3.3 1.6.15 1.6.16
միմոսութիւն noun   [2]
    միմոսութիւն 2.4.1
    միմոսութեան 2.4.0
մինչեւ adverb   [1]
    մինչեւ 1.5.12
միշտ adverb   [2]
    միշտ 1.5.10 5.2.10
միջին adjective   [1]
    միջին 1.4.2
միջնորդ adjective   [1]
    միջնորդաւ 1.6.7
միջոց noun   [2]
    միջոցք 1.1.6
    միջոցաց 5.3.5
միս noun   [1]
    միսք 1.5.5
միտ noun   [8]
    միտք 1.6.13 2.4.1 3.1.6 3.1.16 4.3.2 5.9.1
    մտաց 1.6.13 5.8.1
միտատարին noun   [1]
    միտատարենէ 1.5.8
մնամ verb   [1]
    մնալով 5.1.8
մշտապուխ adjective   [1]
    մշտապուխ 5.7.0
մշտակայիմ verb   [1]
    մշտակային 1.3.2
մշտակացութիւն noun   [2]
    մշտակացութիւն 1.3.1
    մշտակացութենէ 5.8.2
մշտնջենաւոր adjective   [1]
    մշտնջենաւորի 5.9.6
մոլորակ noun   [4]
    մոլորակք 1.3.5
    մոլորակաց 1.4.4 1.5.12 1.6.17
մորթ noun   [1]
    մորթք 1.5.5
յաղագս preposition   [33]
    յաղագս 1.0.0 1.1.0 1.2.0 1.3.0 1.4.0 1.5.0 1.6.0
    1.6.17 2.0.0 2.1.0 2.2.0 2.3.0 2.4.0 2.5.0 3.0.0
    3.1.0 3.2.0 3.3.0 4.0.0 4.1.0 4.2.0 4.3.0 5.0.0
    5.1.0 5.2.0 5.3.0 5.4.0 5.5.0 5.6.0 5.7.0 5.8.0
    5.9.0 5.9.5
յայտ adjective   [2]
    յայտ 2.5.3 3.1.4
յայտնապէս adverb   [1]
    յայտնապէս 2.5.3

յայտնեմ verb   [2]
        յայտնին 5.3.6
        յայտնեցաւ 5.1.10
յայտնութիւն noun   [1]
        յայտնութիւն 2.5.2
յանգեմ verb   [2]
        յանգին 5.3.1
        յանկին 3.1.3
յաջողութիւն noun   [1]
        յաջողութեան 2.1.1
յառաջ adverb   [1]
        յառաջ 5.3.9
յառաջադասութիւն noun   [1]
        յառաջադասութեան 2.3.4
յառաջտեսութիւն noun   [1]
        յառաջտեսութիւն 1.6.13
յատկապէս adverb   [1]
        յատկապէս 4.2.9
յատուկ adjective   [9]
        յատուկ 4.2.3 4.2.7 4.2.10 4.2.11 4.2.14 5.1.8
        յատկի 4.2.7 4.3.5
        յատկէ 4.2.13
յարակցեմ verb   [1]
        յարակցեալ 4.1.1
յարակցութիւն noun   [1]
        յարակցութեան 4.1.2
յարածգական adjective   [1]
        յարածգական 5.4.6
յարանունաբար adverb   [1]
        յարանունաբար 4.2.13
յատ noun   [2]
        յատ 2.3.4 2.3.5
յատրուած noun   [1]
        յատրուած 1.5.5
յաւէտ adjective   [2]
        յաւէտ 1.1.3 4.2.11
յաժարեմ verb   [1]
        յաժարել 3.1.13
յաժարութիւն noun   [1]
        յաժարութիւն 1.6.12
յափտեան noun   [3]
        յափտեան 6.1.1
        յափտեանս 5.9.6
        յափտենից 5.9.6
յափտենական adjective   [1]
        յափտենականէ 5.8.2
յետոյ adverb   [1]
        յետոյ 5.1.6
յղովութիւն noun   [1]
        յղովութեան 4.2.10
յղովումն noun   [3]
        յղովման 4.2.4 4.2.5 5.5.2
յոյն noun   [1]
        յունաց 1.4.8

յոյս noun		[1]

    յուսոյ 1.6.16

յորդորումն noun   [1]

    յորդորման 2.3.6

յորժամ conjunction   [1]

    յորժամ 2.5.1

յոքնակի adverb   [1]

    յոքնակի 5.4.8

ն   article   [559]

    ն 1.1.1(4x) 1.1.3(3x) 1.1.4(7x) 1.1.5 1.1.6 1.1.7(6x) 1.2.3(3x)
1.2.4(3x) 1.3.1(3x) 1.3.2(3x) 1.3.3(4x) 1.3.4(3x) 1.3.5(8x)
1.4.2(4x) 1.4.3(3x) 1.4.4(4x) 1.4.5 1.4.7(9x) 1.4.8(4x) 1.4.9(5x)
1.4.10(6x) 1.5.1(2x) 1.5.2 1.5.3 1.5.4(2x) 1.5.5(2x) 1.5.6(6x)
1.5.7(5x) 1.5.8(5x) 1.5.9 1.5.10(3x) 1.5.11(4x) 1.5.12(8x)
1.5.13(6x) 1.5.14(2x) 1.6.2(2x) 1.6.3(2x) 1.6.4(3x) 1.6.5(3x)
1.6.6(2x) 1.6.7(8x) 1.6.8(4x) 1.6.9(3x) 1.6.10(5x) 1.6.11
1.6.12(2x) 1.6.13(2x) 1.6.14(2x) 1.6.15(6x) 1.6.16 1.6.17(3x)
1.6.18(4x)
2.0.0 2.1.0 2.1.1(8x) 2.2.0 2.2.1 2.2.2(5x) 2.2.3(2x) 2.3.0
2.3.1(2x) 2.3.2 2.3.3 2.3.5(3x) 2.3.6 2.3.7(7x) 2.4.1 2.4.2(4x)
2.5.1 2.5.3(4x) 2.5.4 2.5.5
3.0.0 3.1.1 3.1.2 3.1.3(3x) 3.1.4(6x) 3.1.6(4x) 3.1.7(2x)
3.1.8(2x) 3.1.9(5x) 3.1.10(3x) 3.1.11 3.1.12(4x) 3.1.13(6x)
3.1.14(6x) 3.1.16(2x) 3.2.1(5x) 3.2.2 3.2.3 3.3.2
4.1.0 4.1.1(6x) 4.1.2(5x) 4.1.3(12x) 4.2.2(3x) 4.2.3 4.2.5(9x)
4.2.6 4.2.7(3x) 4.2.8 4.2.10(5x) 4.2.11(3x) 4.2.12 4.2.13(2x)
4.2.14(2x) 4.2.15(9x) 4.3.1(2x) 4.3.2(3x) 4.3.3(2x) 4.3.5(3x)
5.1.1(4x) 5.1.2(2x) 5.1.3 5.1.4(5x) 5.1.5(3x) 5.1.6(4x) 5.1.7
5.1.8(5x) 5.1.9(2x) 5.1.10(4x) 5.2.2(2x) 5.2.3(5x) 5.2.4(4x)
5.2.5(2x) 5.2.6(4x) 5.2.7(8x) 5.2.8(2x) 5.2.9(3x) 5.2.10(2x)
5.2.11(3x) 5.2.12(6x) 5.3.1(3x) 5.3.2 5.3.3(4x) 5.3.4(2x)
5.3.5(4x) 5.3.6(6x) 5.3.7(4x) 5.3.8(3x) 5.3.9(4x) 5.4.1(2x)
5.4.2(2x) 5.4.3(2x) 5.4.4 5.4.6(4x) 5.4.7(2x) 5.4.8 5.5.1(6x)
5.5.2 5.5.3(3x) 5.5.4(4x) 5.5.5(7x) 5.6.1(7x) 5.6.2 5.6.3(2x)
5.7.0 5.7.1 5.7.2(8x) 5.7.3(6x) 5.7.4(3x) 5.8.1(3x) 5.8.2
5.9.1(3x) 5.9.2(4x) 5.9.3(2x) 5.9.4(4x) 5.9.5 5.9.6(3x)
5.9.7(9x)

նա   demonstrative pronoun   [8]

    նմանէ 4.2.5

    նոցա 2.5.3(2x) 2.5.4(2x) 2.5.5 5.1.8 5.3.2

նազատ adjective   [1]

    նազատ 2.5.3

նախ adverb   [2]

    նախ 3.1.1 5.4.5

նախադասութիւն noun   [3]

    նախադասութիւն 3.2.1
    նախադասութիւնս 5.2.7
    նախադասութենէ 3.2.1

նախադրեմ verb   [1]

    նախադրի 2.3.1

նախադրութիւն noun   [1]

    նախադրութիւն 2.3.4

նախանձ noun   [1]

    նախանձ 1.5.10

նախդասութիւն noun   [1]
    նախդասութեամբ 5.1.1
նախդիր noun   [1]
    նախդիր 2.3.5
նախերգութիւն noun.   [2]
    նախերգութեան 2.3.6
    նախերգութեամբ 4.3.1
նախկին adjective   [5]
    նախկին 4.2.10 4.3.2 5.3.6
    նախկնի 4.2.2 4.3.1
նախկնութիւն noun   [1]
    նախկնութեամբ 5.1.6
նաւավարեմ verb   [2]
    նաւավարի 2.3.5
    նաւավարիլ 3.1.4
նաւսրութիւն noun   [1]
    նաւսրութեան 5.7.3
նեարդ noun   [1]
    նեարդք 1.5.5
ներածեմ verb   [1]
    ներածեն 5.2.5
ներածութիւն noun   [2]
    ներածութեանց 5.1.1
    ներածութեամբ 3.2.3
ներարհեստ noun   [1]
    ներարհեստի 5.2.9
ներգոյ adjective   [1]
    ներգոյս 2.3.2
ներգործեմ verb   [2]
    ներգործեն 5.2.5
    ներգործեալք 5.7.1
ներգործութիւն noun   [2]
    ներգործութեան 1.5.10
    ներգործութեանց 5.1.1
ներկայ adjective   [1]
    ներկայում 5.2.5
ներկուտ adjective   [1]
    ներկուտ 2.3.2
ներհակաբար adverb   [1]
    ներհակաբար 4.3.1
ներքին adjective   [2]
    ներքին 2.5.4
    ներքինս 4.2.5
ներքոկացի adjective   [1]
    ներքոկացեաց 3.2.1
նիստ noun   [1]
    նիստ 4.2.13
նիւթ noun   [38]
    նիւթ 1.1.2 1.6.2 1.6.11 5.1.6 5.5.4 5.6.2 5.6.3 5.7.1(4x) 5.7.4
    5.9.1
    նիւթս 5.7.1
    նիւթի 1.5.3 5.4.5 5.4.6 5.7.0 5.7.2 5.7.3 5.8.1
    նիւթոյ 1.4.4 1.5.2 1.5.3 1.5.4 1.5.12 1.5.13 1.6.6 5.1.6(2x)
    5.4.5 5.4.6 5.7.2
    նիւթէ 5.7.4

նիւթից 1.5.7 5.3.8
նիւթոց 1.5.11 1.6.7

նիւթական adjective [2]
նիւթական 5.4.1
նիւթականաց 1.5.14

նման adjective [4]
նման 3.1.1 3.1.12
նմանք 1.6.5
նմանից 5.5.1

նմանութիւն noun [3]
նմանութիւն 3.1.5 3.1.12 3.1.13

նշանակ noun [8]
նշանակ 3.1.4 3.1.9 4.1.3
նշանակք 1.6.7(3x) 1.6.18 4.1.3

նոյն pronoun [12]
նոյն 1.1.1 1.3.2(2x) 1.3.4 1.6.4 5.1.2 5.1.4 5.1.9
նորին 1.2.3
նմին 1.6.18 5.4.4 5.5.3

նոյնպէս adverb [2]
նոյնպէս 1.6.4 5.9.6

նոր adjective [1]
նոր 4.3.2

նուագեմ verb [1]
նուագել 5.7.2

նուագութիւն noun [2]
նուագութիւն 4.3.4
նուագութեան 5.5.2

նուրբ adjective [1]
նուրբ 1.5.6

շաբաթ noun [1]
շաբաթք 5.3.2

շաղկապ noun [1]
շաղկապ 2.3.4

շարաբանութիւն noun [2]
շարաբանութիւն 3.2.1
շարաբանութենէ 3.2.1

շարաբառութիւն noun [1]
շարաբառութեամբ 3.2.3

շարագրեմ verb [1]
շարագրին 5.2.12

շարադրական adjective [1]
շարադրականէ 5.5.5

շարադրելի adjective [2]
շարադրելի 5.5.5(2x)

շարադրեմ verb [4]
շարադրի 2.2.3 2.3.6
շարադրեալ 4.1.3(2x)

շարադրութիւն noun [6]
շարադրութիւն 1.1.5
շարադրութեան 1.6.8 2.3.3
շարադրութեամբ 2.2.1 2.3.4 5.5.4

շարամանութիւն noun [1]
շարամանութեան 4.2.9

շարառնութիւն noun [1]
շարառնութեան 1.5.4

շարասութիւն noun   [1]
    շարասութիւն 3.2.1
շարժումն noun   [37]
    շարժումն 1.6.11 5.1.6(2x) 5.5.1 5.5.4 5.6.2 5.6.3 5.7.1(3x)
    5.7.3 5.7.4 5.9.1
    շարժման 1.5.13 1.6.4 1.6.5 3.3.1 4.3.4 5.4.5(2x) 5.4.6 5.7.0
    5.7.2 5.7.3 5.8.1
    շարժմանէ 5.1.6 5.3.8 5.4.6 5.7.2 5.7.4
    շարժմամբ 1.1.1 3.1.6
    շարժմունք 5.7.1
    շարժմունս 1.6.17 2.5.4 5.7.1
    շարժմամբք 1.1.5
շարունակ noun   [3]
    շարունակ 4.2.11(2x) 5.3.7
շարունակութիւն noun   [1]
    շարունակութեան 5.3.7
շաւիղ noun   [3]
    շաւիղ 1.6.18
    շաւեղս 1.2.4 1.3.4
շաւշափեմ verb   [1]
    շաւշափի 1.5.12
շեղ adjective   [1]
    շեղ 1.6.18
շէկ adjective   [1]
    շէկ 1.5.6
շնորհ noun   [1]
    շնորհս 1.5.10
շուրջ adverb   [3]
    շուրջ 1.1.4 1.3.4 3.1.11
շտեմարան noun   [3]
    շտեմարան 2.5.3(2x)
    շտեմարանս 2.5.3
շտեմարանապիակ adjective   [1]
    շտեմարանապիակ 2.5.4
շրջապայ adjective   [6]
    շրջապայ 1.6.17
    շրջապայէ 1.5.12
    շրջապայից 1.4.4 1.6.18 5.3.1 5.3.2
շրջապայիմ verb   [2]
    շրջապային 1.1.7 1.3.5
շրջապայութիւն noun   [2]
    շրջապայութեան 5.2.2
    շրջապայութեամբ 1.3.4
շրջան noun   [7]
    շրջանք 1.0.1 1.3.1 1.6.17 5.3.2
    շրջանս 1.3.3 1.3.5
    շրջանաց 1.3.0
շրջանակ noun   [1]
    շրջանակք 5.3.3
շրջումն noun   [1]
    շրջումն 2.4.2
ոլորումն noun   [1]
    ոլորումն 5.3.1
ոլորտ noun   [2]
    ոլորտս 1.1.5

ողորտք 5.3.3
ողորմածութիւն noun [1]
ողորմածութեան 5.9.5
ումն indefinite pronoun [1]
ումանք 5.8.2
ոյժ noun [1]
ուժոյ 1.5.12
ոչ adverb [62]
չ 5.3.4
ոչ 1.2.3 1.2.4(2x) 1.3.3(2x) 1.4.3 1.5.3(2x) 1.5.4(2x)
1.5.14(2x) 1.6.6(4x) 1.6.8 2.5.4 3.1.7(2x) 3.1.11 3.1.12
4.2.2(2x) 5.1.3 5.1.4 5.1.5(2x) 5.2.1 5.2.4 5.2.5(2x) 5.2.7
5.2.8 5.2.10 5.2.11 5.2.12 5.3.3 5.3.6(2x) 5.3.9 5.4.1(3x)
5.4.4(2x) 5.5.3(2x) 5.6.3(2x) 5.8.2 5.9.1(6x) 5.9.2(2x) 5.9.3
ոչինչ 5.8.2
ոտոգանեմ verb [1]
ոտոգանել 1.6.2
ուկր noun [1]
ուկերք 1.5.5
ուտն noun [2]
ուտից 1.4.10 2.3.3
որ relative pronoun [213]
ո՞ր 3.1.4(2x) որ 1.1.2 1.1.4 1.1.5(3x) 1.1.6(2x) 1.2.2 1.2.3
1.3.1 1.3.3(2x) 1.4.3(4x) 1.4.5(2x) 1.4.6(2x) 1.4.7(4x) 1.4.8
1.4.10 1.5.3 1.5.4 1.5.10(2x) 1.5.11(2x) 1.5.13 1.5.14 1.6.1(3x)
1.6.4 1.6.5 1.6.6(4x) 1.6.14 1.6.17(2x) 1.6.18
2.2.3 2.3.5(6x) 2.5.2 2.5.3 2.5.4
3.1.1 3.1.3 3.1.4(3x) 3.1.7(2x) 3.1.10(2x) 3.1.16 3.2.1
4.1.1(4x) 4.1.3(2x) 4.2.2(4x) 4.2.4(2x) 4.2.5(3x) 4.2.6(2x)
4.2.7(4x) 4.2.8 4.2.9 4.2.11(4x) 4.3.1(4x) 4.3.2 4.3.4 4.3.5(2x)
5.1.1(2x) 5.1.2(3x) 5.1.3 5.1.5(4x) 5.1.6(2x) 5.2.1 5.2.3(2x)
5.2.4(2x) 5.2.5 5.2.7 5.2.11 5.2.12 5.3.1 5.3.2 5.3.3 5.3.4 5.3.5
5.3.6(2x) 5.3.9 5.4.1(4x) 5.4.2(2x) 5.4.4(4x) 5.4.6(2x) 5.4.7
5.4.8 5.4.8 5.5.2(3x) 5.5.3(5x) 5.5.5(3x) 5.6.4(2x) 5.7.0
5.7.1(2x) 5.7.4 5.9.1(2x) 5.9.4(3x) 5.9.7 5.9.8
որոյ 1.6.10 2.5.4
որում 5.9.6
որմէ 1.5.5 1.5.10 1.5.12 2.5.3 3.1.4 3.1.8 5.1.7(2x) 5.2.9
որով 1.6.10
որք 1.2.3 1.3.4 1.3.5 1.4.4 3.1.5 3.1.11 3.3.2 4.2.4 5.2.10
5.2.11 5.3.2(2x) 5.3.3(2x) 5.3.5 5.3.6
որս 1.1.7 1.3.4 1.6.14 5.3.1
որովք 5.9.7
որակ noun [3]
որակ 4.2.8 4.2.14
որակի 4.2.15
որակութիւն noun [1]
որակութեան 4.3.5
որդի noun [1]
որդւոյ 5.9.5
որգայթ noun [1]
որգայթից 1.5.11
որոշեմ verb [2]
որոշի 4.2.2
որոշեալ 5.1.6

որոշիչ noun   [1]
    որոշիչ 5.1.10
որոշումն noun   [11]
    որոշումն 1.5.11 1.6.10 3.3.2 5.1.8 5.8.1
    որոշման 4.2.0 4.2.1 5.5.4
    որոշմամբ 5.1.7
    որոշմունք 1.6.13
    որոշմանց 1.6.18
որպէս conjunction   [2]
    որպէս 1.6.6 5.8.2
որպիսի adjective   [1]
    որպիսի 3.1.2
ութ number   [1]
    ութ 2.3.4
ուղեղ noun   [1]
    ուղղոյ 1.5.5
ունակաւրէն adverb   [1]
    ունակաւրէն 4.3.1
ունակութիւն noun   [2]
    ունակութիւն 4.2.12
    ունակութեան 4.2.14
ունայն adjective   [15]
    ունայն 1.6.11 5.5.4 5.6.2 5.6.3 5.8.1
    ունայնի 1.1.1 1.3.1 5.3.8 5.4.6 5.7.3 5.8.0 5.8.2
    ունայնէ 1.1.2 5.4.6 5.7.3
ունայնագոյն adjective   [2]
    ունայնագոյն 5.9.2
    ունայնագունից 5.9.2
ունիմ verb   [10]
    ունի 1.1.1 2.5.4 4.2.5
    ունին 4.2.11(2x)
    ունէր 1.6.17 4.2.8 4.2.11 4.2.15 5.9.2
ուռուցումն noun   [2]
    ուռուցմամբ 1.1.6
    ուռուցմանց 1.6.7
ոս noun   [1]
    ոսք 1.4.7
ոսումն noun   [1]
    ոսմանց 5.9.8
ոսումնական adjective   [1]
    ոսումնական 3.2.2
ուստի adverb   [7]
    ուստի 1.1.5 1.3.2 1.5.1 1.5.10 1.6.15 3.1.2 3.1.4
ուր adverb   [4]
    ուր 4.2.1(2x) 4.2.8 4.2.15
ուրկութիւն noun   [1]
    ուրկութիւնք 1.5.8
ոք indefinite pronoun   [2]
    ոք 5.2.1
    ումեքէ 1.6.6
չար adjective   [17]
    չար 1.6.11 5.1.1 5.1.2 5.1.4(3x) 5.1.5(4x) 5.1.7 5.1.10 5.9.1
    չարի 5.1.4 5.1.6(2x) 5.1.10
չարութիւն noun   [1]
    չարութեան 2.2.1

չափի noun   [7]
    չափք 1.0.1 1.4.1 1.6.17 5.3.1 5.3.5
    չափուց 1.4.0 5.4.6
չափատրեմ verb   [1]
    չափատրել 2.1.1
չափեմ verb   [2]
    չափի 1.4.4
    չափին 2.4.1
չորեքանկիւնի adjective   [1]
    չորեքանկիւնի 1.1.5
չորեքին adjective   [3]
    չորեցունց 1.3.4 1.4.4 1.6.6
չորրեակ noun   [3]
    չորրեկի 5.9.1 5.9.4
    չորրեակք 5.9.7
չորրորդ numeral ordinal   [4]
    չորրորդ 1.1.4 5.1.2 5.2.8 5.3.8
չորք number   [18]
    չորք 1.5.1 4.1.1 4.2.12 5.7.2
    չորս 1.6.7 1.6.9 3.1.1 3.1.2 3.1.6 4.2.3 4.2.10 5.1.1 5.1.5
    չորից 1.4.1 1.6.3 3.1.6 5.1.7
    չորիւք 5.3.6
պակատբար adverb   [1]
    պակատբար 4.3.1
պակասեմ verb   [2]
    պակասի 5.5.2
    պակասել 1.5.12
պադպաշումն noun   [1]
    պադպաշմունք 1.4.2
պաճարեմ verb   [1]
    պաճարել 2.1.1
պաճարող adjective   [1]
    պաճարող 1.1.5
պաշտատ noun   [1]
    պաշտատ 3.1.11
պաշտատնեայ noun   [1]
    պաշտատնեայ 3.1.11
պատառ noun   [5]
    պատառք 4.2.10
    պատառից 3.1.3 5.3.7(2x) 5.3.9
պատառեմ verb   [2]
    պատառին 5.2.8
    պատառիլ 1.5.13
պատառումն noun   [19]
    պատառումն 1.5.11 4.2.1(3x) 4.2.6 5.6.1(3x)
    պատառմունս 1.6.18 5.1.3
    պատառման 5.4.3 5.5.3 5.6.2(2x) 5.6.4
    պատառմանէ 4.2.2 5.1.5
    պատառմամբ 1.5.11
    պատառմանց 5.2.8
պատասխանական adjective   [1]
    պատասխանական 3.2.3
պատասխանի noun   [1]
    պատասխանեաւ 3.2.2

պատերազմ noun [2]
   պատերազմի 1.5.11
   պատերազմունք 1.5.10
պատժեմ verb [1]
   պատժելով 1.5.10
պատիւ noun [1]
   պատիւ 5.9.6
պատճառ noun [9]
   պատճառ 1.1.6 1.5.12 1.5.13 1.6.10 3.1.16 4.3.1 5.1.7(2x)
   5.5.4
պատմութիւն noun [2]
   պատմութիւն 2.3.7
   պատմութեանց 2.3.2
պատշաճական adjective [2]
   պատշաճական 2.1.1(2x)
պատշաճեմ verb [1]
   պատշաճին 5.3.2
պատուեմ verb [1]
   պատուեն 3.1.6
պարագայ noun [1]
   պարագայից 3.1.4
պարագայիմ verb [2]
   պարագայի 3.1.3 3.1.4
պարանոց noun [1]
   պարանոց 1.4.7
պարզ adjective [6]
   պարզ 3.1.12 4.1.3 5.5.4 5.5.5(2x)
   պարզէ 5.5.5
պարզաբար adverb [1]
   պարզաբար 5.5.1
պարզութիւն noun [1]
   պարզութեան 2.3.3
պարունակ noun [2]
   պարունակս 1.2.4 1.3.3
պարունակեմ verb [3]
   պարունակեալ 1.1.1 1.1.3 1.3.3
պարս name [1]
   պարսից 1.4.7
պարսաւեմ verb [1]
   պարսաւել 2.3.7
պարտ noun [2]
   պարտ 2.5.3 3.1.1
պարփակող adjective [1]
   պարփակող 1.1.3
պէս adverb [2]
   պէս 1.5.7(2x)
պէսպէս adjective [1]
   պէսպէս 1.5.13
պիթագորեան noun [1]
   պիթագորեանք 3.1.6
պիտակաբար adverb [6]
   պիտակաբար 1.6.6 1.6.7 1.6.8 2.4.1 5.1.2 5.1.3
պիտանացու adjective [4]
   պիտանացու 1.0.0 1.6.17

պիտանացու 5.6.3
պիտանացուք 1.0.1

պղնձոտ adjective [1]
պղնձոտ 1.5.6

պնդեմ verb [1]
պնդի 1.5.10

ջերմութիւն noun [1]
ջերմութեան 1.5.12

ջիլ noun [1]
ջիլք 1.5.5

ջուր noun [11]
ջուր 1.4.6 2.5.3 2.5.4
ջուրս 1.1.5 2.5.3 2.5.4
ջրոյ 2.5.2
ջուրց 2.5.4
ջրոց 1.1.5 2.5.4
ջրովք 1.1.5

ջրայարկ noun [2]
ջրայարկի 1.1.3 1.3.3

ջրհոս noun [3]
ջրհոս 1.4.6 1.4.10 1.4.11

ս article   [32]
ս 1.1.4(2x) 1.1.5(2x) 1.1.6(2x) 1.2.2 1.3.1 1.3.3 1.3.4 1.4.1
1.4.4(2x) 1.6.4 3.1.5 3.1.8 3.1.9 3.1.10 3.1.12 3.1.16 4.2.0
4.2.3 4.3.5 5.2.2 5.2.4(2x) 5.2.9 5.3.3 5.3.4 5.9.3(2x) 5.9.8

սա demonstrative pronoun [16]
սորա 1.3.5 4.3.5 5.2.1 5.2.3 5.2.5 5.2.9
սոսա 5.3.7
սոցա 2.5.3 3.1.3 5.2.1
սոցանէ 1.4.2 1.4.3 1.5.7 1.6.3 1.6.6 5.1.6

սակս preposition [1]
սակս 1.6.7

սահման noun [28]
սահման 3.1.3 3.1.4(2x) 5.1.2 5.1.9 5.9.3
սահմանս 1.2.2 1.3.5 1.6.17 5.2.4 5.3.8
սահմանի 3.1.1 5.1.3 5.1.4
սահմանաւ 1.6.11 4.2.5
սահմանք 1.1.7 1.4.4 1.6.12 1.6.18 3.1.5 3.1.7 5.2.2 5.3.6 5.9.8
սահմանաց 3.1.0 3.1.16 5.2.6

սահմանադրեմ verb [1]
սահմանադրի 5.5.2

սահմանական adjective [11]
սահմանական 1.6.9 1.6.11 3.1.2 5.2.6 5.5.1(2x) 5.5.3(4x)
սահմանականի 5.5.5

սահմանեմ verb [8]
սահմանի 1.1.7 1.6.6 3.1.10 4.2.5 5.5.2
սահմանին 5.2.11 5.9.7
սահմանեցան 5.2.9
սահմանեալ 5.1.7

սարավի noun [1]
սարավի 2.5.3

սատ adjective [2]
սատ 1.4.2 1.6.3

սեաւ adjective [2]
սեաւ 1.4.2 1.6.3

սեռ noun [23]
    սեռ 4.1.2(2x) 4.2.3 4.2.4 4.2.5(3x) 4.2.10
    սեռս 4.2.8
    սեռի 1.3.1 1.6.5 4.2.5 4.3.5
    սեռէ 3.1.3 5.5.1 5.5.2
    սեռք 1.0.1
    սեռից 1.0.0 1.4.3 1.6.17 5.2.1 5.9.7
    սեռիւք 5.1.9

սեռականագոյն adjective [1]
    սեռականագոյնք 4.2.4

սեռանամ verb [1]
    սեռանայ 4.2.5

սերմանիք noun [1]
    սերմանեաց 1.5.12

սերմն noun [2]
    սերման 4.2.4
    սերմանս 1.6.2

սեաւամաղձութիւն noun [1]
    սեաւամաղձութենէ 1.5.8

սէր noun [1]
    սիրոյ 1.6.16

սիրելութիւն noun [1]
    սիրելութիւն 3.1.5

սիրեմ verb [1]
    սիրել 3.1.15

սիրտ noun [2]
    սիրտ 1.1.5 1.5.13

սկիզբն noun [25]
    սկիզբն 1.6.11 5.3.5 5.4.1(6x) 5.4.2(3x) 5.4.3 5.4.4(3x) 5.4.5 5.4.6 5.4.8(2x) 5.9.1
    սկզբան 5.1.1 5.2.4 5.2.5 5.4.0 5.4.7

սկսանիմ verb [1]
    սկսանին 5.3.2

սկումն noun [2]
    սկման 5.6.3(2x)

անունդ noun [1]
    աննդեան 2.2.2

անուցիչ noun [2]
    անուցիչք 1.6.1
    անուցչաց 1.6.2

սողուն noun [1]
    սողնոց 2.2.2

սոյն pronoun [1]
    սոցին 1.5.13

սովորութիւն noun [1]
    սովորութեան 2.2.2

սուտ adjective [1]
    սուտ 4.2.9

սուրբ adjective [3]
    սուրբ 5.9.6(3x)

սպիտակ adjective [2]
    սպիտակ 1.4.2 1.6.3

ստեղծումն noun [2]
    ստեղծումն 1.5.3
    ստեղծմանց 1.6.5

ստոյգ adjective [1]
    ստոյգ 5.2.8
ստորադաս adjective [1]
    ստորադասիւ 1.6.15
ստորադասութիւն noun [2]
    ստորադասութիւն 3.2.1
    ստորադասութենէ 3.2.1
ստորադրական adjective [1]
    ստորադրական 3.1.3
ստորական adjective [1]
    ստորական 3.1.1
ստորասութիւն noun [4]
    ստորասութիւն 1.6.12 4.2.9
    ստորասութեան 3.2.3
    ստորասութեամբ 4.3.1
ստորին adjective [2]
    ստորին 1.4.2
    ստորնոց 1.6.6
ստորոգեմ verb [4]
    ստորոգին 5.2.3
    ստորոգեցաւ 5.1.5
    ստորոգեալ 3.2.1
    ստորոգեցելոյ 3.2.1
ստորոգութիւն noun [6]
    ստորոգութիւն 4.2.3 5.2.7
    ստորոգութիւնս 1.6.10
    ստորոգութեան 4.2.0
    ստորոգութեանց 4.2.8 4.3.5
ստուար adjective [1]
    ստուար 1.5.6
ստուգաբանութիւն noun [4]
    ստուգաբանութեան 2.3.2 3.1.6 5.4.2
    ստուգաբանութեամբ 3.1.15
ստուեր noun [4]
    ստուեր 5.1.7
    ստուերէ 5.1.7 5.1.8(2x)
սրունք noun [1]
    սրունք 1.4.9
սքանչելագործութիւն noun [1]
    սքանչելագործութիւնք 1.5.14
վաղագոյն adjective [1]
    վաղագոյն 4.3.2
վայր noun [1]
    վայրս 1.3.4
վանգ noun [3]
    վանգի 4.1.2
    վանգիւ 4.1.1
    վանգից 2.3.3
վասն preposition [9]
    վասն 1.1.3 1.6.17 3.1.2 3.1.7(3x) 4.2.6 5.2.8 5.3.9
վասն զի conjunction [1]
    վասն զի 5.1.2
վարդապետական adjective [1]
    վարդապետականի 1.6.10

վարդապետութիւն noun [1]
    վարդապետութեան 4.3.3
վարեմ verb [4]
    վարին 1.3.4 5.1.6
    վարեալք 1.2.3
    վարիլ 5.3.8
վարումն noun [6]
    վարման 2.3.3 5.1.7 5.1.8 5.3.9
    վարմանէ 1.1.7 5.1.7
վարք noun [4]
    վարք 1.5.10
    վարս 2.2.1
    վարուց 2.4.2 5.3.3
վեհագոյն adjective [2]
    վեհագոյն 5.2.9
    վեհագունի 2.1.1
վերաբերեմ verb [1]
    վերաբերին 4.3.3
վերաբերութիւն noun [3]
    վերաբերութիւն 1.6.10 4.3.3
    վերաբերութեան 4.3.4
վերագնամ verb [1]
    վերագնացեալ 1.1.5
վերագոյն adjective [3]
    վերագոյն 1.5.4 5.2.3
    վերագոյնք 5.3.7
վերադասական adjective [1]
    վերադասականաց 1.6.6
վերական adjective [1]
    վերական 3.1.1
վերատեսութիւն noun [1]
    վերատեսութեան 5.2.5
վերին adjective [3]
    վերին 1.4.2(2x)
    վերնով 1.1.3
վերլուծական adjective [2]
    վերլուծական 1.6.9 3.3.2
վերլուծութիւն noun [1]
    վերլուծութեան 3.3.0
վերծանութիւն noun [1]
    վերծանութիւն 2.3.2
վերնագոյն adjective [1]
    վերնագոյնս 4.2.5
վերջին adjective [3]
    վերջին 3.1.10 5.3.6 5.4.5
վեց number [8]
    վեց 1.0.1 1.1.1 1.4.11 2.3.2 3.1.5 3.1.7(2x) 4.3.4
վեցեակ noun [3]
    վեցեակ 1.6.15
    վեցեկի 5.9.1
    վեցեակք 5.9.7
վեցերորդ numeral ordinal [1]
    վեցերորդ 1.1.6
վնաս noun [1]
    վնաս 2.5.4

վտիտ adjective [1]
    վտիտ 1.5.6

տամ verb [2]
    տալ 1.1.4 1.6.18

տառ noun [2]
    տառք 4.3.2
    տառից 2.3.3

տասն number [1]
    տասն 4.2.8

տասնեակ noun [1]
    տասնեակք 3.1.9

տարածումն noun [1]
    տարածմամբ 1.3.4

տարբերեմ verb [2]
    տարբերի 3.2.2 5.1.1

տարբերութիւն noun [3]
    տարբերութիւն 4.2.3 4.2.6
    տարբերութեան 4.3.5

տարորոշ adjective [2]
    տարորոշ 4.2.11(2x)

տարրական adjective [1]
    տարրական 1.6.7

տեղական adjective [1]
    տեղական 3.2.2

տեղեկութիւն noun [1]
    տեղեկութիւն 2.3.2

տեղի noun [9]
    տեղի 1.4.2 2.3.7 4.2.11(2x)
    տեղւոյ 1.4.1 3.3.1 4.3.4
    տեղեաց 1.1.7 1.6.18

տեղխանամ verb [1]
    տեղխանալ 5.1.8

տեսակ noun [46]
    տեսակ 1.6.5 4.1.2(2x) 4.2.3 4.2.4 4.2.5(2x) 4.2.10 5.2.7
    5.3.4
    տեսակս 1.1.1 1.3.1 1.4.3 1.5.2 1.6.7 1.6.9 3.1.1 3.1.2 3.1.9
    4.2.4 4.3.4 5.1.1 5.3.5
    տեսակի 1.6.5 4.3.3 4.3.5 5.1.5 5.3.4
    տեսակք 1.5.1 1.6.2 2.3.1 3.3.2 4.1.1 4.2.1 4.2.12 4.3.5 5.6.1
    տեսակաց 1.4.3 1.6.7 3.1.9 5.2.1 5.5.1 5.9.7
    տեսակաւք 5.1.9 5.3.3 5.3.6

տեսակագոյն adjective [1]
    տեսակագոյնք 4.2.4

տեսական adjective [8]
    տեսական 1.6.9 1.6.10 3.1.1 3.1.14 4.3.5 5.4.1
    տեսականի 1.6.13
    տեսականէ 4.1.0

տեսականամ verb [1]
    տեսականայ 4.2.5

տեսանելի adjective [2]
    տեսանելի 1.6.3
    տեսանելեաց 1.6.3

տեսանեմ verb [2]
    տես 2.5.1 2.5.2

տեսիլ noun [2]
> տեսիլս 1.6.3
> տեսլենէ 1.6.8

տեսարան noun [1]
> տեսարանի 2.3.7

տեսուած noun [1]
> տեսուածս 4.3.2

տեսութիւն noun [5]
> տեսութեամբ 5.2.11 5.3.9 5.4.6
> տեսութիւնք 4.3.2 5.9.1

տէր noun [2]
> տէր 2.5.5 5.9.6

տիրագոյն adjective [1]
> տիրագոյն 4.2.10

տկարութիւն noun [1]
> տկարութենէ 2.4.1

տնաւրէնութիւն noun [1]
> տնաւրէնութեան 1.2.2

տնաւրինական adjective [5]
> տնաւրինական 1.6.9 2.0.1 2.1.1(2x)
> տնաւրինականի 2.1.0

տնտեսական adjective [2]
> տնտեսական 2.1.1(2x)

տումիչ noun [1]
> տումիչք 5.9.8

տուն noun [2]
> տանց 1.1.7 1.3.5

տունկ noun [2]
> տնկոց 1.6.2 2.2.3

տապատրեմ verb [1]
> տապատրեալ 1.3.1

տապատրութիւն noun [2]
> տապատրութիւն 1.3.1
> տապատրութեան 1.3.2

տրամաբանական adjective [2]
> տրամաբանական 1.6.9 3.2.2

տրամաբանեմ verb [1]
> տրամաբանեալք 5.7.1

տրամաբանութիւն noun [2]
> տրամաբանութեան 3.2.0
> տրամաբանութեամբ 3.1.2

տրամագիծ adjective [1]
> տրամագծի 1.1.1

տրամադրութիւն noun [2]
> տրամադրութեան 4.2.14
> տրամադրութեամբ 5.3.1

տրամախոհութիւն noun [1]
> տրամախոհութիւն 1.6.13

տրամանկիւնի adjective [2]
> տրամանկիւնի 1.6.16
> տրամանկիւնիք 1.6.15

տրամատեմ verb [1]
> տրամատեալ 5.1.5

ցամաք noun [1]
> ցամաքի 1.1.5

ցամաքային adjective [1]
    ցամաքայինս 1.5.2
ցամաքումն noun [1]
    ցամաքումն 5.7.2
ցանկութիւն noun [2]
    ցանկութիւն 1.5.10 1.6.12
ցաւ noun [1]
    ցաւոց 1.5.13
ցատակից adjective [1]
    ցատակից 1.4.7
ցոյլ noun [3]
    ցոյլ 1.4.5 1.4.7 1.4.11
ցուրտ adjective [1]
    ցրտոյ 1.5.8
ցուցական adjective [1]
    ցուցական 3.2.3
ցուցանեմ verb [2]
    ցուցանի 4.2.4
    ցուցեալ 5.3.2
ցուցումն noun [1]
    ցուցմանէ 3.1.4
ցրուեմ verb [1]
    ցրուեալ 1.3.4
ցրտումն noun [1]
    ցրտումն 5.7.2
փակեմ verb [2]
    փակեալ 1.1.4 1.1.5
փաղանուն adjective [1]
    փաղանուն 3.3.1
փաղատութիւն noun [4]
    փաղատութիւնս 4.3.2
    փաղատութեան 4.1.2
    փաղատութեամբ 4.1.1
    փաղատութեանց 2.3.3
փայլածու noun [1]
    փայլածու 1.3.5
փայլումն noun [1]
    փայլմունք 1.4.2
փառասիրութին noun [1]
    փառասիրութին 1.5.10
փառատրեմ verb [1]
    փառատրեալ 5.9.6
փառք noun [2]
    փառք 5.9.6 6.1.1
փիլիսոփայական adjective [1]
    փիլիսոփայական 5.9.8
փիլիսոփայ noun [1]
    փիլիսոփայից 5.9.8
փոխանակ preposition [1]
    փոխանակ 2.3.5
փոխեմ verb [2]
    փոխի 1.2.3
    փոխին 1.2.4
փորուած noun [1]
    փորուած 1.1.6

քննեմ verb   [3]
        քննեալ 2.4.1
        քննել 3.1.10 3.1.15
քննութիւն noun   [1]
        քննութեանց 5.9.3
քսանութ number   [1]
        քսանութիւք 5.3.3
...*ուման* noun   [1]
        ...*մանց* 5.3.5

TRILINGUAL LISTS

1. *By Armenian*

This and the following two lists contain the proposals made of possible Greek terms reflected by the Armenian words in the text of Pseudo-Zeno.

Armenian	English	Greek	Ref.
ազդումն	influence	ἐνέργεια	1.0.1
ազդումն	influence	ἐνέργεια	1.6.0
ախտ	property	πάθος	4.2.14
այլայլակ	differently	ἑτεροῖος	1.5.3
անբան	irrational	ἄλογος	4.2.4
անզգայուն	non-perceptive	ἀναίσθητος	4.2.4
անթուելի	innumerable	ἀναρίθμητος	1.5.4
անկենդանի	non-living	ἄψυχος	4.2.4
անկրական	impassible	ἀπαθής	1.5.4
անյեղլի	unchanging	ἄτρεπτος	1.5.3
անմարմին	bodiless	ἀσώματος	4.2.4
անմարմնաբար	in a bodiless way	ἀσωμάτως	1.5.3
անչափ	without measure	ἀμέτρως	1.4.3
ապացուցական	demonstrating	ἀποδεικτικός	1.6.9
ապացուցական	probative	ἀποδεικτικός	3.2.1
ատենական	forensic	δικανικός	2.3.7
արածկական	imperfect	παρατατικός	5.4.6
արարչական	qualitative [creative]	ποιητικός	5.5.1
արտաբերութիւն	bringing forth	ἐκφορά	1.5.1
արտադատութիւն	separating forth	ἔκκρισις	1.5.1
արտադրութիւն	giving forth	ἔκδοσις	1.5.1
արտաքոյ	from outside	θυράθεν	1.5.3

Armenian	English	Greek	Ref.
բաժանական	divisible	διαιρετικός	1.6.9
բախխունճական	deliberative	συμβουλευτικός	2.3.7
բանական	reasonable	λογικός	1.6.9
բանական	possessed of reason	λογικός	4.2.4
բանական	reasonable	λογικός	1.6.9
բանական	reasonable	λογικός	1.6.12
բառ	word	λέξις	2.3.3
բարառնական	that which causes character	ἠθοποιητικός	2.2.3
բարեխառնութիւն	good mixture	εὐκρασία	1.5.12
բարեխառնութիւն	a balanced blending	ἰσόρροπος εὐκρασία	1.5.7
բարոյական	moral	ἠθικός	1.6.9
բժշկական	healing	ἰατρικός	1.5.1
բժշկականութիւն	medicine	ἡ ἰατρική	1.5.5
բնական	the natural	φύσις	1.2.3
բնութիւն	nature	φύσις	5.5.0
գիտութիւն	knowledge	γνῶσις	1.6.13
գործնական	practical	πρακτικός	1.6.9
դասատրութիւն	ordering	διάταξις	5.3.7
դասիմ	arrange	τάσσω	4.2.5
դատումն	judgement	κρίσις	2.3.2
դիր	position	θέσις	1.0.1
դիր	position	θέσις	1.1.0
դրութիւն	position	θέσις	4.2.12
ենթակայ	substrate	τὸ ὑποκείμενον	4.2.5
եկամուտ	the external things	τὰ ἔξωθεν	1.5.13
եղանակ	modification	τρόπος	1.5.7
երբ	when	ποτε	4.2.15
երկակենցաղ	amphibious	ἀμφίβιος	1.5.2
զաւրութիւն	power	δύναμις	1.0.1
զաւրութիւն	power	δύναμις	1.5.0
զգայուն	perceptive	αἰσθητός	4.2.4
ընդունելութիւն	participle	μετοχή	2.3.5

Armenian	English	Greek	Ref.
թիւ	number	ἀριθμός	1.4.3
թուականութիւն	calculation	ἀριθμητικός	3.1.7
ժամանակ	time	χρόνος	4.3.2
ի ձեռն խնդրականին	inquiry	διαζητικός not LS	4.1.0
ի ներքոյ	under	ὑπό	4.2.5
իմաստական	sophistical	σοφιστικός	1.6.9
իր	thing	πρᾶγμα	2.0.1
լինելութիւն	generation	γένεσις	1.5.3
խառնակցութիւն	mixture	σύμμιξις	1.5.3
խառնուած	mixture	κρᾶσις	1.5.5
խնդիր	question	ζήτημα	5..4.2
խոնաւային	moist	ὑγρός	1.5.2
խորհուրդ	plan	βουλή	1.5.10
կարգ	rank	τάξις	1.0.1
կարգ	rank	τάξις	1.2.0
կացրդական	declamatory	πανηγυρικός	2.3.7
կենդանի	living	ἔμψυχος	4.2.4
կողմն	place	χώρα	1.5.2
համեստական	moderate	σώφρων	2.1.1
հնագոյն	more ancient	πρεσβύτερος	4.3.2
հմտութիւն	practice	ἐμπειρία	2.3.1
հմտութիւն	practical	ἐμπειρία	2.3.1
ձեւ	shape	σχῆμα	1.4.3
մակազդ	related	συγγενής	2.3.5
մակացելի	erudition	ἐπιστήμη	1.6.9
մակացութիւն	erudition	ἐπιστήμη	3.1.5
մակացութիւն	knowledge	ἐπιστήμη	4.2.12
մարմին	body	σῶμα	4.2.4
միմոսութիւն	mimetic representation	μίμησις	2.4.0
յատուկ	particular	ἴδιος	4.2.3
յեղումն	change	τροπή	5.4.6
շարադրութիւն	composition	σύνθεσις	2.3.3

Armenian	English	Greek	Ref.
շրջան	orbit	κύκλος	1.0.1
շրջան	orbit	κύκλος	1.3.0
ունակութիւն	condition	ἕξις	4.2.12
ունակութիւն	condition	ἕξις	4.2.14
ունայն	the void	τὸ κενόν	1.1.1
ունայն	the void	τὸ κενόν	1.1.2
ուղեղ	the brain	ἐγκέφαλος	1.5.5
ուր	where	που	4.2.15
չափ	measure	μέτρον	1.0.1
պատժեմ	punish	κολάζω	1.5.10
պիտակաբար	improperly	καταχρηστικῶς	2.4.1
սահմանական	definitive	ὁριστικός	1.6.9
սահմանական	determined	ὡρίσμενος	5.5.1
սեռ	kind	γένος	1.0.1
սեռ	genus	γένος	4.2.5
սեռականագոյն	most generic	γενικώτατος	4.2.4
ստեղծումն արտաքոյ	creation from outside	κτίσις ἔξωθεν	1.5.3
վաղագոյն	earlier	πρότερος	4.3.2
վարք կենացն	styles of life	ἤθη τοῦ βίου	1.5.10
վերլուծական	analytical	ἀναλυτικός	1.6.9
տարբերութիւն	difference	διαφορά	4.2.3
տարբերութիւն	difference	διαφορά	4.2.6
տեսակ	species	εἶδος	1.5.1
տեսակագոյն	most specific	εἰδικώτατος	4.2.4
տնտերինական	administrative	οἰκονομικός	1.6.9
տրամաբանական	dialectical	διαλεκτικός	1.6.9
վանկառութիւն	syllable	σύλληψις	2.3.3
ցանկութիւն	desire	ἐπιθυμία	1.5.10
քաղաքական	political	πολιτικός	1.6.9
քերթած	literary work	ποίημα	2.3.2

2. *By Greek*

Greek	Armenian	English	Ref.
αἴσθησις	*զգայութիւն*	sense perception	4.2.12
αἰσθητός	*զգայուն*	perceptive	4.2.4
ἄλογος	*անբան*	irrational	4.2.4
ἀμέτρως	*անչափ*	without measure	1.4.3
ἀμφίβιος	*երկակենցաղ*	amphibious	1.5.2
ἀναίσθητος	*անզգայուն*	non-perceptive	4.2.4
ἀναλυτικός	*վերլուծական*	analytical	1.6.9
ἀναρίθμητος	*անթուելի*	innumerable	1.5.4
ἀπαθής	*անկրական*	impassible	1.5.4
ἀποδεικτικός	*ապացուցական*	demonstrating	1.6.9
ἀποδεικτικός	*ապացուցական*	probative	3.2.1
ἀριθμητικός	*թուականութիւն*	calculation	3.1.7
ἀριθμός	*թիւ*	number	1.4.3
ἀσώματος	*անմարմին*	bodiless	4.2.4
ἀσωμάτως	*անմարմնաբար*	in a bodiless way	1.5.3
ἄτρεπτος	*անյեղլի*	unchanging	1.5.3
ἄψυχος	*անկենդանի*	non-living	4.2.4
βουλή	*խորհուրդ*	plan	1.5.10
γένεσις	*լինելութիւն*	generation	1.5.3
γενικώτατος	*սեռականագոյն*	most generic	4.2.4
γένος	*սեռ*	kind	1.0.1
γένος	*սեռ*	genus	4.2.5
γνῶσις	*գիտութիւն*	knowledge	1.6.13
διαζητικός not LS	*ի ձեռն խնդրականին*	inquiry	4.1.0
διαιρετικός	*բաժանական*	divisible	1.6.9
διαλεκτικός	*տրամաբանական*	dialectical	1.6.9
διάταξις	*դասաւորութիւն*	ordering	5.3.7
διαφορά	*տարբերութիւն*	difference	4.2.3
διαφορά	*տարբերութիւն*	difference	4.2.6
δικανικός	*ատենական*	forensic	2.3.7
δύναμις	*զաւրութիւն*	power	1.0.1

Greek	Armenian	English	Ref.
δύναμις	զաւրութիւն	power	1.5.0
εἰδικώτατος	տեսակագոյն	most specific	4.2.4
εἶδος	տեսակ	species	1.5.1
ἔκδοσις	արտադրութիւն	giving forth	1.5.1
ἔκκρισις	արտադատութիւն	separating forth	1.5.1
ἐκφορά	արտաբերութիւն	bringing forth	1.5.1
ἔκχυσις	արտահոսութիւն	flowing forth	1.5.1
ἐμπειρία	հմտութիւն	practice	2.3.1
ἐμπειρία	հմտութիւն	practical	2.3.1
ἔμψυχος	կենդանի	living	4.2.4
ἐνέργεια	ազդումն	influence	1.6.0
ἐνέργεια	ազդումն	influence	1.0.1
ἕξις	ունակութիւն	condition	4.2.14
ἕξις	ունակութիւն	condition	4.2.12
ἐπιθυμία	ցանկութիւն	desire	1.5.10
ἐπιστήμη	մակացելի	erudition	1.6.9
ἐπιστήμη	մակացութիւն	erudition	3.1.5
ἐπιστήμη	մակացութիւն	knowledge	4.2.12
ἑτεροῖος	այլայլակ	differently	1.5.3
τὰ ἔξωθεν	եկամուտ	the external things	1.5.13
εὐκρασία	բարեխառնութիւն	good mixture	1.5.12
ζήτημα	խնդիր	question	5..4.2
ἤθη τοῦ βίου	վարք կենացն	styles of life	1.5.10
ἠθικός	բարոյական	moral	1.6.9
ἠθοποιητικός	բարառնական	that which causes character	2.2.3
θέσις	դիր	position	1.1.0
θέσις	դիր	position	1.0.1
θέσις	դրութիւն	position	4.2.12
θυράθεν	արտաքոյ	from outside	1.5.3
ἡ ἰατρική	բժշկականութիւն	medicine	1.5.5
ἰατρικός	բժշկական	healing	1.5.1
ἴδιος	յատուկ	particular	4.2.3
ἰσόρροπος εὐκρασία	բարեխառնութիւն	a balanced blending	1.5.7
καταχρηστικῶς	պիտակաբար	improperly	2.4.1

Greek	Armenian	English	Ref.
τὸ κενόν	ունայն	the void	1.1.2
κρίσις	դատումն	judgement	2.3.2
κολάζω	պատժեմ	punish	1.5.10
κρᾶσις	խառնուած	mixture	1.5.5
κτίσις ἔξωθεν	ստեղծումն արտաքոյ	creation from outside	1.5.3
κύκλος	շրջան	orbit	1.3.0
κύκλος	շրջան	orbit	1.0.1
λέξις	բառ	word	2.3.3
λογικός	բանական	reasonable	1.6.9
λογικός	բանական	possessed of reason	4.2.4
λογικός	բանական	reasonable	1.6.9
λογικός	բանական	reasonable	1.6.12
μετοχή	ընդունելութիւն	participle	2.3.5
μέτρον	չափ	measure	1.0.1
μίμησις	միմոսութիւն	mimetic representation	2.4.0
ξηρός	ցամաքային	dry	1.5.2
οἰκονομικός	տնաւրինական	administrative	1.6.9
ὁριστικός	սահմանական	definitive	1.6.9
πάθος	ախտ	property	4.2.14
πανηγυρικός	կացրդական	declamatory	2.3.7
παρατατικός	արածգական	imperfect	5.4.6
ποίημα	քերթած	literary work	2.3.2
ποιητικός	արարչական	qualitative [creative]	5.5.1
πολιτικός	քաղաքական	political	1.6.9
ποτε	երբ	when	4.2.15
που	ուր	where	4.2.15
πρᾶγμα	իր	thing	2.0.1
πρακτικός	գործնական	practical	1.6.9
πρεσβύτερος	հնագոյն	more ancient	4.3.2
πρόγνωσις	յառաջգիտութիւն	prescience	1.6.13
πρότερος	վաղագոյն	earlier	4.3.2
σοφιστικός	իմաստական	sophistical	1.6.9
συγγενής	մակագդ	related	2.3.5
σύλληψις	վաղառութիւն	syllable	2.3.3

Greek	Armenian	English	Ref.
συμβουλευτικός	*բախխոճական*	deliberative	2.3.7
σύνθεσις	*շարադրութիւն*	composition	2.3.3
σχῆμα	*ծեւ*	shape	1.4.3
σῶμα	*մարմին*	body	4.2.4
σώφρων	*համեստական*	moderate	2.1.1
τάξις	*կարգ*	rank	1.2.0
τάξις	*կարգ*	rank	1.0.1
τάσσω	*դասիմ*	arrange	4.2.5
τροπή	*յեղումն*	change	5.4.6
τρόπος	*եղանակ*	modification	1.5.7
ὑγρός	*խոնաւային*	moist	1.5.2
ὑπό	*ի ներքոյ*	under	4.2.5
τὸ ὑποκείμενον	*ենթակայ*	substrate	4.2.5
φύσις	*բնական*	the natural	1.2.3
φύσις	*բնութիւն*	nature	5.5.0
χρόνος	*ժամանակ*	time	4.3.2
χώρα	*կողմն*	place	1.5.2
ὡρίσμενος	*սահմանական*	determined	5.5.1

3. *By English*

English	Greek	Armenian	Ref.
administrative	οἰκονομικός	*տնաւրինական*	1.6.9
amphibious	ἀμφίβιος	*երկակենցաղ*	1.5.2
analytical	ἀναλυτικός	*վերլուծական*	1.6.9
more ancient	πρεσβύτερος	*հնագոյն*	4.3.2
arrange	τάσσω	*դասիմ*	4.2.5
a balanced blending	ἰσόρροπος εὐκρασία	*բարեխառնութիւն*	1.5.7
bodiless	ἀσώματος	*անմարմին*	4.2.4
in a bodiless way	ἀσωμάτως	*անմարմնաբար*	1.5.3
body	σῶμα	*մարմին*	4.2.4
the brain	ἐγκέφαλος	*ուղեղ*	1.5.5
bringing forth	ἐκφορά	*արտաբերութիւն*	1.5.1
calculation	ἀριθμητικός	*թուականութիւն*	3.1.7
change	τροπή	*յեղումն*	5.4.6
that which causes character	ἠθοποιητικός	*բարաննական*	2.2.3
composition	σύνθεσις	*շարադրութիւն*	2.3.3
condition	ἕξις	*ունակութիւն*	4.2.14
condition	ἕξις	*ունակութիւն*	4.2.12
creation from outside	κτίσις ἔξωθεν	*ստեղծումն արտաքոյ*	1.5.3
declamatory	πανηγυρικός	*կացրդական*	2.3.7
definitive	ὁριστικός	*սահմանական*	1.6.9
deliberative	συμβουλευτικός	*բաղխորհական*	2.3.7
demonstrating	ἀποδεικτικός	*ապացուցական*	1.6.9
desire	ἐπιθυμία	*ցանկութիւն*	1.5.10
determined	ὡρίσμενος	*սահմանական*	5.5.1
dialectical	διαλεκτικός	*տրամաբանական*	1.6.9
difference	διαφορά	*տարբերութիւն*	4.2.3
difference	διαφορά	*տարբերութիւն*	4.2.6
differently	ἑτεροῖος	*այլայլակ*	1.5.3
divisible	διαιρετικός	*բաժանական*	1.6.9
dry	ξηρός	*ցամաքային*	1.5.2
earlier	πρότερος	*վաղագոյն*	4.3.2

English	Greek	Armenian	Ref.
erudition	ἐπιστήμη	մակացութիւն	3.1.5
the external things	τὰ ἔξωθεν	եկամուտ	1.5.13
flowing forth	ἔκχυσις	արտահոսութիւն	1.5.1
forensic	δικανικός	ատենական	2.3.7
generation	γένεσις	լինելութիւն	1.5.3
most generic	γενικώτατος	սեռականագոյն	4.2.4
genus	γένος	սեռ	4.2.5
giving forth	ἔκδοσις	արտադրութիւն	1.5.1
good mixture	εὐκρασία	բարեխառնութիւն	1.5.12
healing	ἰατρικός	բժշկական	1.5.1
impassible	ἀπαθής	անկրական	1.5.4
imperfect	παρατατικός	արտաձգական	5.4.6
improperly	καταχρηστικῶς	պիտակաբար	2.4.1
influence	ἐνέργεια	ազդումն	1.6.0
influence	ἐνέργεια	ազդումն	1.0.1
innumerable	ἀναρίθμητος	անթուելի	1.5.4
inquiry	διαζητικός not LS	ի ձեռն խնդրականին	4.1.0
irrational	ἄλογος	անբան	4.2.4
judgement	κρίσις	դատումն	2.3.2
kind	γένος	սեռ	1.0.1
knowledge	γνῶσις	գիտութիւն	1.6.13
knowledge	ἐπιστήμη	մակացութիւն	4.2.12
literary work	ποίημα	բերթած	2.3.2
living	ἔμψυχος	կենդանի	4.2.4
measure	μέτρον	չափ	1.0.1
medicine	ἡ ἰατρική	բժշկականութիւն	1.5.5
mimetic representation	μίμησις	միմոսութիւն	2.4.0
mixture	κρᾶσις	խառնուած	1.5.5
mixture	σύμμιξις	խառնակցութիւն	1.5.3
moderate	σώφρων	համեստական	2.1.1
modification	τρόπος	եղանակ	1.5.7
moist	ὑγρός	խոնաւային	1.5.2
moral	ἠθικός	բարոյական	1.6.9
the natural	φύσις	բնականն	1.2.3

English	Greek	Armenian	Ref.
non-living	ἄψυχος	անկենդանի	4.2.4
non-perceptive	ἀναίσθητος	անզգայուն	4.2.4
number	ἀριθμός	թիւ	1.4.3
orbit	κύκλος	շրջան	1.3.0
orbit	κύκλος	շրջան	1.0.1
ordering	διάταξις	դասատրութիւն	5.3.7
from outside	θυράθεν	արտաքոյ	1.5.3
participle	μετοχή	բնդունելութիւն	2.3.5
particular	ἴδιος	յատուկ	4.2.3
perceptive	αἰσθητός	զգայուն	4.2.4
place	χώρα	կողմն	1.5.2
plan	βουλή	խորհուրդ	1.5.10
political	πολιτικός	քաղաքական	1.6.9
position	θέσις	դիր	1.1.0
position	θέσις	դիր	1.0.1
position	θέσις	դրութիւն	4.2.12
possessed of reason	λογικός	բանական	4.2.4
power	δύναμις	զաւրութիւն	1.0.1
power	δύναμις	զաւրութիւն	1.5.0
practical	ἐμπειρία	հմտութիւն	2.3.1
practical	πρακτικός	գործնական	1.6.9
practice	ἐμπειρία	հմտութիւն	2.3.1
prescience	πρόγνωσις	յառաջգիտութիւն	1.6.13
probative	ἀποδεικτικός	ապացուցական	3.2.1
property	πάθος	խիտ	4.2.14
punish	κολάζω	պատժեմ	1.5.10
qualitative [creative]	ποιητικός	արարչական	5.5.1
question	ζήτημα	խնդիր	5..4.2
rank	τάξις	կարգ	1.2.0
rank	τάξις	կարգ	1.0.1
reasonable	λογικός	բանական	1.6.9
reasonable	λογικός	բանական	1.6.9
reasonable	λογικός	բանական	1.6.12
related	συγγενής	մակագգ	2.3.5

English	Greek	Armenian	Ref.
separating forth	ἔκκρισις	*արտադատութիւն*	1.5.1
shape	σχῆμα	*ձեւ*	1.4.3
sophistical	σοφιστικός	*իմաստական*	1.6.9
species	εἶδος	*տեսակ*	1.5.1
most specific	εἰδικώτατος	*տեսակագոյն*	4.2.4
styles of life	ἤθη τοῦ βίου	*վարք կենացն*	1.5.10
substrate	τὸ ὑποκείμενον	*ենթակայ*	4.2.5
syllable	σύλληψις	*վաղառութիւն*	2.3.3
thing	πρᾶγμα	*իր*	2.0.1
time	χρόνος	*ժամանակ*	4.3.2
unchanging	ἄτρεπτος	*անյեղլի*	1.5.3
under	ὑπό	*ի ներքոյ*	4.2.5
the void	τὸ κενόν	*ունայն*	1.1.2
the void	τὸ κενόν	*ունայն*	1.1.1
when	ποτε	*երբ*	4.2.15
where	που	*ուր*	4.2.15
without measure	ἀμέτρως	*անչափի*	1.4.3
word	λέξις	*բառ*	2.3.3

NEOLOGISMS IN PSEUDO-ZENO

Words marked with an asterisk were already noted by Xač'ikyan.

առնդդէմ	§5.3.1
առինչունակապէս	§4.3.1
արտատրութիւն	§1.5.1 (*NBH*)
բաղկանաց	§5.1.1; 5.2.5
բանատրութիւն	§1.6.18; 5.9.4 (*NBH* only բանատու)
*գռուզ	§1.5.6
դիւրացուցանելի	§2.4.2 (*NBH* դիւրացուցանեմ only)
*եռակարբ	§1.4.2; 4.2.4; 5.6.4; 5.8.1 (*NBH*)
*երկմանաբար	§1.6.15
*զանազանիչք	§4.3.5
*էագոյն	§5.9.2
ընդկողմանումն	§4.2.13
*ընդկայութիւն	§4.2.13
*խոնատումն	§5.7.2
*կարճաբառութիւն	§3.2.2 (*NBH* կարճաբանութիւն only)
*կացադրութիւն	§1.6.10 (*NBH* կացուրդ, կացրդական)
*համեստական	§2.1.1 (*NBH*)
*Հատղական	§5.6.4
*Հատադիմակայ	§1.1.6 (*NBH*)
*Հատրանական	§3.2.3 (*NBH* Հատարան: only in Շիր.)
*Հատուցական	§3.2.3
*Հիմնական	§5.4.1
Հնարական (միտք = μεθοδική νους)	§3.1.16
միմոսութիւն	§2.4.0; 2.4.1 (*NBH* միմոս only)
*միտատար	§1.5.8
*մշտակացութիւն	§1.3.1; 5.8.2
ներարհեստ	§5.2.9 (ἐντέχνος province of art, furnished or invented by art)
*շարանութիւն	§1.5.4
*շարասութիւն	§3.2.1
շտեմարանափակ	§2.5.4
*ունակարէն	§4.3.1
*պադպաջմունք	§1.4.2
*պղնձոտ	§1.5.6
*սերանամ	§4.2.5
վերադասականաց	§1.6.6 etc.
ցրտումն	§5.7.2

There are also words which are rare and are recorded by *NBH* only from Pseudo-
Zeno and one other source. Such are:

անամանակ	§5.4.7 (Pseudo-Zeno and Narekacʻi)
անվայր	§5.8.2 (Pseudo-Zeno and Narekacʻi)
արտադատութիւն	§1.5.1 (Pseudo-Zeno and Xorenacʻi)
յառաջադատութիւն	§2.3.4 (Pseudo-Zeno and Grammar, Movses Qertoł)
բարատնականն	§2.2.3 (Pseudo-Zeno and David, *Prol.*)

MAIN TYPES OF VARIANTS

This list presents the main types of variants discussed in the Textual Commentary. The numbers refer to paragraphs of the Textual Commentary.

Abbreviation by omission of final syllables 1.4.11
amenayn "all", addition or omission of 2.3.5
Case, alternation of nominative and genitive 1.6.11
Dittography 1.6.3, 1.6.8, 1.6.13. 4.2.5
Graphic corruptions *g— d* 1.1.3, *l — š* 1.1.5, *n — v* 2.3.3, *p' — x* 5.1.2, *t — wr* 1.5.6, *y — c'* 1.1.4
Graphic similarities, corruption caused by 1.2.1, 1.2.4, 1.3.4, 1.4.6
Haplography 1.3.2, 4.2.1, 4.2.7
Homoeoteleuton 1.2.3, 1.4.2, 1.5.7, 1.6.11, 1.6.14, 1.6.15, 1.6.16, 2.3.3, 2.3.4, 4.2.4, 5.2.8
Nouns, variation of abstract and concrete 1.1.4
Omission of *žē* 1.5.12
Phonetic variant, *g — k'*, etc. 1.0.1
Prepositions, omission of *ĕst* 1.4.3
Prepositions, variation of *ĕnd — i* 2.5.3, *ĕst — z-* 1.2.3, *ew — qanzi — zi* 4.2.1
Privative *an-*, addition or omission of 1.1.1
Verbs, singular for plural 1.1.1
Verbs, variation of present indicative — infinitive 1.2.4

PHILOSOPHIA ANTIQUA

A SERIES OF STUDIES ON ANCIENT PHILOSOPHY

EDITED BY

J. MANSFELD, D.T. RUNIA
AND J.C.M. VAN WINDEN

1. Verdenius, W.J. and Waszink, J.H. *Aristotle on Coming-to-Be and Passing-Away*. Some Comments. Reprint of the 2nd (1966) ed. 1968. ISBN 90 04 01718 6

7. Saffrey, H.D. *Le περὶ φιλοσοφίας d'Aristote et la théorie platonicienne des idées nombres*. 2ème éd. revue et accompagnée du compte-rendu critique par H. Cherniss. 1971. ISBN 90 04 01720 8

13. Nicolaus Damascenus. *On the Philosophy of Aristotle*. Fragments of the First Five Books, Translated from the Syriac with an Introduction and Commentary by H.J. Drossaart Lulofs. Reprint of the 1st (1965) ed. 1969. ISBN 90 04 01725 9

14. Edelstein, L. *Plato's Seventh Letter*. 1966. ISBN 90 04 01726 7

15. Porphyrius. *Πρὸς Μαρκέλλαν*. Griechischer Text, herausgegeben, übersetzt, eingeleitet und erklärt von W. Pötscher. 1969. ISBN 90 04 01727 5

17. Gould, J.B. *The Philosophy of Chrysippus*. Reprint 1971. ISBN 90 04 01729 1

18. Boeft, J. den. *Calcidius on Fate*. His Doctrine and Sources. 1970. ISBN 90 04 01730 5

19. Pötscher, W. *Strukturprobleme der aristotelischen und theophrastischen Gottesvorstellung*. 1970. ISBN 90 04 01731 3

20. Bertier, J. *Mnésithée et Dieuchès*. 1972. ISBN 90 04 03468 4

21. Timaios Lokros. *Über die Natur des Kosmos und der Seele*. Kommentiert von M. Baltes. 1972. ISBN 90 04 03344 0

22. Graeser, A. *Plotinus and the Stoics*. A Preliminary Study. 1972. ISBN 90 04 03345 9

23. Iamblichus Chalcidensis. *In Platonis dialogos commentariorum fragmenta*. Edited with Translation and Commentary by J.M. Dillon. 1973. ISBN 90 04 03578 8

24. Timaeus Locrus. *De natura mundi et animae*. Überlieferung, Testimonia, Text und Übersetzung von W. Marg. Editio maior. 1972. ISBN 90 04 03505 2

26. Gersh, S.E. *Κίνησις ἀκίνητος*. A Study of Spiritual Motion in the Philosophy of Proclus. 1973. ISBN 90 04 03784 5

27. O'Meara, D. *Structures hiérarchiques dans la pensée de Plotin*. Étude historique et interprétative. 1975. ISBN 90 04 04372 1

28. Todd, R.B. *Alexander of Aphrodisias on the Stoic Physics*. A Study of the *De Mixtione* with Preliminary Essays, Text, Translation and Commentary. 1976. ISBN 90 04 04402 7

29. Scheffel, W. *Aspekte der platonischen Kosmologie*. Untersuchungen zum Dialog 'Timaios'. 1976. ISBN 90 04 04509 0

30. Baltes, M. *Die Weltentstehung des platonischen Timaios nach den antiken Interpreten*. Teil 1. 1976. ISBN 90 04 04720 4

31. Edlow, R.B. *Galen on Language and Ambiguity*. An English Translation of Galen's *De Captionibus* (On Fallacies), With Introduction, Text and Commentary. 1977. ISBN 90 04 04869 3

34. Epiktet. *Vom Kynismus.* Herausgegeben und übersetzt mit einem Kommentar von M. Billerbeck. 1978. ISBN 90 04 05770 6

35. Baltes, M. *Die Weltentstehung des platonischen Timaios nach den antiken Interpreten.* Teil 2. Proklos. 1979. ISBN 90 04 05799 4

37. O'Brien, D. *Theories of Weight in the Ancient World.* Four Essays on Democritus, Plato and Aristotle. A Study in the Development of Ideas 1. Democritus: Weight and Size. An Exercise in the Reconstruction of Early Greek Philosophy. 1981. ISBN 90 04 06134 7

39. Tarán, L. *Speusippus of Athens.* A Critical Study with a Collection of the Related Texts and Commentary. 1982. ISBN 90 04 06505 9

40. Rist, J.M. *Human Value.* A Study in Ancient Philosophical Ethics. 1982. ISBN 90 04 06757 4

41. O'Brien, D. *Theories of Weight in the Ancient World.* Four Essays on Democritus, Plato and Aristotle. A Study in the Development of Ideas 2. Plato: Weight and Sensation. The Two Theories of the 'Timaeus'. 1984. ISBN 90 04 06934 8

44. Runia, D.T. *Philo of Alexandria and the Timaeus of Plato.* 1986. ISBN 90 04 07477 5

45. Aujoulat, N. *Le Néo-Platonisme Alexandrin: Hiéroclès d'Alexandrie.* Filiations intellectuelles et spirituelles d'un néo-platonicien du Ve siècle. 1986. ISBN 90 04 07510 0

46. Kal, V. *On Intuition and Discursive Reason in Aristotle.* 1988. ISBN 90 04 08308 1

48. Evangeliou, Ch. *Aristotle's Categories and Porphyry.* 1988. ISBN 90 04 08538 6

49. Bussanich, J. *The One and Its Relation to Intellect in Plotinus.* A Commentary on Selected Texts. 1988. ISBN 90 04 08996 9

50. Simplicius. *Commentaire sur les Catégories.* Traduction commentée sous la direction de I. Hadot. I: Introduction, première partie (p. 1-9, 3 Kalbfleisch). Traduction de Ph. Hoffmann (avec la collaboration d'I. et P. Hadot). Commentaire et notes à la traduction par I. Hadot avec des appendices de P. Hadot et J.-P. Mahé. 1990. ISBN 90 04 09015 0

51. Simplicius. *Commentaire sur les Catégories.* Traduction commentée sous la direction de I. Hadot. III: Préambule aux Catégories. Commentaire au premier chapitre des Catégories (p. 21-40, 13 Kalbfleisch). Traduction de Ph. Hoffmann (avec la collaboration d'I. Hadot, P. Hadot et C. Luna). Commentaire et notes à la traduction par C. Luna. 1990. ISBN 90 04 09016 9

52. Magee, J. *Boethius on Signification and Mind.* 1989. ISBN 90 04 09096 7

53. Bos, E.P. and Meijer, P.A. (eds.) *On Proclus and His Influence in Medieval Philosophy.* 1992. ISBN 90 04 09429 6

54. Fortenbaugh, W.W., et al. (eds.) *Theophrastes of Eresos.* Sources for His Life, Writings, Thought and Influence. 1992. ISBN 90 04 09440 7 *set*

55. Shankman, A. *Aristotle's* De insomniis. A Commentary. ISBN 90 04 09476 8

56. Mansfeld, J. *Heresiography in Context.* Hippolytos' *Elenchos* as a Source for Greek Philosophy. 1992. ISBN 90 04 09616 7

57. O'Brien, D. *Théodicée plotinienne, théodicée gnostique.* 1993. ISBN 90 04 09618 3

58. Baxter, T.M.S. *The Cratylus.* Plato's Critique of Naming. 1992. ISBN 90 04 09597 7

59. Dorandi, T. (Hrsg.) *Theodor Gomperz. Eine Auswahl herkulanischer kleiner Schriften (1864-1909).* 1993. ISBN 90 04 09819 4

60. Filodemo. *Storia dei filosofi. La stoà da Zenone a Panezio* (PHerc. 1018). Edizione, traduzione e commento a cura di T. Dorandi. 1994. ISBN 90 04 09963 8

61. Mansfeld, J. *Prolegomena.* Questions to be Settled Before the Study of an Author, or a Text. 1994. ISBN 90 04 10084 9

62. Flannery, s.J., K.L. *Ways into the Logic of Alexander of Aphrodisias.* 1995. ISBN 90 04 09998 0

63. Lakmann, M.-L. *Der Platoniker Tauros in der Darstellung des Aulus Gellius*. 1995.
ISBN 90 04 10096 2

64. Sharples, R.W. *Theophrastus of Eresus*. Sources for his Life, Writings, Thought and Influence. Commentary Volume 5. Sources on Biology (Human Physiology, Living Creatures, Botany: Texts 328-435). 1995. ISBN 90 04 10174 8

65. Algra, K. *Concepts of Space in Greek Thought*. 1995. ISBN 90 04 10172 1   66. Simplicius. *Commentaire sur le manuel d'Épictète*. Introduction et édition critique de texte grec par Ilsetraut Hadot. 1995. ISBN 90 04 09772 4

67. Cleary, J.J. *Aristotle and Mathematics*. Aporetic Method in Cosmology and Metaphysics. 1995. ISBN 90 04 10159 4

68. Tieleman, T. *Galen and Chrysippus on the Soul*. Argument and Refutation in the *De Placitis* Books II-III. 1996. ISBN 90 04 10520 4

69. Haas, F.A.J. de. *John Philoponus' New Definition of Prime Matter*. Aspects of its Background in Neoplatonism and the Ancient Commentary Tradition. 1997.
ISBN 90 04 10446 1

71. Andia, Y. de. *Henosis*. L'Union à Dieu chez Denys l'Aréopagite. 1996.
ISBN 90 04 10656 1

72. Algra, K.A., Horst, P.W. van der, and Runia, D.T. (eds.) *Polyhistor*. Studies in the History and Historiography of Ancient Philosophy. Presented to Jaap Mansfeld on his Sixtieth Birthday. 1996. ISBN 90 04 10417 8

73. Mansfeld, J. and Runia, D.T. *Aëtiana*. The Method and Intellectual Context of a Doxographer. Volume 1: The Sources. 1997. ISBN 90 04 10580 8

74. Slomkowski, P. *Aristotle's* Topics. 1997. ISBN 90 04 10757 6

75. Barnes, J. *Logic and the Imperial Stoa*. 1997. ISBN 90 04 10828 9

76. Inwood, B. and Mansfeld, J. (eds.) *Assent and Argument*. Studies in Cicero's *Academic Books*. Proceedings of the 7th Symposium Hellenisticum (Utrecht, August 21-25, 1995). 1997. ISBN 90 04 10914 5

77. Magee, J. (ed., tr. & comm.) *Anicii Manlii Severini Boethii* De divisione liber. Critical Edition, Translation, Prolegomena, and Commentary. 1998.
ISBN 90 04 10873 4

78. Olympiodorus. *Commentary on Plato's* Gorgias. Translated with Full Notes by R. Jackson, K. Lycos & H. Tarrant. Introduction by H. Tarrant. 1998.
ISBN 90 04 10972 2

79. Sharples, R.W. *Theophrastus of Eresus*. Sources for his Life, Writings, Thought and Influence. Commentary Volume 3.1. Sources on Physics (Texts 137-223). With Contributions on the Arabic Material by Dimitri Gutas. 1998.
ISBN 90 04 11130 1

80. Mansfeld, J. *Prolegomena Mathematica*. From Apollonius of Perga to Late Neoplatonism. With an Appendix on Pappus and the History of Platonism. 1998.
ISBN 90 04 11267 7

81. Huby, P. *Theophrastus of Eresus*. Sources for His Life, Writings, Thought and Influence. Commentary Volume 4. Psychology (Texts 254-327). With Contributions on the Arabic Material by D. Gutas. 1999. ISBN 90 04 11317 7

82. Boter, G. *The* Encheiridion *of Epictetus and Its Three Christian Adaptations*. Transmission and Critical Editions. 1999. ISBN 90 04 11358 4

83. Stone, M.E. and Shirinian, M.E. *Pseudo-Zeno. Anonymous Philosophical Treatise*. Translated with the Collaboration of J. Mansfeld and D.T. Runia. 2000.
ISBN 90 04 11524 2